FAITHFUL WITNESSES

United Methodist Theology of Mission

By John Edward Nuessle
Assistant General Secretary
General Board of Global Ministries

Study Guide

By Diana L. Hynson
Director of Learning and Teaching Ministries
General Board of Discipleship

THE BASIC RESOURCE BOOK
OF THE ACADEMY OF MISSION RENEWAL

A Mission Education Program of Leadership Development
from the Mission Education Program Area
General Board of Global Ministries
The United Methodist Church

Copyright © 2008 General Board of Global Ministries

A publication of the General Board of Global Ministries, The United Methodist Church

ISBN 978-1-933663-19-7

Library of Congress Control Number 2007941443

TABLE OF CONTENTS

ACKNOWLEDGEMENTS 5

WELCOME 7

PREFACE 9

CHAPTER ONE: INTRODUCTION TO THEOLOGY OF MISSION 13
Essay 1: Why a Theology of Mission, Anyway? It Is Grace Upon Grace 16
Essay 2: What Is Mission? *Missio Dei*—Mission Is God's Mission for the
    Coming Kingdom 23
Essay 3: Where and When Is Mission? From Missions to Mission 29
Essay 4: Who Is Mission? Our Call, Journey, and Incarnation in the
    Global Ministries of the Church 37
Essay 5: How Do We Understand Mission? "Doing" Theology 44

CHAPTER TWO: SCRIPTURE 51
Essay 6: On Fire in Mission: Witnessing *Is* Discipleship *Is* Witnessing 53
Essay 7: In Deep Water Fishing for Other Fish:
    Mission as Leadership Development 59
Essay 8: Why We Care: Humanitarian Needs, Theological Answers 66
Essay 9: Going Into the Spokes of the Wheel:
    Eliminating Barriers to the Kingdom 71

CHAPTER THREE: TRADITION 79
Essay 10: From Everywhere to Everywhere: The Dimensions of Mission 81
Essay 11: Organizing to Beat the Devil: The United Methodist Connection 90
Essay 12: No More Children for Calamity 98
Essay 13: The Feet of the Messenger: Servanthood in God's Mission 104

CHAPTER FOUR: EXPERIENCE 111
Essay 14: Equipping the Body for Mission Through Mission Education 113
Essay 15: Paddling the Canoe Together: The Experience of Partnership 121
Essay 16: Coming Home to Abundant Life 128
Essay 17: Justice Is "Done" by Loving Kindness and Walking Humbly 135

CHAPTER FIVE: REASON 141
Essay 18: God Is Doing a New Thing:
       Missionaries From Everywhere, to Everywhere 143
Essay 19: The Bread of Life, Food for the Journey 149
Essay 20: Being the "Glocal" Church in the 21st Century:
       The World Is Our Parish 156
Essay 21: No Canning Jars in the Kingdom:
       Stewardship Is the Bread of Heaven Meant for All 166

RESOURCES: BIBLIOGRAPHY AND SONG SUGGESTIONS 173

STUDY GUIDE 183
       Introduction 184
       Six-Session Study 190
       Two- to Three-Day Retreat 218
       One-Day Event 241
       Appendix 251

ACKNOWLEDGEMENTS

I offer this work to the Glory of God, that it may encourage the whole Church to move into God's Mission—the *missio Dei*—fully and fruitfully. It comes from the collective efforts of a great many people over a number of years. And so, I give my sincere thanks for the following people:

Duane Sarazin, Diane Tombough, and David Wilson: the General Board of Global Ministries directors who first conceived the need for this project in 2001;

The General Board of Global Ministries Cabinet and Mission Education directors, for their support for this project ever since that beginning;

The General Board of Global Ministries team on the Academy of Mission Renewal, past and present: Jorge Domingues, Sam Dixon, David Wu, Una Jones, S T Kimbrough, Jr., Carol Thompson, Marisa Villarreal, Cheryl Trent, Jorge Lockward, and Jodi Cataldo, all of whom have given significant time, creativity, and energy to this new Mission Education program for the denomination;

In addition to the above, many other General Board of Global Ministries staff persons for their assistance and encouragement, including Barbara Wheeler, Kim Lehmann, Lisa Katzenstein, Michelle Scott, Jong Sung Kim, Amanda Brummer Choi, Becky Louter, Brenda Connelly, Stephen Goldstein, and Edith Gleaves;

My extended family, the Buzckowski and Nuessle families, for the graceful and hospitable use of an Adirondack home sanctuary for a wonderful summer of restful and fruitful writing;

The editorial and design staff and consultants of the General Board of Global Ministries Communications unit, Darcy Quigley, Sean Grandits, Terri Chang, Susan B. Glattstein, Hal Sadler and Brenda Carr, who shaped and molded this conceptual idea into a real, live book;

The wonderfully talented Christian educator, Dr. Diana Hynson, from the staff of the General Board of Discipleship, who faithfully and enthusiastically took on this project with grace and creativity, and who enabled us to move forward at a very critical moment in God's *Kairos* time, producing an effective and exciting study guide; and

More than anyone else, my spouse, Ginena Dulley Wills, who, with significant mission leadership in her personal and professional life, has encouraged, motivated, and loved me to the place in my life where I have been able to engage in this work.

John Edward Nuessle

WELCOME TO THE ACADEMY
OF MISSION RENEWAL

*A Mission Education Program of Leadership Development
from the Mission Education Program Area,
General Board of Global Ministries*

The Academy of Mission Renewal arose from discussions among the directors of the General Board of Global Ministries' Mission Education program area as they recognized the need for a program of mission education for clergy, centered on the theology of mission, to be carried out by annual conference leadership with resources from Global Ministries. This was quickly expanded to include all who, through your church-related offices or personal interests, are called to more fully understand God's Mission.

The Academy is neither a place nor a program, but is envisioned as an opportunity for United Methodists to expand our understandings of mission theology from a United Methodist framework, and to empower you to engage your congregation in God's Mission. We look for partnerships among church organizations to create organized settings for reflection on mission and mission theology using resources prepared by the General Board of Global Ministries Mission Education unit. These settings may be through local congregations, districts, or annual conference agencies.

As a continuing education experience, programs may be implemented by the various church bodies or committees, or by interested participants themselves. Events may be offered in varying time lengths, and would occur within either the conference, a district, or a local arena, utilizing local and regional leadership. The events are to be tailored to the needs and interests of each group, recognizing our great diversity in style and level of missional involvement.

The benefits to the whole Church from these ongoing programs will be a medium for disseminating theological understandings and mission education concepts and practices throughout our Church. This firm foundation of Methodist missiology will enable congregations to have greater mission interest and involvement.

Faithful Witnesses is the first resource book of the Academy of Mission Renewal. It offers concepts of the theology and practice of mission involvement and seeks to assist you in developing a sound theology of the *missio Dei*—that is, what God's Mission is and why we are called into mission—giving you the language and understanding of how to engage your congregations in what mission is, and what it means to be the faithful witnesses of the Gospel through the Church in mission.

Future resources such as this will enable further and deeper study into United Methodist missiology, with an emphasis on specific missional issues and opportunities. You will want to visit the Academy of Mission Renewal pages on the General Board of Global Ministries' website, where you will find these additional resources listed and previewed as they become available, along with comments and suggestions from participating groups and conference leaders for using the materials in your setting.

The Academy of Mission Renewal webpages will also have significant benefits to assist you in engaging in group study, in your local congregation, district, or annual conference. We welcome you to this community of United Methodist missiologists!

ACADEMY OF MISSON RENEWAL
http://academyofmissionrenewal.org
Mission Education Program Area, General Board of Global Ministries
475 Riverside Drive, New York, New York 10115

PREFACE

WHY!

"What?" is the question for the Natural Sciences.
"Where?" is the question for the Physical Sciences.
"When?" is the question for the Historical Sciences.
"Who?" is the question for the Social Sciences.
"How?" is the question for the Engineering Sciences.

But "Why?" is the whole topic of the theological sciences. It is the almost unknowable human question of theology. However, from a faith perspective, "Why?" becomes "Why!" Why do we do what we do? Why, indeed! Theological inquiry moves the question of "Why?" toward a faithful response to life with an emphatic statement of "Why!" Why does the world need to be the way it is? Why is there suffering and confusion and conflict? Why are not more of the peoples of the world moving together for the common good, with a secure hope in God's eternal care? Theology has been called faith seeking understanding. A theology of mission is this faith seeking to understand the what, where, when, who, how, and why! of the Church's involvement throughout the whole world. We in United Methodism call this the global ministries of the church.

This study will help immerse you in a contemporary understanding of mission, yet it recognizes that the church is immersed in ministry already. We will study the Scriptures, hear of the ecumenical history of the modern missionary movement, and engage in discussion with one another, as well as with ourselves personally, to craft a shared theology of mission, through this basic resource book for the Academy of Mission Renewal. This is a United Methodist General Board of Global Ministries program of continuing education in our denomination, for everyone who seeks an active theology of mission in the 21st century. This resource offers concepts on the theology and practice of mission involvement for United Methodists, as you seek to develop a clear understanding of the *missio Dei*—what God's Mission is and why we are called into mission by God—which will give you the language and understandings to engage your congregation in what mission is, and what it means to be the church in mission. Through God's Mission we are connecting the church as faithful witnesses.

This resource book and accompanying study guide offer an analysis of missiology, as well as concepts of mission education, through an organized opportunity for reflection on mission and mission theology from the United Methodist perspective. The book has five major chapters that in total have 21 sub-chapters or essays, plus an annotated resources section and the accompanying study guide. The resources section includes a list of books for further and deeper study into missiology, from both historic and contemporary writers. Also, there is a listing of hymn and song suggestions to accompany each of the essays. Music is both an intellectual and emotive experience to help us understand the totality of mission, thus these are offered to enhance your personal and group study. The study guide has three models for use as an Academy of Mission Renewal in several possible settings (which are described more fully in the introduction to the study guide).

The first chapter presents the United Methodist understanding of mission, using historical and contemporary sources with an emphasis on the United Methodist tradition coming from a Wesleyan background. The next four chapters each develop this mission theology using the Theological Task from *The Book of Discipline*, illumined by the Four Mission Goals of the General Board of Global Ministries. As the Theological Task states: "Wesley believed that the living core of the Christian faith was revealed in Scripture, illumined by tradition, vivified in personal experience, and confirmed by reason." Thus you will find Scripture, Tradition, Experience, and Reason, the sources of theology in the Wesleyan understanding, integrated through these Four Mission Goals, which together express our United Methodist methodology for engaging in God's Mission.

The Four Mission Goals, formulated by the volunteer directors of the General Board of Global Ministries over the past three quadrennia, express in concise form the mission responsibilities of Global Ministries as set forth in *The Book of Discipline of The United Methodist Church*, and in the specific program mandates adopted by the General Conference. Each of these goals is implemented through specific program strategies approved by the board of directors and carried out in cooperation with annual conferences and other mission partners across the global connection. Together these are a summary statement of the directions of United Methodists as we move together into the 21st century in God's Mission.

The Four Mission Goals of the General Board of Global Ministries are:

1. Make Disciples of Jesus Christ

We will witness by word and deed among those who haven't heard or heeded the Gospel of Jesus Christ. We will initiate, facilitate, and support the creation and development of communities of faith that seek, welcome, and gather persons into the body of Christ and challenge them to Christian discipleship. Where direct proclamation is not permitted, a caring presence becomes the means of Christian witness.

2. Strengthen, Develop, and Renew Christian Congregations and Communities

We will work mutually with mission partners in common growth and development of spiritual life, worship, witness, and service.

3. Alleviate Human Suffering

We will help to initiate, strengthen, and support ministries to the spiritual, physical, emotional, and social needs of people.

4. Seek Justice, Freedom, and Peace

We will participate with people oppressed by unjust economic, political, and social systems in programs that seek to build just, free, and peaceful societies.

By using the "lens" of the United Methodist Theological Task (Scripture, Tradition, Experience, and Reason) to view these Four Mission Goals, a core and foundation for our United Methodist theology of mission emerges, which will shape our common calling in God's Mission. You are invited to enter into this study to engage your mind and your heart, as you move more fully into this high calling as faithful witnesses to the love of God in Christ Jesus, so that the "Why?" of life may become a resounding "Why!" in your mission and ministry throughout all of God's world.

CHAPTER ONE

INTRODUCTION TO THEOLOGY OF MISSION

The Why, What, Where, When, Who, and How of Mission

This first chapter of the study engages us in the background of missiology as a function of theology. The rationale for a theology of mission, as well as the modern history of the mission movement, will form the foundation for engaging in the Theological Task from the United Methodist missiological perspective in the next four parts of the study.

ESSAY 1: *Why a Theology of Mission, Anyway? It Is Grace Upon Grace*

John 1:16-17: Grace upon grace, as the expression of incarnation.

John 3:16: For God so loved the world that he gave his only son.

"As the Word became flesh and lived among us, and we have seen his glory…full of grace and truth; so too from his fullness we have all received, grace upon grace. For God so loved the world…." Global ministries are the church's expression of God's grace and love, for the salvation of the whole world; our expression of God's love for and care of the whole earth and all peoples. Our theology of mission is grace upon grace.

ESSAY 2: *What is Mission?* Missio Dei—*Mission is God's Mission for the Coming Kingdom*

Matthew 6:10: "Your Kingdom come. Your will be done, on earth as it is in heaven."

Mark 1:14-15: "The time is fulfilled, and the kingdom of God has come near…"

Luke 17:20-21: "The kingdom of God is not coming with things that can be observed…For, in fact, the kingdom of God is among you."

Jesus prayed, "your will be done, on earth as it is in heaven." For, "the time is fulfilled, and the kingdom of God has come near…" And, "the kingdom of God is not coming with things that can be observed…For, in fact, the kingdom of God is among you." This is the *missio Dei*—mission is God's Mission, through which we participate in the coming reign of God.

ESSAY 3: *Where and When is Mission? From Missions to Mission*

John 20:21-22: God sends Jesus, Jesus sends disciples; the connecting of mission.

Acts 10:34-35: All are acceptable to God.

"Jesus said to them again, 'Peace be with you. As the Father has sent me, so I send you.'" "Then Peter began to speak to them: 'I truly understand that God shows no partiality, but in every nation anyone who fears him and does what is right is acceptable to him.'" Here we have gone from missions to mission, which is expressed as the global ministries of the church—how we connect the whole church in God's Mission, sent into the entire world, which includes next door, for all are acceptable to God. You can't separate geography and timeframe in mission, thus the term "global ministries" implies both *where* and *when*.

ESSAY 4: *Who is Mission? Our Call, Journey, and Incarnation in the Global Ministries of the Church*

Isaiah 6:1-8: "Here I am, send me," and 43:1-2: Called you by name.

Luke 9:23-27: Pick up your Cross and follow.

2 Corinthians 4:7: Treasure in earthen vessels/common clay pots.

John 1:1 and 14: "And the Word became flesh and lived among us."

"Whom shall I send, and who will go for us?" And I said, "Here am I; send me!" And he said, "Go…" Mission is not a "vacation" from reality, but rather a vocational call to serve as Christ's representative in the world. Your call to global ministries, and the calling of the whole church, is a theology of incarnational mission; mission as the way of Christ.

ESSAY 5: *How Do We Understand Mission? Doing Theology*

Deuteronomy 18:18: A prophet speaking God's words among the people.

Psalm 119:33-34: Teach us, O Lord.

Mark 1:21-28 (Luke 4:31): Teaching as one having authority.

"They were astounded at [Jesus'] teaching, for he taught them as one hav-ing authority, and not as the scribes." Christian theology is not just made-up ideas, but there are specific sources for us to use in checking the reality of any response to life. The question of theological authority is a real issue for the church, and we do have real sources of theological authority for use in checking the reality of any response to life.

ESSAY 1

Why a Theology of Mission, Anyway?
It Is Grace Upon Grace

John 1:16-17: Grace upon grace, as the expression of incarnation.

John 3:16: For God so loved the world that he gave his only son.

"As the Word became flesh and lived among us, and we have seen his glory…full of grace and truth; so too from his fullness we have all received, grace upon grace. For God so loved the world…" Global ministries are the church's expression of God's grace and love, for the salvation of the whole world; our expression of God's love and care of the whole earth and all peoples. Our theology of mission is grace upon grace.

Grace Upon Grace

> Amazing Grace, how sweet the sound that saved a wretch like me.
> I once was lost, but now I'm found, was blind but now I see.[1]

The great sage of baseball and life, Yogi Berra, stated that, "You can see a lot by observing."[2] When we take the time and energy to observe the world about us, we can truly see quite a bit that helps us understand what we believe. The world is, at one and the same time, both infinitely complex, and amazingly simple. All of it, however, is the creative act of an extravagant God who has offered us much more than we can ever appreciate, or even totally enjoy and use. As we observe "What God hath wrought" (Numbers 23:23, KJV) in this wonderful creation, we can see in the infinite genius of the creator of the universe, who also created you and I, the complex interrelationships of nature and all human society and culture. Annie Dillard is one writer who calls us to observe and appreciate the magnificent extravagance of this creation, when she writes:

> If the landscape reveals one certainty, it is that the extravagant gesture is the very stuff of creation. After the one extravagant gesture of creation in the first place, the universe has continued to deal exclusively in extravagances, flinging intricacies and colossi down aeons of emptiness, heaping profusions on profligacies with ever-fresh vigor.[3]

God was not lavish just at the initial act of creation, but has continued in these wildly extravagant offerings to us throughout all time. We see the abundance of the world and the fullness of our lives, and it would seem that the only possible response to all that we observe is thankfulness and joy. And yet…why do we seem to be preoccupied with the troubles and difficulties of this life? It is a matter of faith. God's grace is wildly abundant but requires us to be observant with our seeing, using the eyes of faith. With these eyes we can celebrate a beautiful day spent in a natural setting or a family gathering, as well as a day in service to someone stricken in a hospital bed, or offering life-giving food to a child in an African refugee camp, or sharing the Good News of God's love in Christ Jesus with a Bible study among a group of new Christians in Southeast Asia. All these experiences of life are grace-filled moments, as we see by observing.

This is grace. Today itself is grace, the free gift and gifts of God. We cannot make this day happen, for it comes as a gift. We can place ourselves in the pathway of God's grace. We can look for the evidence of it. We can openly receive it. We can see a lot by observing, as Yogi said, but we cannot manufacture grace nor manipulate its presence. God, in God's most gracious manner, does not require anything from us for the grace of this day to come into our lives, just that we be aware and open, that we seek and then we will find (paraphrase of Matthew 7:7). Graciously wonderful days abound in life, and if one is truly open to their possibility, they can even be found in the midst of what may seem to be trials and tribulations. Grace is the profoundly wonderful blessing that is available to all simply because we are, and are in God's creation.

Grace upon grace is what we have received from the fullness of God's incarnation in Jesus Christ (John 1:16). Grace stacked up on top of more grace. Life itself is a grace-filled experience, as we seek what God is doing in the world. As we so gloriously sing Charles Wesley's most Methodist of hymns:

O for a thousand tongues to sing my great Redeemer's praise,
The glories of my God and King, the triumphs of his grace![4]

Grace can be triumphant. It is not so much a passive feeling of pleasant gifts from God as it is the active divine presence in the world. Grace is the very nature of God and of God's interaction with the world, human and natural. We observe this foundation of our faith so well-expressed in what may be the most widely known of scriptural verses:

"For God so loved the world that he gave his only Son, so that everyone who believes in him may not perish but may have eternal life. Indeed, God did not send the Son into the world to condemn the world, but in order that the world might be saved through him (John 3:16-17).

By grace God loves the whole world, and offers the world the divine presence through the incarnation of Christ, not to condemn but to save. This, then, is the foundation for our theology of mission: to point the peoples of the world toward the gracious free gift of love and acceptance in Jesus Christ, and for us, as the body of Christ, to live the reality of God's loving presence in the world. Christ, who as the Word was God (John 1:1) and came to live among us full of grace and truth (John 1:14), is the incarnation of this loving presence that is the basis of mission, for "God so loved the world." God loves the world so much that God has chosen to dwell among us that we all might perceive the glory of this grace-filled gift. God in Christ makes the divine dwelling here among us and we have received "grace upon grace" because of this missionary presence of God.

Grace is the fullness of God's presence, heaped upon us and all in the world. God loves the whole world, first and foremost, and to this world we are called to proclaim this loving grace in word and deed. Grace is everywhere visible if we but see by observing in our own lives. As the contemporary writer theologian Frederick Buechner states,

> I am thinking of grace. I am thinking of the power beyond all power, the power that holds all things in manifestation, and I am thinking of this power as ultimately a Christ-making power, which is to say a power that makes Christs, which is to say a power that works through the drab and hubbub of our lives to make Christs of us before we're done....[5]

The Need for Theology of Mission

The life of the church of Jesus Christ is not to be a mere human organization, but a divinely empowered instrument of God's grace, as St. Francis is said to have sung, "Lord make me an instrument of thy Peace..." and then follows with that well-known graceful prayer of self-giving love. We will miss the power and the life-giving purpose of Christian faith if we limit our arena of concern and knowledge to only those persons we live among or meet along our journey.

Grace is found in the body and blood of Christ, given in love for the whole world, all at once. To comprehend the fullness of John 3:16-17 we must seek to grasp the truth that the most important people are those we do not know and will likely never meet. They are all of those for whom Christ died and was raised to new life, not just ourselves and those we know and live among. This is grace upon grace, freely available to all. The global ministries of the church are the processes and methods by which we attempt to be with God in mission among all peoples and in all places at all times. To limit our field of ministry to a particular congregation or any geographic or thematic entity is to miss the limitless power of divinity that is incarnate in the world. Literally, we need to see the world through eyes of faith, observing all that God offers us in every time and place. We must live the truth of John 3:16-17, living for the whole world.

We, as United Methodists, do not have a clear and sound theology of mission when we think and act as if faith is a matter of our personal concern and the concerns of individuals we come in contact with. This often leads us to engage in what we call mission, but we do not understand why we do what we do. Too many congregations are in the world, but seem to fail to observe what is happening around them in the whole world. Our vision, our sight, is limited by our lack of observation.

To move the church to be the instrument of grace in the world we must consider what we believe about the world and God's Mission as the purpose of the church. We need to be clear about missiology, which is "the study of the church's mission especially with respect to missionary activity."[6] For the church to fully become God's instrument of grace in the world, whether locally, regionally, nationally, or internationally, we need to understand clearly and to state clearly our theology of mission.

Margaret Wheatley, and her colleague Myron Kellner-Rodgers, are secular business consultants who attempt to assist corporations with new understandings about human organizational theory. In a book entitled *A Simpler Way*, they write their observations that life itself is inherently organized, and the world about us—natural or human—will organize itself whether we do anything about it or not.

> We work from the premise that if we can know our beliefs, we can then
> act with greater consciousness about our behaviors…we have found that
> belief is the place from which true change originates.[7]

As Wheatley understands human life, it is only by knowing what we believe that we can change our actions. The world, it seems, will indeed seek organization if simply left alone. It may or may not be an organization that we would want or desire, but it will happen. Our task is to be observant about this natural organization, and to be creative in how we find meaning for life's activities in this, and how we seek to use and adapt it.

The organization of natural life is more like play than what we call work, and so also is the theological task. It is more organic and growth-oriented than mechanistic, that is, more like a plant or flower than a lawn mower. "This world of a simpler way has a natural and spontaneous tendency toward organization. It seeks order."[8] As stated in the Book of Genesis:

> In the beginning when God created the heavens and the earth, the earth was a formless void and darkness covered the face of the deep, while a wind from God swept over the face of the waters. Then God said, "Let there be light"; and there was light. And God saw that the light was good; and God separated the light from the darkness. God called the light Day, and the darkness he called Night. And there was evening and there was morning, the first day (Genesis 1:1-5).

Chaos, the formless void and churning waters of the deep, covered all that existed. Creation is the act of bringing order to this chaos, and thus organization occurs. Not in a mechanical or imposed way, but in a simpler, more organic and natural way. We call this natural way—the beginning of life—Creation. It grows and changes, coming forth from the Divine Creator, "in whom we live and move and have our being," as Paul quoted ancient Greek poets in Acts 17:28, to support the Christian theology of the one creator God as opposed to many gods. This simpler, creative approach to understanding human organizational behavior is thus not a pantheistic, secular notion of business techniques, but comes from orthodox Christian theology.

Organization is at the very heart of Christian theology, and our theology of mission. Yet, if we look at the vast variety of missional activities being carried out by congregations and individuals in The United Methodist Church, it certainly does not seem to be organized, or to have a theological focus. Rather, it looks to be a haphazard and chaotic understanding of what Christian mission is, and why we engage in all this work. Various church bodies are moving to and fro in disconnected activities, with little awareness of what each of the others is doing, and even less communication among them. There is little recognition of the ongoing work of mission of our denomination over the past two centuries, with the result that quite a few new "wheels" are being reinvented.

The reality is that Christians in general, and North American Christians in particular, have a tremendous record of engaging the world with mission strategies and methodologies. We get things done. We get things done almost everywhere, as Jesus summoned the disciples in Matthew 28:19 and Acts 1:8. However, when we face situations that confront our notions of how best to get this work done, or when we simply can't accomplish what we have chosen to "do," we tend to get frustrated, or angry, or lose enthusiasm for that great work we set out to do.

And difficult it will be. Materials for the building can't get from the major city up into the mountain village. It is seemingly impossible to obtain visas for our national mission partners to visit the United States with their wonderful stories of our cooperative work. Missionaries, overwhelmed by the tasks they face in a violent culture reeling from the negative effects of economic globalization, do not communicate frequently with their supporting congregations. The difficult situations are as many as the congregations of our denomination who are faithfully seeking to be in mission. Many lack a sound theology of mission to carry us through the difficult pathways of mission. However, as Margaret Wheatley understands from a similarly difficult corporate business arena, when we understand our beliefs we can more effectively change our behaviors.

Through the resource book you are reading, the General Board of Global Ministries seeks to invite mission leaders in our church to struggle with what God's Mission is in our day and in each of our congregations. Not just what we should do, but more importantly why it is we engage in all the great activities we organize for our churches.

Why mission? *What* is mission? *Where* and *when* is mission happening in our day? *Who* is called to engage in missional activity? *How* do we know what this mission is? These are the primary questions that this study will attempt to address, so that you may struggle with your understanding of mission, and then bring these into the life of your congregation, your district, and your annual conference.

The call of this book is not for an externally mechanistic approach to organizing mission work, but for an organic, growth-oriented, and creational understanding of *what* we "do" in mission, based upon *who* we "are," as the body of Christ called to advance the coming reign of God in all the world. Not as much a matter of *where*, but of *when*; and also knowing that mission is always carried out in the world by *who*, from a specific theological stance that describes *how* to so engage the world. We, all believers, are thus called to participate in the *missio Dei*—God's Mission in the world—as faithful witnesses to the fullness of God's grace.

Concepts to Consider

1. Why is theology the foundation of missional involvement?

2. How is it that you can love persons you do not know and will not meet?

3. What have you "observed" about mission by "seeing" with the eyes of faith?

Notes for ESSAY 1

[1] *United Methodist Hymnal* (Nashville, TN: United Methodist Publishing House, 1989), #378.

[2] Spoken on October 24, 1963 at the Savoy Hilton Hotel in New York City in a press conference that introduced Berra as the new baseball Yankee manager in 1963, succeeding Ralph Houk: "I've been with the Yankees 17 years, watching games and learning. You can see a lot by observing."

[3] Annie Dillard, *Pilgrim at Tinker Creek*, Bantam Books, 1st edition (New York: Random House Bantam, 1975), p. 10.

[4] *United Methodist Hymnal* (Nashville, TN: United Methodist Publishing House, 1989), #57.

[5] Frederick Buechner, *The Alphabet of Grace* (New York: The Seabury Press, 1970), p. 11.

[6] *Merriam-Webster Collegiate Dictionary*, 11th Edition, 2003.

[7] Margaret J. Wheatley and Myron Kellner-Rodgers, *A Simpler Way* (San Francisco: Berrett-Koehler, 1996), pp. 2-3.

[8] Ibid., p. 6.

ESSAY 2

What Is Mission? Missio Dei – *Mission Is God's Mission for the Coming Kingdom*

Matthew 6:10: "Your Kingdom come. Your will be done, on earth as it is in heaven."

Mark 1:14-15: "The time is fulfilled, and the kingdom of God has come near…"

Luke 17:20-21: "The kingdom of God is not coming with things that can be observed….For, in fact, the kingdom of God is among you."

Jesus prayed, "your will be done, on earth as it is in heaven." For, "the time is fulfilled, and the kingdom of God has come near…" And, "the kingdom of God is not coming with things that can be observed….For, in fact, the kingdom of God is among you." This is the *missio Dei*—mission is God's Mission, through which we participate in the coming reign of God.

Missio Dei

The 1910 World Conference on Mission and Evangelism in Edinburgh, Scotland was a watershed missiological event, which eventually produced not only the World Council of Churches and the major impetus for the 20th-century ecumenical movement, but also the progress toward the creation of missiology as an academic discipline within Christian seminaries. The great realization and call from this meeting was that the world *could* be evangelized for Christianity, and that Christians and churches could do this together.

The 20th century, however, lumbered forward through two world wars, the advent of nuclear weapons, the creation and dissolution of the Communist world, and the subsequent cultural domination by the United States of many other cultures, with some Muslim resentment of this fact. In this same time period, missiology and the church-sponsored activities of mission wandered from a triumphalistic and somewhat militaristic culture of missionary activity, on through the rise of "Two-Thirds-World" Christian churches (with the numeric and cultural erosion of Christian churches in the "North" and "West"), to a global-village sense of everyone as missionary, with mission being every-thing we do as Christians. But if mission is everything, what *is* mission?

The concept of *missio Dei*—the Mission of God, or God's Mission—came to the fore in the ecumenical world mission conferences of the 1950s and 1960s. It became the clear call to The United Methodist Church through the 1986 theology of mission statement of the General Board of Global Ministries, entitled "Partnership in God's Mission." It remains the most agreed-upon understanding of what mission is in the context of the church engaging the world with a missionary calling. Mission is not so much what we do as who we are. We are the church of Jesus Christ that participates in what God is doing in the world.

Karl Barth, the 20th-century German theologian speaking at a conference in 1932, may have been the first to refer to mission as an activity of God by the very nature of God. *Missio Dei* as a concept, while not the phrase itself, was first expressed at the Willingen conference of the International Missionary Council in 1952, albeit with some controversy. This arose from the shift in missional thinking from the Christendom-based understanding of the church, to a more universal view that Christian faith was being lived out throughout the whole earth. *Missio Dei* primarily refers to the purposes and activities of God in and for the whole world. God is in mission by virtue of the Incarnation of Christ, in that God sent the Son into the world (again, John 3:16). Thus the very nature of the church as the visible body of Christ in the world is to be in mission, as God in Christ is in mission.

> Those who are sought out, gathered together, and transformed by Christ are the Church. Their very existence, therefore, springs from God's sending forth of His son. In this sense "mission" belongs to the life of the Church....Whatever else ought to be said about the structure, life, and purpose of the Church, this one thing must be said: that "mission" is woven into all three and cannot be separated out from any one without destroying it. When God says to the Church, "Go forth and be my witness," [note: cf. Matthew 28, Acts 1:8] He is not giving the Church a commission that is added to its other duties; but a commission that belongs to its royal charter (covenant) to be the Church.[1]

The missional activities of the Church are an expression of the identity of the church, rather than simply a response to need or a desire to expand the church. The mission of the church is to participate in what God is already, and has always been, about in the world. This is the natural extension of the basic Christian theology of incarnation. God is preveniently present in the world (grace) through the Son, Jesus Christ, who proclaimed the kingdom/reign of

God in word and deed, and remains in the world by the power and presence of the Holy Spirit (cf: the General Board of Global Ministries' *Partnership in God's Mission* theology statement). Both the *missio Dei* and the kingdom are what God "does"—and the church is empowered by the Holy Spirit to participate in both, for God's Mission is the visible manifestation of the in-breaking kingdom of God, and is most clearly seen in Christ Jesus.

Philip Potter, noted missiologist and former general secretary of the World Council of Churches, in describing this understanding of mission as the *missio Dei*, puts it clearly before us, saying that, "Quite simply—and quite profoundly— what this phrase [*missio Dei*] means to assert is that *mission is God's, not ours*. This was stated in the same way by the International Missionary Council meeting in Ghana in 1958 ('The Christian world mission is Christ's, not ours')."[2]

Dr. Potter describes four significant consequences of this statement. First, he states that the church is not the center and goal of mission but rather the means and instrument of mission. We participate in what God is doing in God's world. We are servants of the Servant of the world, Jesus Christ. The church is not the kingdom, but as the late Lesslie Newbigin, a missionary bishop of the Church of South India and the most well-known 20th-century missiologist, also asserted, the church is a sign of that kingdom which is always breaking into the world in new and different ways.[3] Therefore, there is no one way, method, model, or strategy for calling attention to God's in-breaking reign.

Second, if God is so engaged with the world, we must be also. That is to be listening to the world's agenda and be in constant dialogue and interaction with the world about us, in order to be an authentic witness to God's Mission. Third, this means that the whole world, barring no nation or peoples, is the venue for mission. And last, in this engagement the church needs to be constantly renewed as we call the world to repentance and renewal. "Mission is not only concerned with the conversion of others, but with the conversion of God's people."[4]

The Church's Mission

The core of mission is, then, participation in the *missio Dei* rather than in any specific programs or activities. Church extension, helping people in need, and providing access to education or health-care are not mission. Church planting is a methodology of mission, not the point of mission. Volunteers in Mission are a methodological construct of the contemporary church, not the purpose of mission. Disaster response after hurricanes or floods, and the resettlement of political or economic refugees are all crucial and vital activities of the church of Jesus Christ, and all point toward the reality of the kingdom, but none of these are the heart, soul, and driving force of mission. It is the prevenient grace of God, expressed as *missio Dei*—God's Mission—which is the reason we engage in any of these activities as Christians.

J. Andrew Kirk, former professor at the School of Mission and World Christianity at the Selly Oak Colleges in Birmingham, United Kingdom, believes the problem is precisely this, that the church, or more appropriately local congregations in the church, do not understand what mission is:

> First, there is confusion over the nature of mission. For far too long in the Western world it has been perceived as something which is done overseas, in places where the Church is not yet established or perceived to be still in its youth. People still betray their thinking by talking about "going to the mission field", meaning somewhere else where the Gospel is needed. At best, mission is thought of as a vital *activity* of the Church, one among others; mission as the essential *being* of the Church has not yet been properly recognized.[5]

United Methodist Bishop Sudarshana Devadhar writes of this as the difference between *theocentric* and *ecclesiocentric* mission.[6] *Theocentric* mission is centered on God—*missio Dei*—and is a participation in the reign of God in our midst. *Ecclesiocentric* mission is concerned with expanding the organization of the church, often by undercutting or eliminating other religious groups, Christian as well as other faith communities. The former is about the quality of life and relationships with the divine experience for all. The latter is about numbers, of persons, buildings, and finances, as well as protecting all of these. *Theocentric* mission embraces all persons, and by invitation offers grace. "Offer them Christ," the words of John Wesley to Thomas Coke as he left for the Americas, is *theocentric* mission. *Ecclesiocentric* mission is about us and our self-experience of the activities. *Theocentric* mission is about God and selfless service of others, Christian or not.

Bishop Newbigin likewise understands "evangelism" and "proselytism" to be different activities; the former as a Christian call in God's Mission, while the latter is an effort to grow numbers for a group. As conversion is the work of the Holy Spirit, and not of human effort, our call is to proclaim the Gospel, in Word and Deed, without regard to church growth.[7] Or more simply, as is attributed to the Sri Lankan Methodist missiologist, D. T. Niles, "Evangelism is just one beggar telling another beggar where to find bread."

The *missio ecclesia*—Mission of the church—is to be in and for the world as an instrument of God's Mission, not as an end unto itself or for self-preservation, but to bear witness to the reign of God. The mission of the church is not God's Mission, but to participate in God's Mission. The agenda of the mission of the church must not be for itself, but be the agenda of *missio Dei*. Thus an understanding of *missio Dei*, which is our mission theology, is crucial as we continually seek to understand God's Mission in our day and in the changing world.

God's Mission is the ongoing expression of the actions of the Trinity in and for all of life. *Missio Dei* is love and grace under the reign of God, which, as Jesus stated, is "at hand"—within our grasp, yet not fully revealed (Matthew 4:17; Mark 1:15; Luke 17:20-21). The mission of the church is to center on announcing this reign of God as a present and future reality that is the "at-handedness" of the kingdom of God. It is all about living into the kingdom, which is a reality more than an activity or an action. Again, Bishop Newbigin states, "I have insisted that the Church's message is about the kingdom. The Church is called to be a sign, foretaste, and instrument of God's kingly rule."[8]

While our denominational mission statement, found in *The Book of Discipline*, is biblically and theologically on track, the problem with the phrase "making disciples for Jesus Christ" is our understanding of the source and origin of the "making." This is all right as long as we understand that we are the messengers of God's already-occurring actions far more than we are the actors or "doers" of God's Mission. All of our activities must proclaim the reality of God's coming kingdom that is, in fact, breaking into the world already through our very proclamation of this reality. Also, all of these proclamations, in word and deed, must exhibit the reality of God's reign that is described by Jesus in the Beatitudes (cf. Matthew 5:1-12).

The church must also never engage in an effort to simply be an outpost of the coming kingdom. We are to be authentically in the world, as God is incarnate in the world. Wilbert Shenk, a Reformed missiologist, suggests that, at best, a Christian culture is an ambiguous understanding from both biblical and historical grounds. He harkens to John Wesley, Soren Kierkegaard, Karl Barth, and H. Richard Niebuhr, who all sought to move the church away from the notion of creating a Christian world in which to live, as opposed to being Christian in the world. Identity for the church is not found in separateness, but in finding the reign of God through the lives of God's people everywhere. (Luke 17:21: "For, in fact, the kingdom of God is among you.") The church exists to serve the *missio Dei*, and has this as its essential purpose. Shenk believes, however, that the church of modern Western culture is living out of the bygone era of "Christendom," which was a church without a missional ethos, and now the church must be renewed in mission to be the authentic body of Christ. "The sole source for renewal of the church is the *missio Dei* as the basis for its life in relationship to the world."[9] Mission is God's Mission, *missio Dei*. It's about the reign of God, present now and yet to be revealed. "The time is fulfilled, and the kingdom of God has come near…" (Mark 1:15).

By our activities in mission we become the signposts of this coming reign of God. The Church in mission is always pointing toward what God has done and continues to do in the world, by leading persons to participate in this grace-filled life. That is, to engage in the *missio Dei*, God's Mission, is to connect the church as faithful witnesses to the reign of God that is constantly breaking into the world.

Concepts to Consider

1. What are church-centered mission activities and what are God-centered mission activities that you have encountered?
2. How is it different for you to think of mission as God's Mission rather than our activities?
3. Where have you experienced God's Mission "at hand," but beyond your grasp?

Notes for ESSAY 2

[1] From Willingen Conference, 1952, quoted by Thomas, *Classic Texts*, p. 241.

[2] Philip Potter, *Life In All Its Fullness* (Grand Rapids, MI: William B. Eerdmans, 1982), p. 71.

[3] Lesslie Newbigin, *A Word in Season* (Grand Rapids, MI: William B. Eerdmans, 1994), p. 44.

[4] Potter, op. cit., pp. 73-74.

[5] J. Andrew Kirk, *What Is Mission?* (Minneapolis: Fortress Press, 2000), p. 20.

[6] Sudarshana Devadhar, "A Religiously Pluralistic Society," in *Christian Mission in the Third Millennium*, Charles Cole, ed. (New York: General Board of Global Ministries, 2005), p. 159.

[7] Newbigin, op. cit., p. 45.

[8] Ibid., p. 44.

[9] Wilbert Shenk, *Write The Vision* (Valley Forge, PA: Trinity Press International, 1995), p. 32.

ESSAY 3

Where and When Is Mission?
From Missions to Mission

John 20:21-22: God sends Jesus, Jesus sends disciples; the connecting of mission.

Acts 10:34-35: All are acceptable to God.

"Jesus said to them again, 'Peace be with you. As the Father has sent me, so I send you.'" "Then Peter began to speak to them: 'I truly understand that God shows no partiality, but in every nation anyone who fears him and does what is right is acceptable to him.'"

We have gone from missions to mission, which we understand as the global ministries of the church—how we connect the whole church in God's Mission, sent into the entire world, which includes next door, for all are acceptable to God. You can't separate geography and timeframe in mission, thus the term "global ministries" involves both *where* and *when*.

All Are Acceptable to God

"What God has made clean, you must not call profane" (Acts 10:15).

"Then Peter began to speak to them: 'I truly understand that God shows no partiality, but in every nation anyone who fears him and does what is right is acceptable to him'" (Acts 10:34-35).

Luke's telling of how the Jerusalem church came to accept Gentile believers into the fold is perhaps the heart and soul of the Book of Acts. It was nothing less than a conversion experience for Peter and the other Jewish leadership of the fledgling church, as they moved from the theological understanding of the chosen status of the Hebraic people to the new vision of God's salutary grace freely given to all the world. This is the significant event that moves the church into mission mode.[1]

Peter, in a vision from God, comes to understand that there are no "unclean" persons, meaning that all people are acceptable to God and are to be included within the Christian community. This realization is not just one that moves the church to mission in other geographic realms, but also into the understanding that humanity is chosen by God, not a particular group, and as all persons are thus "chosen" by God, so too must the church proclaim the reign of God and all its benefits to all persons, in all situations, in all places. We are to engage in global ministries. "Mission is no longer thought of as the Church's activity overseas or in another culture. The mission frontier is not primarily a geographic one, but one of belief, conviction, and commitment."[2] Bishop Newbigin often commented on the "salt water myth" in mission, and consistently stated that mission is not necessarily a matter of crossing over an ocean, but it does mean crossing over to meet and serve the Other. Mission does not necessarily mean leaving one's own country, but it does mean entering into the Other's world, and sharing the Gospel in that context and within those persons' understandings of life and their worldview.

In fact, Newbigin asserts, the whole world is now Christian. There is no longer a "Christendom" from which mission work may be launched, as was understood at Edinburgh in 1910. The center from which we are called to move into mission is now worldwide.

> ...the whole base of mission is now in every country. This means we must move the Christian missionary enterprise out of the colonial era into a radically new situation....What is needed is the widespread and deep recovery throughout the churches, old and young alike, of the truth that to be a Christian is to be part of a universal fellowship in which all are committed to participation in Christ's reconciling work for the whole world. The traditional picture of the missionary enterprise has been of the lonely pioneer going out from the secure citadel of Christendom into the world of heathendom. Today the picture must be redrawn. It must be the picture of one universal family present in almost every land, possessing the secret of reconciliation to God through Jesus Christ and offering that secret to all nations and peoples.[3]

From Missions to Mission to Global Ministries

When most people think of the mission of the church they tend to think, either consciously or unconsciously, of geography. We go on mission, as earlier stated. The whole commentary on the early Church in the Book of Acts seems to be about going from here to there. "Where is mission?" is both a right question and a question filled with controversy in the church today. In fact the term itself is somewhat controversial. Very often in the church the term "missions" is used to refer to all that this book is concerned with. This term 'missions,' however, makes us think of this missional enterprise as a straight-line programmatic activity of a local congregation of the church. Conversely, the "mission" of the Church, as an extension or corollary to the *missio Dei*—God's Mission—is the way we become faithful witnesses to God's coming reign by connecting the Church (*koinonia*) to God's Mission.

This mission of the Church can most clearly be stated as the "global ministries" of the church. That is: engaging in a variety of whole body-of-Christ relationships within a variety of levels and pathways throughout the whole world, so that we are interconnected and interdependent within these interrelationships. The global ministries of the Church are the ongoing expressions of the reality of the reign of God breaking into our world, present and yet to be fulfilled in God's time (*kairos*). These expressions are a proclamation in word and deed across the human-made barriers of culture, which separate humanity from one another and therefore also from God, as we are all together created in God's image.

Global ministries is not just a nice name for a church agency, any more than is discipleship, higher education, or church and society. Global ministries is an understanding of the universal call to preach, teach, heal, free, and unify the whole world with the whole Gospel of Jesus Christ. Global ministries is connecting the church in mission, which is the Mission of God, *missio Dei*.

This connectional view of mission is stated by Jesus in John's Gospel, as he says, "As the Father has sent me, so I send you." When he had said this, he breathed on them and said to them, "Receive the Holy Spirit" (John 20:22). Global Ministries is this connecting concept, as the missionary God sends Jesus, who then sends the disciples, connecting the church in mission with and to the whole world.

Bishop Newbigin notes that for many in church leadership in the mid- to late-20th century there was a feeling that "the age of missions has ended."[4] This was a result of the realization of: 1) the end of Western colonial power and the rise of independent nations in the developing world; 2) the emergence of a global civilization (the global village concept) because of advanced technology in travel and communications; and 3) the explosive growth of Christianity in the "newer" churches that were begun out of the missionary enterprise of the 19th and 20th centuries, that now have autonomy of leadership and organization.

The age of missions has ended. We have gone through several decades of discussion, confusion, rancorous debate, and struggles concerning the most appropriate and effective strategies for global ministries. And that is the point. Missions, the plural use of the term, has to do with strategy and methodology.

The 21st century will be the call once more to participate in God's Mission, the *missio Dei*, through global ministries, rather than through humanly devised efforts to extend our ecclesiastical organizations.

Missions began to be an intentional "program" of the church because of what the Scottish missiologist, Andrew Walls, refers to as "the Great Maritime Migration."[5] Around the year 1500, persons began to move out from Europe to establish new homes—and political colonies—in many lands of the earth. This vast migration of peoples went on until the middle of the 20th century, when the migration began to happen in reverse. The Western world moved from a crusading model of mission—that of using the force of military power or economic reality—to that of the "foreign missionary" model. The high point of this missionary model was experienced at the World Missionary Conference held in Edinburgh, Scotland in 1910 (previously discussed in this study). This history-making conference, chaired by the great Methodist layman and mission statesman John R. Mott, was an attempt to bring together an ecumenical community whose goal was to Christianize the "heathen lands" within the century.

Thomas Thangaraj notes that nearly all of the persons at this great conference were either white European or American men, and also that persons engaged in missionary efforts within Europe or America were explicitly excluded.[6] Yet even as they met, there was a lingering notion that "Christendom" as a home base for spreading the Christian gospel to all nations was itself breaking apart. "The analysts of 1910, living in an age of seaborne communications, held a maritime view of the church and of the world. The carriers of the gospel crossed the seas in order to fulfill their task."[7] Even though the ecumenical organization that this conference called into being was in fact created, and resulted eventually in the formation of the World Council of Churches in 1948, two world wars and the rise of indigenous nation-states in the former colonies all led to a further realization that new understandings of mission were necessary. After many centuries of emigration, and then a new immigration from those colonized lands, much of Europe, as well as the United States, could be identified as post-Christian, while in the newer nations of the South the faith was growing exponentially.

This recognition fully came forth from the International Missionary Council at its world conference held in Willingen, Germany, in 1952 (also referred to previously in this study). This body, the predecessor to the World Council of Churches Division of World Mission and Evangelism, expresses that theological premise that mission is God's Mission—the *missio Dei*—which means that mission extends from God's sending of the Son, Jesus Christ, and the consequent sending of the disciples into all the world. Mission is what the Church is, more than what the Church does, so that mission that was once strictly a matter of geography had become more a matter of crossing cultures with the Gospel than of crossing salt water in a ship. "The map of the Christian Church, its demographic and cultural makeup, changed more dramatically during the 20th century than (probably) in any other since the first." [8]

Engaging in the "missions" of the church was no longer needed, or even helpful, with the newly emerging world of the late 20th century. To include all Christians in God's Mission meant that the Church must jettison its geographic strategies of taking the Gospel to new lands and among new peoples, and move forward with an inclusive "global ministries," using the grace-filled lives of Christians everywhere. The Church, as it engages in the *missio Dei*, will literally follow God around the world, identifying the divine activities already existing, and in so doing become that sign and instrument of God's in-breaking reign. The *where* of mission has to a great extent become the *when* of mission.

Newbigin makes three main observations concerning this changing reality of mission in the 21st century.[9] He notes that this has all come about, to a large extent, for three reasons. First, the loss of international political power in the Western nations due to the rise of nation-states in the South, bringing to the world stage more north/south struggles for political, economic, and social recognition. Second, the renaissance of other world religions such as Hinduism and Islam, with growing numbers of adherents and influence in the world changing how Western religious faith is viewed around the world. And, third, the rise of influence of the "younger" Christian churches because of their explosive numerical growth. These are the churches that came into being as a result of the missionary efforts of the 19th century, as well as those which are indigenous Christian movements.

In addition, the churches of the South and East having endured great persecution and hardship may best be fitted for the next centuries' Christian leadership in the world. "Theology is one area in which that leadership may be necessary. Theology is about making Christian decisions. It is the effort to think about faith in a Christian way." [10] As the churches of the developing world seek to understand their call and their identity, the theological task for mission seems to be at low ebb in the Western church. Andrew Walls candidly states:

> The Western theological academy is at present not well placed for leadership in the new situation. It has been too long immersed in its local

33

concerns and often unaware of the transformation that has taken place in the church....Its intellectual maps are pre-Columbian; there are vast areas of the Christian world of which they take no account.[11]

And so, not only has geography been made virtually irrelevant for the mission of the Church, the global nature of the 21st-century Church will call for a significant shift in understanding of where, and when, we are in mission.

The Third Church

As there is the Third World, so also there is the Third Church, with the explosive growth of Christianity in the developing world among both Western-established churches and indigenous Christian and neo-Christian communities. Roman Catholic missiologist Karl Muller, after listing the many statistics on the growth of both population and Christian adherence in developing nations, notes that it is not just a matter of numbers, but of a kind of new paradigm in mission. "Taking a closer look, however, we see that here we are dealing with a phenomenon that is more than a matter of statistics; an essential theological shift and change of emphasis is taking place."[12] It may well be the kind of paradigm shift akin to the experience of the early Church in Acts 10.

Not only is geography not a real issue any more, as previously stated, but the churches in the developing world are now missional churches, sending missionaries to countries other than their own. Bishop Newbigin believes that, "An increase in the foreign missionary activity of the younger churches will help to put the whole missionary enterprise into a more biblical perspective."[13] As the "young" church of the 1st century came to discover, so now the "young" churches of the 21st century are learning that to be a church in mission, both with their own land and beyond their boundaries, is the very nature of Christianity. And the "boundaries" are not just geographic, but situational.

A contemporary German Franciscan theologian, Walbert Bühlmann, writing in *The Coming of the Third Church*, first coined this term to describe the socio-religious reality of the newly developing church in the developing world.[14] He turns the socio-political conceptualization of First World, Second World, and Third World around a bit, by referring to the First Church as the Orthodox Churches in Eastern Europe and Asia (as they were still within the Communist sphere when his book was written); the Second Church as the Western Church, both Protestant and Roman Catholic of Europe and North America under the influence of capitalism; and then the Third Church as that of the Christian churches in the developing or Third World. "We are in the middle of a process of change as a result of which the Church, at home in the western world for almost 2,000 years will, in a short time, have shifted its centre of gravity into the Third World, where its adherents will be much more numerous."[15]

Fr. Bühlmann identifies several characteristics of this Third Church. First, there is a dynamism, or energy for the faith, just when it seems that the Church in the West seems to be slow, lethargic, and tired, from its association with secularism. Second, these churches are often being organized through base Christian communities, and other "grassroots" movements, which offer significant leadership to the laity. Third, they are in daily struggles with the world about them and across the globe, as they deal with economic, political, and social issues of injustice and oppression, to bring a vibrant and reality-based understanding of the Gospel. He would suggest that all three of these characteristics are mostly lacking within the older or more established churches of the West. It seems to be that these characteristics are also evident in the biblical account of the early Church in the Book of Acts. Thus Newbigin's observation is accurate, that this new reality in the *where* of mission is a return to our biblical heritage, and we now enter the era of the *when* of mission. "When" is the appropriate time for a particular activity to begin, and "when" does it need to be involved? "When" do we end a program and "when" do we move forth into new endeavors? *Kairos*— God's timing—is the missional motivation in the 21st century, rather than a geographic cure for our identity-challenged Western Church. The *Koinonia*— community and fellowship of the Church—lives and moves and "has being" within the *Kairos* of the coming reign of God. For the European and North American Church this is a significant change in our thinking, which will continue to cause us to reevaluate our mission organizations, strategies, and methodologies for engaging in the *missio Dei*.

Concepts to Consider

1. Where have you seen global ministries happening in time?
2. When have you been aware of a place of mission?
3. What does it mean that the newly developing Third Church is numerically becoming the majority church worldwide?

Notes for ESSAY 3

[1] For a more complete analysis of this, see Charles E. Van Engen, "Peter's Conversion," in Robert L. Gallagher and Paul Hertig, eds. *Mission in Acts: Ancient Narratives in Contemporary Context*, American Society of Missiology Series (Maryknoll, NY: Orbis Books, 2004), p. 133ff.

[2] Kirk, op. cit., p. 24.

[3] Lesslie Newbigin, *A Word in Season* (Grand Rapids, MI: William B. Eerdmans, 1994), pp. 12-13.

[4] Lesslie Newbigin, *The Mission and Unity of the Church*, published lectures (Grahamstown, South Africa: Rhodes University, 1960), p. 7.

[5] Andrew Walls, in Stephen W. Gunter, and Elaine A. Robinson, eds. *Considering The Great Commission* (Nashville: Abingdon Press, 2005), pp. 7-8.

[6] M. Thomas Thangaraj, *The Common Task* (Nashville: Abingdon, 1999), pp. 12-13.

[7] Walls, op. cit., p. 12.

[8] Ibid., pp. 14-15.

[9] Newbigin, *A Word in Season*, op. cit., pp. 7-11.

[10] Walls, op. cit., p. 18.

[11] Ibid., p. 19.

[12] Karl Muller, *Mission Theology: An Introduction* (Nettetal, Germany: Steyler Verlag—Wort und Werk, 1987, distributed in the US by Divine Word Seminary, Techny, IL), p. 177.

[13] Newbigin, *A Word in Season*, op. cit., pp. 12-13.

[14] Walbert Bühlmann, *The Coming of the Third Church* (Slough, England: St Paul Publications, 1976, also published under same title by Orbis Books, Maryknoll, NY, 1978).

[15] Ibid., p. 20.

ESSAY 4

Who Is Mission? Our Call, Journey, and Incarnation in the Global Ministries of the Church

Isaiah 6:1-8: "Here I am, send me," and 43:1-2: Called you by name.

Luke 9:23-27: Pick up your Cross and follow.

2 Corinthians 4:7: Treasure in earthen vessels/common clay pots.

John 1:1 and 14: "And the Word became flesh and lived among us."

"Whom shall I send, and who will go for us?" And I said, "Here am I; send me!" And he said, "Go...." Mission is not a "vacation" from reality, but rather a vocational call to serve as Christ's representative in the world. Your call to global ministries, and the calling of the whole Church, is a theology of incarnational mission; mission as the way of Christ.

Here I Am, Send Me

Mission is about going from here to there, even if the here and the there have changed in this age from a geographic notion to thematic missional realities in our day. It is no longer about the "saltwater myth," as missiologist David Bosch states,[1] and yet there is still the basic foundation that to be engaged in the *missio Dei* is a call to get up and *go*. When Isaiah had that terrible and wonderful encounter with the Lord in the Temple, and responded affirmatively to God's call to be sent, God then said...*go*.

Previously we have discussed the *where* of mission, and that *where* has many interesting locations, some of which are human situations more than geographic locations, and are in a sense more a matter of *when* than *where*. But to get to any situation or location or timely event, someone must go. "Who will go for us?" God asks in a most pleading and inquisitive tone. Are you ready to go? Are you prepared to be in mission? Mission, in which we tend to focus on the why, what, how, and where, is mostly about *who*. And you are the who! Mission always comes down to your response to God's call to the *missio Dei*. God will be in mission because God is, by nature, mission. God created the world and continues to be totally involved in the world, even to the point of sending God's only Son for the sake of the whole world (cf. John 3:16-17). As missiologist Dr. Philip Potter wrote, "The God of the Bible is a missionary God, a God who sends.

God sent Abraham and Sarah. God sent Moses and Miriam. God sent Jesus and the Holy Spirit. God sent the Apostles through the power of the Son and the Spirit. God so loved the world he *sent* his only Son...."[2] It is always someone who is sent, someone who goes.

Here I am, Lord. Is it I, Lord? I have heard you calling in the night.
I will go, Lord, if you lead me. I will hold your people in my heart.

Call

Going for God in mission is a matter of hearing the call to participate in the *missio Dei* through a lifelong journey as a faithful witness to the living Lord Jesus Christ. The preacher and author Frederick Buechner is best known for his profound commitment to hearing God speak to each of us through our very lives, and calling us to awareness as faithful witnesses to life itself:

Listen to your life. See it for the fathomable mystery that it is. In the boredom and pain of it no less than the excitement and gladness: touch, taste, smell your way to the Holy and hidden heart of it because in the last analysis all moments are key moments and life itself is Grace.[3]

As mission is more than anything else an expression of the grace of God, so it is in our life that we experience and understand that grace. We hear the call to proclaim this grace and to live it out among all peoples within our lives. God calls each of us by name and claims us as the conduits of the *missio Dei* (Isaiah 43:1: "Do not fear, for I have redeemed you; I have called you by name, you are mine"). In understanding this call as movement, Buechner suggests that we are to go where we most need to go, and to go where we are most needed.[4] The call to mission is this combined comprehension of both our grace-filled heart's desire, and of what most needs to be done in the world. Neither alone will be the fulfillment of the *missio Dei*. It is in the convergence of who we are as persons created in God's image, as well as the universal yet specifically local needs of God's world, through which we fully participate in what God is about in this world. These together constitute our call to mission.

Clara Biswas is a United Methodist missionary serving in Cambodia, but is originally from Bangladesh. She served in the slums of her homeland for many years before she was offered the opportunity to become an international missionary, first in Japan and then in Cambodia. She remembers her reluctance to go, because she felt she was not theologically trained, and because she always thought that missionaries came from the Western world, not a developing nation. She said to herself, "I'm a simple person who works with the poorest, low caste, 'untouchable' people. What can I do as a missionary?"

But as she studied the Scriptures concerning God's call of Moses and Isaiah, she heard the call of God in her life in Bangladesh, and responded "Here am I, Send me." She now ministers among the children of Phnom Penh, in a program called "Light at the Dump Sites." The dumpsite is a place that many people, including children, pick over the trash for things to sell in order to survive for their daily living. As a missionary in the newly developed United Methodist Mission in Cambodia, Clara seeks to bring some light to the lives of these children as she helps them to learn English, gospel stories, gospel songs, and other activities such as games. In the midst of her life she understood both her need to go in service to others, and the profound need of these children; to go where she most needed to go and where she was most needed. This is the call to God's Mission that we must hear through our lives and the life of the church. As a professional educator she is offering a helping hand and a loving life to children living in Phnom Penh City's garbage dump. Clara brings educational programs and modest nutritional supplements, with Gospel singing, stories, and games. She also visits, in hospitals and homes, those who have the AIDS virus, and those who care for them.

She says of all this, "Walking into the narrow, muddy and filthy alleys, one easily observes people who have fallen into the cracks of helplessness and misery. A few, surely, are able to swim out to the shore. Realities, though, depict many who are sinking and waiting to be touched and reached physically, emotionally, ...spiritually, the children particularly."

Clara also discovered the reality of what the prophet Isaiah assures us—that while acting on this call to "go" may be very difficult personally, as God's messengers and ambassadors of the *missio Dei*, we will be cared for along the way. The prophet proclaims, "When you pass through the waters, I will be with you; and through the rivers, they shall not overwhelm you; when you walk through fire you shall not be burned, and the flame shall not consume you" (Isaiah 43:2). Whatever life throws at you as you follow God in mission, you will be guided and protected from the swirling rivers and the blazing fire. Clara thrives in the dump of Phnom Penh, as she brings light to the little ones of the Lord.

The voice of God is calling its summons in our day;
Isaiah heard in Zion, and we now hear God say:
"Whom shall I send to succor my people in their need?
Whom shall I send to loosen the bonds of shame and greed?"[5]

Journey

"Then he said to them all, "If any want to become my followers, let them deny themselves and take up their cross daily and follow me" (Luke 9:23).

This personal call to "go" is a journey throughout a lifetime. Yet it is not a *vacation* from our daily living, but a *vocation* as a servant of Christ. Mission must not be seen as just a trip or a program or activity within the life of your congregation, but rather a wholly holy, holistic identity as the body of Christ. Mission is a daily walk as one who comprehends oneself as living in the world for the sake of the whole world, regardless of your daily activities. The Book of Acts, the mission history of the early Church, has journey as a central motif.[6] The disciples move out from Jerusalem to Samaria to the Hellenistic world of Asia Minor, and on to Rome and beyond. While they move geographically they also move out in ever-widening circles from the Jewish community to God-fearing Gentiles to secular Greeks and Romans, including within the church all persons—male and female, slave and free, persons with handicapping conditions, and the wealthy and powerful.

Mission is being on a journey of faith, going from here to there each day ("jour," the Anglo-French root of journey, means "the day"). How far can one go in a day? That is a practical and spiritual question to answer. How will you spend your time during the day? Just going from here to there? Or engaged in God's movement and in God's time for that day?

Jesus stated to the disciples that to follow him means to pick up the cross and go (Luke 9:23). This surely is a sacrifice, but it also means to participate in movement, to be on a journey. It was suggested by the Rev. J. Alexander Findlay, a British Methodist pastor of the early 20th century, and quoted by the noted Methodist missiologist, D. T. Niles, that among the nomadic peoples of the Middle East, the Greek word, *stauros* (used in Luke 9:23, as well as Mark 8:34, 10:21, and Matthew 10:38, 16:24), which is translated as "cross" in the New Testament, could mean simply a stick upright in the ground.[7] While *stauros* did refer to the cross of crucifixion, it could also be meant to describe a tent peg. When the nomadic tribal leader gave orders to move the community, he would say, "pick up the cross (tent peg) and follow me." To pick up the cross is a matter of sacrifice, but it is also a matter of moving on in a journey. God is calling us to get up and go, to move the tents of our lives and be prepared to follow Christ into other places, ideas, and concepts of mission.

Picking up your cross or your tent pegs in life, and going on this missional journey is not always a matter of either going where you want to go, or even knowing where you are going. As the writer to the Hebrews stated, Abraham went on mission not knowing where God was sending him: "By faith Abraham obeyed when he was called to set out for a place that he was to receive as an inheritance; and he set out, not knowing where he was going" (Hebrews 11:8). We journey to places and situations because of the need, as God speaks that need, not necessarily because of our own wishes and desires. Our desire is to faithfully serve, to bloom not only where we are planted but also where we are transplanted to. The Psalmist says, "For I am your passing guest, an alien, like all my forebears" (Psalm 39:12). We journey on in mission, following Christ into the changing needs of the world, and into places that God calls the Church to proclaim the coming reign of God, for we are called to be Christ in this world.

Incarnation

"In the beginning was the Word and the Word was with God and the Word was God....And the Word became flesh and lived among us" (John 1:1 and 14).

Just as "the Word became flesh and lived among us" (John 1:14) tells of the incarnation of the creator God as one of our own in this world, so too, as we journey on the missional call we also are sent into the world. Our call and participation in mission is the visible witness to the Incarnation. The term "Christian" was originally meant as a derisive label for one who follows that Jewish teacher who was crucified by the Romans, the one who was a radical rabble-rouser. To be Christian is to be like Christ. To be in mission is to be living in the way of Christ. "God's mission does not come from doing a host of activities, but rather from a prayerful relationship through the empowering of his Spirit. In simpler terms, mission flows from being rather than doing."[8]

If we "are" in mission, being rather than doing, then what is it that makes us the missionary presence of the missionary God? Are we not the same persons as all persons, created in the image of God? Yes, in fact Paul wrote to the Corinthian church to remind them that we are all just humans, and nothing special without God's prevenient grace. "But we have this treasure in clay jars, so that it may be made clear that this extraordinary power belongs to God and does not come from us" (2 Corinthians 4:7). Other translations refer to these as being treasure in earthen vessels, or common clay pots. We are nothing particularly special, though called of God to be in mission. Rather it is the Holy Spirit moving among us as a common connectional people that allows the common clay pots that we are to hold the sacred treasure of the gospel. Dag Hammarskjöld wrote, "I am the vessel. The draught [the drink or the measure of the drink] is God's. And God is the thirsty one."[9] God fills us up, and then quenches the divine thirst for life as we go forth as Christ in mission.

Bishop Newbigin affirms this in that we are called to be in mission in Christ's Way.[10] Because the reign of God is revealed and yet hidden, God uses the community of faith to proclaim the reality of this reign to the world. It is precisely on the hill of Calvary that God's kingdom is most fully revealed in all its hiddenness. The crucifixion of Jesus was not overcome by the Resurrection. Rather the Resurrection proclaimed the victory that *is* the Cross. After 40 days of continued study and reflection, the resurrected Christ gathered the believers, the disciples, on the Mount of the Ascension to be sent out as witnesses of this reality (Acts 1). And so we continue in this great ongoing mission through which we are called to journey into all the world as the visible incarnation of our missionary God. Mission is the faithful witness to the victory of God's reign over all that would enslave, oppress, and prevent life in all its fullness from happening in God's created order. We are the common clay pots whom God fills by the power of the Holy Spirit, to be in mission through the inclusive and ever-present global ministries of the Church.

Concepts to Consider

1. When have you picked up your tent peg in response to God's missional call?
2. How can you assist others to hear God's call to missional involvement?
3. Who are you, as a common clay pot from which God's thirst is quenched?

Notes for ESSAY 4

[1] David J. Bosch, *Transforming Mission, Paradigm Shifts in Theology of Mission* (Maryknoll, NY: Orbis Books, 1991) p. 10.

[2] Potter, op. cit., p. 71.

[3] Frederick Buechner, *Now and Then* (San Francisco: Harper & Row, 1983), p. 87.

[4] Frederick Buechner, *Secrets in the Dark* (San Francisco: HarperCollins, 2006), pp. 39-40.

[5] John Hynes Holmes, *The Voice of God is Calling*, in *The United Methodist Hymnal* (Nashville: The United Methodist Publishing House, 1989), p. 436.

[6] For a more complete analysis of this, see Robert L. Gallagher and Paul Hertig, eds., *Mission in Acts*, op. cit., pp. 12-13.

[7] Quoted by D. T. Niles in *Upon the Earth: The Mission of God and the Missionary Enterprise of the Churches*, Foundations of the Christian Mission, Studies in the Gospel and the World (New York: McGraw-Hill Book Co., 1962), pp. 77-78; taken from J. Alexander Findlay, *A Portrait of Peter* (New York: Abingdon, 1935), p. 130.

[8] Gallagher and Hertig, eds., *Mission in Acts*, op. cit., p. 45.

[9] Dag Hammarskjöld, *Markings* (London: Faber and Faber, 1964, translation by W. H. Auden and Leif Sjoberg, for Alfred A. Knopf, Inc.), p. 88.

[10] Lesslie Newbigin, *Mission in Christ's Way* (New York: Friendship Press, 1987), p. 6.

ESSAY 5

How Do We Understand Mission?
"Doing" Theology

Deuteronomy 18:18: A prophet speaking God's words among the people.

Psalm 119:33-34: Teach us, O Lord.

Mark 1:21-28 (Luke 4:31): Teaching as one having authority.

"They were astounded at [Jesus'] teaching, for he taught them as one having authority, and not as the scribes." Christian theology is not just made-up ideas; there are specific sources for us to use in checking the reality of any response to life. The question of theological authority is a real issue for the Church, and we do have real sources of theological authority for use in checking the reality of any response to life.

Sources of Theology; Authority in Faith

It was a dark and stormy night, as the captain was called to the bridge of the mighty ship. It had all the latest marine technology, yet the officers on deck felt a little uneasy about their exact position, so that the first mate called the captain because the light of what seemed to be another vessel was bearing down upon them directly off the bow. Standard radio communication brought no response from that light ahead, so the captain ordered a signalman to flash a message with the Morse Code light: "This is Captain Wainwright of Her Majesty's Navy. Redirect your course 15 degrees west. The answer came back: "This is Sailor First Class Perkins of the US Coast Guard. Redirect your course 15 degrees east."

Somewhat disturbed by being ordered around by a sailor, the captain sent back: "I command Her Majesty's Ship Portsmouth, a ship of the line. Redirect your course." To which the sailor replied: "I am in charge of this lighthouse. You'd better redirect your course."

Some folks think they have authority in almost any situation, but authority really derives from facts and reality more than your status or place in the world. There is so much information available in the world today, and so many voices calling to us, that determining real authoritative answers is not all that easy, or obvious. I think of the tabloid newspapers in the supermarket check-out lines, with headlines that read: "I sold my baby to UFO aliens," or "Man has world's first head transplant." Many folks think that if it's in print, it must be true. Not so.

Theological issues are no different. There are many interesting notions floating around about what God would have us know. Some of these just keep floating around because we don't take time to seek out the source and authority of the idea.

For example, what is the root of all evil? Money? Not true. The Scripture says, in 1 Timothy 6:10, that the love of money is the root of all kinds of evil. How about Samson? Who cut off his hair? Delilah? Not on your life. Judges 16:19 states that Delilah called another man to come and shave Samson's locks.

Now these may seem picky issues, but they point to the understanding that authority, particularly theological authority, comes not from mere information, or simple knowledge about a subject, but from an intimate connection with the ultimate reality of the Divine, which is based in serious communal prayer, spiritual formation, and study. Paul reminds us in 1 Corinthians 8:1 that, "Knowledge puffs up, but love builds up." He could have said, a little information is a dangerous thing! To really know about God is to be known by God through God's gracious love and our constant connections in worship, prayer, and communal study. Jesus, as Mark's Gospel records in chapter one and the other Synoptics, was recognized as one who taught with authority, not because of special knowledge or information, but because it was clear that he was connected to God. It states there that the people were amazed because Jesus taught with authority and he commanded even the unclean spirits. Jesus had the authority of God, the authority of a prophet, as described in Deuteronomy 18. As this first account of Jesus' ministry also shows us, it was the demons that immediately recognized this authority and they responded to his command to depart from those that they afflicted, calling Jesus as they did so: "The Holy One of God."

Evil listened to Jesus. Evil fled at the command of Jesus. Evil feared Jesus. Why? The word for authority that is used twice in this Gospel text is the Greek word *exousia* (ex-oo-see'-ah), which literally translated means "out of being." Truth, and the authority of it, comes from someone who speaks out of his/her own divinely created being. Truth comes through authentic personhood, which is our created "being" in the image of God. Paul Tillich, the 20th-century theologian, wrote of God as "being itself" or the "Ground of Being," meaning the ultimate personhood or created being from which we all come. Thus, it is from our connection with this divine personhood that we grasp the truth of the Gospel, for mission and all of church life.

We in our day must not accept the tyranny of mere information, but look to real sources for real truth to understand what life is all about. This is not a matter of personal opinion, or what you like or don't like. Theological authority comes through very specific forms of revelation from God, and our seeking to connect in our very being with this revelation.

The Need for a Theology of Mission

The great early-20th-century ecumenical mission conferences were marked by western Protestant denominational leaders gathering to discuss how to best welcome the non-Christian "lands" of the world into the fold. What has come to be called the 1910 Edinburgh Conference, and which ultimately gave birth to the international ecumenical movement and the World Council of Churches, dealt with strategies and methodologies, but this great meeting did not make a clear statement about what mission is, or even suggest a theological rationale for engaging in the strategies which were discussed. This is because the need for mission was presumed to be understood, at least from a minimal biblical call found in "The Great Commission" (Matthew 28:19-20). Thomas Thangaraj states that: "The conversation at Edinburgh was seen primarily as an intra-ecclesial one,"[1] meaning that the church leadership was simply talking to other church leaders about what it should be up to on "the mission field." There have since been a dozen more of these worldwide mission conferences, with increasing involvement of persons from all over the world (truly "ecumenical," from the Greek word, meaning the whole of the inhabited world) and both genders, as well as young adults. There has also been an increasing awareness of the need to think and rethink a theology of mission that speaks not only to the churches of the world, but also to the world about us, concerning the Gospel's call to mission.

All the programs of the General Board of Global Ministries do not arise out of personal notions or even simply good ideas. Rather, using missional theology, Global Ministries has four program goals which together express the United Methodist understanding of God's Mission in and for the world. The theology that these program goals stand upon is the result of "doing" theology in the Wesleyan spirit.

What are the foundations for these missional understandings? One of the greatest contributions to the wider Christian Church from the Methodist tradition is the Wesleyan understanding of foundations, or sources, of theology— which in *The Book of Discipline* are stated as: Scripture, Tradition, Experience, and Reason. This understanding of the sources of the Church's theology has been in our *Book of Discipline* since 1972, and is referred to as "Our Theological Task." The renowned 20th-century missiologist, Bishop Lesslie Newbigin, who happens to have been from the Reformed tradition, writes about these sources as being a very sound foundation and methodology of mission theology.[2]

Scripture—the first, foremost, and beginning of all Christian theology is the written/spoken form of God's Word. These are not the "words" of God, like some kind of journalistic transcript. Rather, the Bible is the humanly recorded account of God's interaction with God's people down through the ages. The Bible contains the Word of God, which is the whole and true message for all of life at all times. Yet because it comes through people from a wide variety of times and cultures it must be constantly studied as a whole and reflected upon by a community in order to bring out the meaning for us today, not simply read in isolation. That is why the Bible is not the only source for theological understanding. And so to understand the Scriptures we must add:

Tradition—God working through the faithful of all ages. The Church is several thousands of years old, going back to the gathering of the Hebraic people in worship of the one God. The Lord has spoken through the prophets, as is stated in Deuteronomy 18, and God will continue to raise up prophets who proclaim the Word. The traditions of the Church through the ages help us to understand how the precepts of the Scriptures have been applied in the past. We are not the first to believe, nor the last. We stand upon the shoulders of all who have gone before us, in all churches around the world. And believe it or not, others will stand upon our shoulders! Thus, we need to be aware of our own:

Experience—which is God speaking through our individual lives and our common life. Each of us is a conduit for God's truth, if we will pay attention to what God is saying to us. Theology has always had a strong autobiographical note. We must pause and reflect upon what is happening to us, in relation to the Bible and what others of the community of faith are saying, now and in past times. You do not determine theological truth as individuals, but our lives are as much a revelation from God as with any person. But to fully understand this, as well as Scripture and Tradition, we must use the most uniquely human faculty with which God has endowed us, namely:

Reason—for this is what ties the four sources of theology together. God has created us with minds, to search, question, analyze, and reflect upon God's Word. Theological reasoning is not always the same as the reasoning of the secular world. That is because the secular world only believes a very small amount of the reality that God presents to us. As Blaise Pascal, the French

Christian philosopher of the 17th century, wrote, "The heart has reasons that reason does not know of" (from his collected writings entitled, *Pensées, 1669*). Yet with this, all theological truth comes through reasoning with our sisters and brothers in constant dialogue and inquiry.

Contextual Theologies and Pluralism

In a world of contending ideologies and faiths, we are called to be enlightened, faithful, and obedient witnesses in word and deed to the revelation of God in Christ, which we have received through Scripture, formed into tradition, mediated by experience, and examined through reason. There is authority for us to rely upon in understanding life and our place in God's creation. These are the sources for comprehending what God's Mission is in our day. Theological truth is very real and knowable, though it is necessary to constantly seek and search for the truth in our ever-changing lives and the world about us.

Karl Muller, a German Roman Catholic theologian, identifies the five basic elements of mission theology as: 1) being based upon the Trinitarian understanding of the nature of God; 2) concerning itself with God's salvation; 3) from within a faith community; 4) while moving into the whole world; 5) among those who have not heard nor heeded the Gospel.[3] These elements, when derived from using the Methodist understanding of the sources of theology, form the foundation for us to *be* in mission as the body of Christ.

To comprehend how we are to be in mission we, as the Church, must engage in the task of discovering anew our theology of mission, based on the recent century's missiological conversations concerning *missio Dei*. Professor Kirk, formerly at the School of Mission and World Christianity of the Selly Oak Colleges in Birmingham, UK, affirms that to be the fully missional Church we are called and created to be, we must be clear about our theological understandings.

> Theology of mission acts, then, as a means of "validating, correcting and establishing on better foundations" the motives and actions of those wanting to be part of the answer to the prayer "Your kingdom come, your will be done on earth as in heaven" (Matthew 6:10).[4]

Using these sources and foundations for theology, so well described as Our Theological Task in *The Book of Discipline*, we can move into our theology of mission. In this book we seek to comprehend the *missio Dei* using the United Methodist Theological Task (sources of theology), in concert with the Four Program Goals of the General Board of Global Ministries to observe how our denomination lives into a sound mission theology through its ongoing global ministries. We will work in each of the four sources of theology from the perspective of each of the Four Program Goals, using contemporary examples of how this theology is being witnessed to in the lives of God's people "in Jerusalem, Judea and Samaria, and to the ends of the earth" (Acts 1:8).

God's Word never changes, even though we do and the world about us does. We live in a new mission age, the age of the global ministries of the whole Church moving into the whole world. And so we are all, each and every one of us, called to be theologians, in conversation and dialogue with all people of faith, using these foundational sources of theology to determine the paths we need to take through life and into a clear understanding of God's Mission in our day. We have this on very good authority from Jesus the Christ, the offspring of God and Savior of the World.

[Note: For the full and complete statement of Our Theological Task, read the entirety of ¶104 in *The Book of Discipline of The United Methodist Church.*]

Concepts to Consider

1. How is theology personal opinion, or a divinely revealed science, or…?
2. Where have you seen the Theological Task at work in your life?
3. What would a mission education program in the church, based on a theology of mission, look like?

Notes for ESSAY 5

[1] Thomas Thangaraj, *The Common Task* (Nashville: Abingdon, 1999), p. 14.

[2] Lesslie Newbigin, *A Word in Season* (Grand Rapids, MI: William B. Eerdmans, 1994), p. 80ff.

[3] Karl Muller, *Mission Theology: An Introduction* (Nettetal, Germany: Steyler Verlag – Wort und Werk, 1987, distributed in US by Divine Word Seminary, Techny, IL), p. 46ff.

[4] J. Andrew Kirk, *What Is Mission?* (Minneapolis: Fortress Press, 2000), p. 21.

CHAPTER TWO

SCRIPTURE

The United Methodist Theological Task states that Scripture is primary, meaning that it contains the core of our living faith and is our beginning point for all theological inquiry. In this chapter we have some of the most revelatory calls to engage in God's Mission found in Scripture, each one viewed through the lens of Global Ministries' Four Mission Goals. We are looking for the primary beginning places for our comprehensive approach to the global ministries of the church.

ESSAY 6: *On Fire In Mission: Witnessing Is Discipleship Is Witnessing*

Scripture understood through Mission Goal 1:
To Make Disciples of Jesus Christ

Goal 1: Making Disciples of Jesus Christ

Acts 1:6-8: Making disciples by being witnesses.

Luke 24:49: Faithful Witnesses.

To be in mission as witnesses is the scriptural call of the global ministries of the church. Participation in God's Mission is a matter of being faithful witnesses to what God is doing in our midst by pointing toward the coming Kingdom, and to make disciples by being disciples.

ESSAY 7: *In Deep Water Fishing for Other Fish: Mission as Leadership Development*

Scripture understood through Mission Goal 2:
To Strengthen, Develop, and Renew Christian Community

Isaiah 43:1-2: I have called you by name.

Luke 5:1-11: Do not be afraid; from now on you will be catching people.

Leadership development is presenting the call to mission service and sending. Just as the disciples were called into mission, we have continued in this call as we develop mission leaders throughout the world, and thereby strengthen, develop, and renew Christian community.

ESSAY 8: *Why We Care: Humanitarian Needs, Theological Answers*

Scripture understood through Mission Goal 3:
To Alleviate Human Suffering

Matthew 25:31-46: Serving the least is serving God.

Mark 9:40-41: The cup of cool water is rewarded.

To understand the spirituality of bread is to grasp the theological basis of mission that to serve the least and the last, those in need in this world who are members of God's family, we are caring for the physical needs of God's people as we would care for Christ himself.

ESSAY 9: *Going Into the Spokes of the Wheel:*
Eliminating Barriers to the Kingdom

Scripture understood through Mission Goal 4:
To Seek Justice, Freedom, and Peace

Isaiah 40:3-5/Luke 3:1-6; Isaiah 58: 6-12: Filling in valleys and lifting yokes of burden from oppressed persons.

Amos 5:21-24; Acts 16:16-24: Justice flowing like waters, as leaders insert their lives to protect others.

Personal sacrifice may be needed in God's Mission to eliminate the barriers to God's Kingdom of justice, freedom, and peace, by being an inclusive Church, and seeking to break down barriers and walls, fill in the valleys and bring down the mountains, building a straight highway for our God.

ESSAY 6

On Fire In Mission:
Witnessing Is *Discipleship* Is *Witnessing*

Scripture understood through Mission Goal 1:
To Make Disciples of Jesus Christ

Acts 1:6-8: Making Disciples by Being Witnesses;
Luke 24:49: Faithful Witnesses

To be in mission as faithful witnesses is the scriptural call to the global ministries of the church. Participation in God's Mission is a matter of being witnesses to what God is doing in our midst, by pointing toward the coming kingdom and making disciples by being disciples.

Being Witnesses Everywhere

The dramatic events that we now call Holy Week were past. For 40 days (that long time in biblical illusion) the tiny community had again walked and talked along the road and in the Upper Room with his amazing presence. They sensed the dramatic climax to these events, as now they all were gathered together on the Mount for what would seem to be a bon voyage party. Jesus was leaving to return to the heavenly Father. Last words were appropriate. But what the disciples said was enough to make Jesus' heart sink. "Lord, is this the time when you will restore the kingdom to Israel?" Had the disciples gone back to square one and not heard anything Jesus had said in three years and then an extra 40 days? The disciples asked about the kingdom, and so one last time Jesus stated the essence of God's missional call upon the newly created church, meaning the disciples gathered in community:

> He replied, "It is not for you to know the times or periods that the Father has set by his own authority. But you will receive power when the Holy Spirit has come upon you; and you will be my witnesses in Jerusalem, in all Judea and Samaria, and to the ends of the earth" (Acts 1:7-8).

Jesus tells the disciples that the kingdom will happen in God's time, and now they are the agents and messengers of this coming reign. *How?* By the divine source of power and motivation that is the Holy Spirit. *What?* The life-long activity and responsibility of witnessing to all that they had seen, heard, and lived. *Where?* Crossing boundaries—locally, nationally, and globally—all at once. It's all about the kingdom!

We do not need to know everything from God, because the truth is God will do whatever God will do, and doesn't need to consult us. Rather, we need to be constantly consulting God by observing much so that we can see what God is doing in the world. Then, empowered by the Holy Spirit, the creating spirit of God that originally moved across the dark waters and the void to bring forth all of life, the community of believers is being empowered to be witnesses to all these things.

And just where is this to occur? Locally, nationally, and internationally. Jerusalem was where the disciples lived. Be a witness to the coming reign of God where you live, for if you don't, then who will? Judea and Samaria make up the national society in which the disciples lived, with a particular awareness of the racial, economic, and cultural barriers between the Jews and the Samaritans. Be a witness in your nation, cutting across these humanly constructed barriers in your culture. And to the ends of the earth, for there is nowhere we must not go to witness to the good news in Jesus Christ. Is there one place for mission? Can we simply go to one spot on the globe and say we have done our duty? Absolutely not. Mission is, as previously stated, not so much a matter of *where*, but of *what* and *why* and *when* and *how* and *who*. The church has focused so much in the past several centuries on where we go and do mission that we have often lost sight of the crucially important call of Christ in this passage. Being Witnesses. With the empowering Holy Spirit we are to be witnesses to the reign of God, everywhere all at once and among all peoples in all situations. Witnessing is a chosen lifestyle as well as a motivational force for transforming the world in God's Mission.

The Fire of Mission

The point here is that as the Church, called to mission by Jesus at the Ascension, we "are" mission, more than we "do" mission. The most well-known illustration of this comes from the 20th-century German theologian, Emil Brunner. In a small book based on lectures given in King's College at the University of London, called *The Word and the World*, Brunner states:

> Mission work does not arise from any arrogance in the Christian Church; mission is its cause and its life. The Church exists by mission, just as a fire exists by burning. Where there is no mission, there is no Church; and where there is neither Church nor mission, there is no faith.[1]

Brunner is here saying that it is of the very nature of Christian faith to share the free gift of God's salvific grace and all that this means. He says that it is as if someone finds a cure for cancer for themselves, and thereby also "would be duty bound to make this remedy accessible to all."[2] He also understands that whether by all this we are referring to mission in other lands or in our home is at best a secondary question. Sharing the Gospel is a matter of spreading the fire that Christ has already brought to the whole earth. "He [sic] who does not propagate this fire shows that he is not burning. He who burns propagates the fire."[3] Jesus was clear that this fire was for all, everywhere, beginning where the disciples were and spreading out to the very ends of the earth. The real issue is that all who believe in the Good News are called now to share this Good News as a characteristic of this belief. Brunner speaks of it being an "urge," because "living faith feels God's purpose as its own."[4] By being Christian we are of necessity and nature a missionary people. We do not exist for ourselves, but for the sake of the world. As "God so loved the world" (John 3:16), so too do we love the world, the whole world and all who are in it. At the core of our being we desire to offer to all the saving Grace of God in Jesus Christ, not to bring any reward or advancement or benefit to ourselves or our organizations, but solely to proclaim to all the wonderful coming reign of God. We are on fire in mission, offering a blazing light from a hilltop for all to see (Matthew 5:14-16).

Being in mission as faithful witnesses is the scriptural call to the global ministries of the church. Participation in God's Mission is a matter of being witnesses to what God is doing in our midst, by pointing toward the coming kingdom and making disciples by being disciples. This is the fire of Mission, that being in mission is the essence of what it is to be the Church of Jesus Christ as recorded in the Acts of the Apostles. There evangelism is understood as witnessing— pointing toward the reality of God in Christ. Acts 17:16-34 is the account of Paul preaching in very secular Athens concerning the "unknown god." Paul perceived evangelistic mission as directing persons toward new life in Christ, where they have already been drawn by the *missio Dei*. He was taken to the Areopagus, meaning the hill or rock of Ares (or Mars), the Greek (Roman) god of war. It was a location of trials in ancient times. Paul was brought here to be better heard by the philosophers and Stoics, for this was a good "theater." He refers to the unknown god, and names this deity as God in Christ, incarnate in the world. God was already at work in Athens, and Paul simply recognized the rich opportunity to evangelize in God's Mission by using local understandings to point the people toward the Lord.

Being Sent

Paul's work was one of several models for mission found in Acts that were used by the fledgling church, which Professor Thomas Thangaraj refers to as *kerygmatic presence.* Thangaraj says that while the term "mission" literally means "being sent," the theological thrust of this was on "being" far more than on "sent."[5] *Kerygmatic presence* is the proclamation of the Good News as the disciples were being witnesses, a way of living the message. *Kerygma* is most often translated as "proclamation" or "preaching," yet as practiced in Acts, this was a holistic presence of the disciples, speaking about the kingdom as well as offering healing, hope, and physical aid. This *kerygma* was experienced at the *koinonia* (fellowship) of the church, extended to *diaconia* (service) to persons of the fellowship in need, and for some the ultimate *marturia* (witnessing through martyrdom) for the faith. *Kerygma* was the mission, the very being and ultimate purpose, of these as the mission of this newly called-out community.

Brunner also writes that *Kerygma* is not preaching of doctrine or right belief, as has often been used in interpretation, but more of the herald's call.

> The herald, the keryx, is a man who in the market-place of a city promulgates the latest decree of the king. He is the living publicity organ of the sovereign's will. The herald makes known what no one could know before: what the king has decreed. It is just this that the Apostles meant by kerygma.[6]

The mission of the Christian community is to live out what God has revealed to us in Jesus Christ, not just in words, as important as this is, but with our whole being. "You shall be my witnesses," Jesus stated. We are to *be* witnesses, not simply engage in witnessing. Being is an essence of reality that is both who you are and what you do as a consequence of this reality. Each Christian is a witness and acts as a witness, and together that is our Christian "being-hood." Discipleship is one term that has been used to describe this, but this has come to be such a localized and personalized notion in the church that we need to reassess its meaning. Witness is the word Luke attributes to Jesus' call to the disciples. The heart of Christian discipleship is the global witnessing to the reality of God's coming reign, in word and deed, with faith in action, which is so much the story of the early church in Acts. Bishop Newbigin states, "It is the acting out by proclamation and by endurance, through all the events of history, of the faith that the Kingdom of God has drawn near. It is the acting out of the central prayer that Jesus taught his disciples to use: Father, hallowed be thy name, thy kingdom come, thy will be done on earth as in heaven."[7]

The global ministries of the Church are the living out of this most significant prayer that we all use nearly every day of our life of faith, so that God's will is *being* done on earth as in heaven, as we witness to God's reign in our midst.

On Fire With Mission in Manila

Jay and Grace Choi are United Methodist missionary pastors in the Philippines. Originally from South Korea, the Chois now bring excitement and new life to inner-city Manila as youth workers. Through the annual "Jesus And Me in the Philippines Annual Conference" (JAMPAC) event, nearly 1,000 young adults gather for worship, praise, Bible study, and fellowship with the Lord through each other. It is a fiesta time, a family experience as the body of Christ, where new Christians are formed in the faith, and then move out into the world as leaders. The Chois say, "JAMPAC is a cradle of reformers and transformers. Once you meet Jesus, once you've tasted the fellowship, then the next step is to step into the world courageously. Whatever the eventual occupations of these young people, they enter their work with faithfulness, spirit, integrity, and honor as children of God." They are on fire with the Spirit, burning as a missional church.

Mongolia Mission Initiative

Sun Lae Kim and Helen Shepherd are United Methodist missionaries witnessing to their faith and seeking to make disciples in a nation that seems to be at the end of the earth to many Americans. They are serving in the Mongolian capital city, Ulaan Baatar, with a new congregation and a new national church in this seemingly remote and un-Methodist environment. The church there is called "The Light UMC," because at the UMC Center in Ulaan Baatar the people gather for prayer every morning. One day, as they were praying and reading the Bible, the first verse of Isaiah chapter 60 came to the congregation in a very powerful way. "Arise and shine for the light has come and the glory of the Lord has risen upon you" (Isaiah 60:1). All the church members who attended the morning prayer that day said, "This is indeed a verse for us, for our church!" The word for light in that verse is *gerelt* in Mongolian. So they named the church "Gerelt United Methodist Church."

The new church center is growing, with two Sunday schools, because of the expanding number of children attending and more and more adults, also. They also have a basketball court, which increases the number of boys over girls. Children and youth have few social experiences, and the new church offers them a safe and enjoyable setting. Many of the boys work for very small sums each day selling newspapers and shining shoes. It is a hard life for the children, and the church under the missionaries' leadership gives them a place to know God's love and grace each and every day. New disciples are being formed in a new land at the end of the earth—or the center of a new church that is offering new light in with a warming fire of mission.

Youth Evangelism in Suburban Atlanta

Duluth, Georgia has become one of the greater metropolitan areas in suburban Atlanta with a growing number of immigrants from Vietnam. The Atlanta Korean United Methodist Church in Duluth has reached out beyond its usual constituency and has started an after-school program to reach out to the Vietnamese youth as one of its community ministries. Although initiated by the local church, this ministry is now being implemented in a partnership with the Southeastern Jurisdictional Asian ministry agency, as well as with the local city agency, exhibiting an exciting connection of the church in mission. The after-school program meets four times a week, and offers music classes, basketball, tutoring services, and Bible studies. An immigrant church reaches out with God's love and grace to bring new Americans into the faith.

By word and deed, in life-enhancing proclamation through a variety of activities, our church is on fire with mission, as faithful witnesses to our living Lord. We are making disciples of Jesus Christ, through the power of the Holy Spirit, by being witnesses, here, there, and everywhere.

Concepts to Consider

1. How does the scriptural call to be a witness inspire you to action?

2. When have you experienced the fire of mission in your congregation?

3. Where have you seen a kerygmatic presence in ministry?

Notes for ESSAY 6

[1] Emil Brunner, *The Word and the World* (New York: Charles Scribner's Sons, 1931), p. 108.

[2] Ibid.

[3] Ibid.

[4] Ibid., p. 109.

[5] M. Thomas Thangaraj, *Common Task* (Nashville: Abingdon, 1999), p. 103.

[6] Brunner, op. cit., p. 109.

[7] Lesslie Newbigin, *The Open Secret*, p. 39.

ESSAY 7

In Deep Water Fishing for Other Fish: Mission as Leadership Development

Scripture understood through Mission Goal 2:
To Strengthen, Develop, and Renew Christian Community

Isaiah 43:1-2: I have called you by name.

Luke 5:1-11: Do not be afraid; from now on you will be catching people.

Leadership development is presenting the call to mission service and sending. Just as the disciples were called into mission, we have continued in this call as we develop mission leaders throughout the world, and thereby strengthen, develop, and renew Christian community.

Called By Name

> But now thus says the Lord, he who created you, O Jacob, he who formed you, O Israel: Do not fear, for I have redeemed you; I have called you by name, you are mine (Isaiah 43:1).

I believe that perhaps the greatest, or at least most primary, biblical truth is that we are not here as human beings just to take up space, but have been created for specific purpose. And this purpose has little to do with ourselves or our own needs and pleasures. The old Westminster Catechism, whatever else its outdated language and simplistic theology has given us, does start right out with the main question: "What is the chief and highest end of man?" and the appropriate answer for all twelve-year-old confirmands to memorize: "Man's chief and highest end is to glorify God, and fully to enjoy him forever."[1] "Enjoy," in this outdated usage, is not so much a pleasurable pursuit as it is participation with God in all of God's work here among us.

God has created and formed us, as were Adam and Eve (Cf. Genesis, chapter 2). This creation is not for our purposes or simply because God was frivolously making "things," but we are formed and fashioned in the manner of a potter creating a pot, and made into specific created beings for God's purposes. Thus, while we are called into mission, we are created even more so, says Isaiah, as missional beings from the very beginning. This creation is ongoing. Creation, according to Isaiah, is an ongoing act of God's divine purposes. The grammatical tense of this passage in Isaiah 43:1 is very much a present reality.

Calling someone by name is an act of creation, and means that we know them personally. Just as Adam named the plants and animals at the beginning of Creation, and thus was the steward and caretaker of these named creatures, so too are we named and claimed by God; "you are mine," says the Lord. This ownership is not so much a matter of enslavement, while it is a call to servanthood, but it is a statement that we are created and formed for God's purposes. We are to be in mission, living out our lives engaged in the work God has set before us. We are called, just as Jesus called his first disciples beside the lake of Gennesaret.

> A charge to keep I have, a God to glorify,
> A never dying soul to save, and fit it for the sky.
> To serve the present age, my calling to fulfill;
> O may it all my powers engage to do my Master's will.[2]

Moving Into Deep Water

> When he had finished speaking, he said to Simon, "Put out into the deep water and let down your nets for a catch."…But when Simon Peter saw it, he fell down at Jesus' knees, saying, "Go away from me, Lord, for I am a sinful man!"…Then Jesus said to Simon, "Do not be afraid; from now on you will be catching people" (Cf. Luke 5:1-11).

Simon encountered the divine presence in Jesus Christ while fishing without much luck, and so felt his own mortality and insecurities in the Lord's presence on that boat. However, as he was called by name, just as Isaiah also heard the Lord, and received a new name, Peter, he in this heard the call to fish for others of God's people. God calls persons like Peter, and you and I, to faithful service each and every day; ordinary getting-on-in-life people who happen to be open to the idea that life is more than just putting one foot in front of the other. People who have the notion that God is a real and a very present experience, and has created us for divine purpose and reason. We are here to work the garden in which we have been planted and till the soil of human existence. We find, like Peter, that to fish for other folk just like us, and so to participate in the coming Kingdom, more of God's creation will be prepared for this new life in our midst.

All this is our vocation, a word from the Latin, "vocare," meaning to call. God calls, and when we're willing to hear, we are moved to action beyond what we would think possible. Vocation is not just for a few select folk, but for all

Christians who have the willingness to understand why we are here. The critical point is, are we listening and expecting to hear God in our life?

First, we must be willing to hear and see the divine call in everyday life. Surely there are special places of God's presence, yet how many of us expect to be moved to new action on any day, and in any place, expecting to hear God speak to you a new path, a new quest in life? God is really here, right now, calling to you. Peter encountered the divine in his occupation, while fishing. He and his coworkers had an unsuccessful fishing trip, which was not only a disappointment, but the realization that he couldn't provide food for himself and his family. While worrying about his own condition, he still was open to new meaning and purpose in life. There on the boat he found the Lord.

Second, we must recognize our basic unworthiness. We will never accomplish anything for God by our own skills and talents, but only by the grace of Jesus Christ and the power of the Holy Spirit working within us. We are unworthy sinners, incapable of anything on our own. But with Christ in us, and doing what God wants us to do, we can accomplish nothing less than miracles, as Peter experienced with that huge catch of fish out in the deep water, where he was afaid to go, and where he least expected to find that treasure.

Third, we then must accept God's forgiveness and grace, and say a resounding "Yes" to God's call. Peter, James, and John left everything, and followed Jesus. Saying yes to God's call in your life is not an easy or even pleasant experience. When Jesus told Peter to put out into the deep water, Peter responded with fear and trepidation. The boat was not large, and Galilee was a dangerous lake, and the fish didn't usually hang around deep water, but in by the shoals, and...the rationalizations go on and on.

To respond to God's call to serve is to spend your life in deep water. It is risky business. You perhaps won't be well liked, and you'll always be misunderstood, except by those few folk who choose to follow Jesus and live in the deep water with you. You will never gain any of the world's riches, and will always be troubled by the notion that you're not really doing any good. Deep water is where we tend to find the *missio Dei*, God's Mission. And yet, it is in the deep water that God is most readily found and that we can be most useful for the kingdom. To look for the Lord's call in your life, listen for that awesome Word of humility and power, and saying yes to God, be sent forth on a journey of faith that will give you the only real reason for living.

Fishing for Leaders for the Kingdom

The leadership development programs of global ministries are a matter of calling the fish-of-the-sea into kingdom service, and then being sent forth to call others into the deep water of mission. We are all sinners, and therefore in ourselves unworthy recipients of God's grace. Leadership for God's reign on earth is not for those who are inherently well qualified. Christian leadership is willing acceptance of God's call to go forth calling others just like yourself into kingdom service.

Just Another Fish-of-the-Sea Seeking Other Fish

Sun Sook Kim is a Korean-American nurse who now serves as a missionary in literacy ministries with The United Methodist Church in the Philippines. Her work takes her into the notorious slum/garbage dump in Manila, called "Smokey Mountain" (because of the underground fires constantly burning there). Here she works with children at the Shalom Children's Learning Center, and tells of a student there from many years ago who went on to college and significant leadership in the church, working with other children in similar conditions. Sun Sook worked with another child, teaching her to read and write, and now she herself is a teacher. Still another such child has gone on to be a community organizer.

Sun Sook originally felt angry and hopeless about the situation of these children-of-the-dump, and not at all sure her work would make a difference in their lives. As she worked there for many years, however, helping them to advance their lives through literacy, she saw how it is the great hope for the future that keeps the families going, and how she is an instrument of God's love and grace in that hope. She felt herself to be just another fish in the sea, but then she began fishing for other fish, and these too have now moved on to fish other seas!

A Missionary Leads Young Leaders

Romeo Del Rosario also serves as a missionary in the Philippines. One of the brightest students he had ever taught at Union Seminary there harbored negative and highly judgmental views of God, rejecting a Wesleyan understanding of a loving and inclusive divine presence in the world. As the semester progressed, Romeo spent time with this student, reflecting on reading and class discussions, and along with other students also engaging him; this future pastor changed his attitude toward himself and others with transformed beliefs of God's image.

The student later told this missionary professor how grateful he was for the understanding and encouragement that Romeo had given him in his faith journey. All of this lets Romeo know the privilege of teaching in the mission setting, and was inspired by what he knew would be this young pastor's impact on congregations and communities he would serve. Leadership development is a crucial aspect of global ministries, as leaders are called out of the church to offer leadership, calling others through church and community.

Scholarships for Leadership Development

Each year the General Board of Global Ministries designates significant funds, (recently in the range of $1.5 million per year) for several hundred mission scholarships. These funds assist women and men from over 50 nations, as well as ethnic minority students in the United States, to further their education in preparation for mission service. Some of these persons may become missionaries, while most serve in their home countries and regions in church and church-related vocations.

An Afro-Latina woman originally from Colombia, now living in the United States, is in a Master's degree program in counseling at the Methodist Theological School in Ohio. Her interests are in developing the skills to support the needs of disenfranchised women and children, and serving within the Hispanic ministry of The United Methodist Church in the United States.

An African-American woman is studying in an M.Div. program in Parish Ministry and Advocacy at Candler School of Theology in Atlanta, Georgia. Originally seeking a law degree, she experienced a turning point in her life that drew her back to the church and pastoral ministry.

A Zambian woman pastor is living and studying in South Africa in a Ph.D. program in Gender and Theology at the University of Kwazulu-Natal. Her goal is to work with different denominations and ethnic groups in the southern part of Africa, sensitizing the churches on issues of sexual violence within the churches and in Christian homes, a situation that has perpetuated the increase of HIV/AIDS in the community.

A woman from The United Methodist Church of Mozambique is in a Bachelor of Science program in Agriculture and Natural Resources at Africa University in Zimbabwe, to work in the field of agriculture for the church. She states that "Mozambique is a country in which poverty is absolute, in spite of having very envious and virgin natural resources in its soil and subsoil. In the battle against poverty, agriculture is on the front-line need for development, because it exists at the base of all sustenance, progress and happiness."

A man from the Methodist Church of Indonesia has entered Ph.D. work in Islamic Studies at the South East Asia Graduate School of Theology in Manila, Philippines. As Indonesia is one of the largest predominately Muslim nations of the world, with a minority Christian population, his goal is to develop holistic ministries, showing God's love to all people through church programs with the Methodist Church in North Sumatra. He knows that Christian mission must be in dialogue with his Muslim neighbors in order to build mutual understanding and promote cooperative work to reform Indonesia for a better life for everyone.

An Afro-Colombian woman pastor of the Methodist Church of Colombia is in the Master's program in Theology at the Fundación Universitaria Seminario Bautista in Cali, Colombia. She is one of eight current students that the Methodist Church has identified for further training. She sees her role as contributing to the growth and development of the emerging church in Colombia and to the social work that accompanies the Wesleyan tradition.

A woman of the Methodist Church of Brazil in Pernambuco is studying for a Bachelor of Science degree in accounting at the Sociedade Pernambucana de Cultura e Ensino. She has previously worked in the Northeast Missionary Conference treasury office for several years, and desires to seek the improvement of the church's resources in northeast Brazil, which is the poorest area of the country.

A pastor of the Methodist Church of Uruguay is a full-time local pastor in Montevideo, Uruguay, and a visiting professor at the Instituto Universitario ISEDET in Argentina, where he is in doctoral studies in missiology. He describes the field of missiology as the academic discipline that connects the missionary practice of the church to theological reflection and urges theology not to lose sight of mission. He will continue his pastoral work and teaching after graduation.

A woman from Port-au-Prince, Haiti, studying pediatric medicine at the Université Quisqueya, Port-au-Prince, seeks to tackle the problem of children's health care in Haiti, where the child mortality rate is 80 percent, and the number of doctors per inhabitants is one in 4,000. She hopes to relieve suffering, help heal, and promote hygiene and preventative care for the most vulnerable in her community.

These are just a sampling of the several hundred students who receive scholarship assistance from the Crusade Scholarship and Leadership Development Grants of the General Board of Global Ministries. Without this aid many of the students would likely not be able to continue with their studies. They are selected from many applicants because it is believed that they will be best able to have the greatest impact in their local churches and communities through the studies that they're undertaking, and thus advance God's Mission. Coming from all regions of the world, as well as from racial and ethnic minorities in the United

States, these Christian scholars are committed to the life and mission of the church, as well as to its ministry to society and the world. The United Methodist Church, through the leadership development programs of the Global Ministries Scholarship Office, offers an opportunity for United Methodists to be in mission with our partners all over the world—those whose hopes, dreams, prayers, and hard work are helping to forge a more peaceful, more just, and healthier tomorrow.

Concepts to Consider

1. Who have you known to follow the scriptural call to mission service?
2. When are risks necessary as you call persons to deep water?
3. What is the difference between fishing for other fish and being a keeper in an aquarium?

Notes for ESSAY 7

[1] Westminster Assembly, *The Westminster Larger Catechism* (Oak Harbor, WA: Logos Research Systems, Inc., 1995).

[2] *The United Methodist Hymnal* (Nashville, TN: United Methodist Publishing House, 1989), #413.

ESSAY 8

Why We Care: Humanitarian Needs,
Theological Answers

Scripture understood through Mission Goal 3: To Alleviate Human Suffering

Matthew 25:31-46: Serving the least is serving God.

Mark 9:40-41: The cup of cool water is rewarded.

To understand the spirituality of bread is to grasp the theological basis of mission that to serve the least and the last, those in need in this world who are members of God's family, we are caring for the physical needs of God's people as we would care for Christ himself.

The Spirituality of Bread

There seems to be a notion in the church, if not also in the wider society, that caring for those in need physically and those in need spiritually are separate and distinct ministries. We speak of the "humanitarian" work of mission, such as aid to communities and individuals during and after a natural disaster, or seeking to offer services to relocated refugees from famine or war. The United Methodist Church has materially responded to the personal and corporate disaster of the attack on the World Trade Center and the Pentagon referred to as "9/11," the awesome destruction of the tsunami in Southeast Asia, and the devastation of entire US communities in hurricanes such as Katrina and Rita in recent years, with a massive outpouring of financial and volunteer resources. We know that engaging in these "humanitarian" response efforts is a high priority among our church members.

And yet, while we see these efforts as an outgrowth of our Christian faith, we do not necessarily consider these ministries to be the same as starting new congregations for new Christians in Senegal or Cameroon, or leading children's Bible classes in Guatemala or Costa Rica. We have compartmentalized our understanding of the *missio Dei* to the point where God's saving grace is administered to different folk in different settings, as if it were a prescription drug for a specific human need. We do not see ourselves as evangelists offering water and food to thirsty and hungry people, or as relief workers sharing the Good News of Jesus Christ. In point of fact these are the same activities as in the *missio Dei*.

The Russian theologian Nikolai Berdyaev puts it most succinctly, saying:

> The question of bread for myself is a material question, but the question
> of bread for my neighbours, for everybody, is a spiritual and a religious
> question. Man does not live by bread alone, but he does live by bread
> and there should be bread for all. Society should be so organized that
> there is bread for all, and then it is that the spiritual question will present
> itself before men in all its depth.[1]

Making the resources of God's creation available for all persons is the ethical, evangelistic, and stewardship call to us as participants in God's Mission.
These missional activities cannot rightly be separated into unrelated tasks, but
are all the same activity from a theological standpoint. God's people are whole
people leading whole, if at times broken, lives. To feed is to heal is to offer peace
is to bring hope is to proclaim salvation. The essential difference between the
humanitarian work of secular and governmental agencies and the relief and
reconstruction efforts of the church is that we as the church are dealing with the
whole lives of persons in crisis, not just the physical, and we offer material aid
because of our faith in God and a realistic hope for a better world. Our goal is
to create healed communities that work for the benefit of all persons, because all
persons are in God's family with us.

The Church Exists for Others, Matthew 25

Dietrich Bonhoeffer, writing from the crucible of a Nazi prison, stated that,
"The church is the church only when it exists for others."[2] This is the same
theological principle that Jesus expressed in the parable of the sheep and goats,
by saying, "Truly I tell you, just as you did it to one of the least of these who are
members of my family, you did it to me" (Matthew 25:40). The Church is called
to exist for others just as God incarnate in Jesus Christ came into the world for
the sake of the whole world...for all others.

At this last discourse in Matthew's gospel prior to the events of "Holy
Week," Jesus is expanding the boundaries of the family of God. We are called to
care for the least and the last, the lost and the lone, precisely because they are
our sisters and brothers. All who are in need are members of God's family, and
thus our immediate siblings. In so offering aid, we are therefore caring for the
head of the family, the King on the heavenly throne, God in Christ himself.
Humanitarian aid or material mission is not that, but is an expression of our
faith in the creator God who created and continues to create us all. It is not a

human-to-human experience, because as Christians we affirm that Christ is the head of the family, and as the incarnation of the creator God we are directly offering life-affirming care to our creator.

Why We Care, Mark 9

> For truly I tell you, whoever gives you a cup of water to drink because you bear the name of Christ will by no means lose the reward (Mark 9:41).

This principle even works in reverse, as those who care for the caregivers, who provide cool water for workers in the kingdom, are counted among the community of faith. They will also be rewarded for aiding all who go by the name of Christ into the world. Caring for the material and physical needs of all people is an act of loving God, the creator, redeemer, and sustainer of all, even when someone does not necessarily understand who this is.

The issue here as we seek to understand the *missio Dei* is that bread for others beyond myself, as well as shelter, clothing, water, medicine, or whatever is needed to sustain life, is a theological and spiritual question for each of us to face. We do not just offer aid when we are emotionally moved by television news broadcasts, or when we personally know a hurting or suffering individual. We care for others' needs because we believe all to be the children of God, our family, and created in the image of God. It is of our very nature to offer aid and assistance whenever we are aware of a need, and to continue with that care long beyond the emotional ties of time or space. The Christian circle of care is as large and lasting as the presence of the incarnate God in the world. To engage in theological and spiritual understanding of God's call to care is of critical importance in our global ministries.

> Where cross the crowded ways of life, where sound the cries of race and clan,
> Above the noise of selfish strife, we hear your voice, O Son of man.
> In haunts of wretchedness and need, on shadowed thresholds dark with fears,
> From paths where hide the lures of greed, we catch the vision of your tears.
> The cup of water given for you still holds the freshness of your grace;
> Yet long these multitudes to view the sweet compassion of your face.[3]

Our Theology of Care

For many in our missionary community, simply doing good work is not the point, as important as it is to offer the cup of cold water, shelter, food, or medical care. They, and we with them, must offer understanding about the physical needs of God's people, as the blanket that surrounds those who care and those cared for. Ronald and Diane Ray have recently retired from many years of service as United Methodist missionaries teaching in Nigeria and Kenya. In Africa the AIDS epidemic has become the AIDS pandemic, sweeping across the continent with death and destruction of personal and communal life. While other professors taught students about the medical issues of HIV/AIDS, Ron realized that he needed to develop a theology of Christian ethics concerning human sexuality and Christian marriage, and thereby also of the disease, by strengthening the understandings of marriage. Diane continues this work at the Women's Center of the theological college in Kenya, focusing on gender awareness and the women's consciousness about their social status and God-given abilities, as well as educating male students on issues of equality.

Our missionaries are responding to the apparent medical tragedy of AIDS by combating the underlying cultural causes of a physical disease with a theology of care and respect for all of God's people. Women in many cultures are the least and the last. To alleviate physical human suffering often requires a theological transformation of a cultural mindset.

Our Theology of Natural Disasters

Soon after the international tsunami disaster in Southern Asia, Methodist pastors in Indonesia told our United Methodist aid workers there that many citizens were hearing misguided statements. There were both fundamentalist Islamic leaders and Western evangelists claiming that this tragedy and the death and destruction of the area was the result of God's negative judgment on the people of Indonesia. Even as UMCOR began to aid in cleanup of the towns and villages, and in providing new housing and infrastructure resources, a program of continuing education for the Methodist pastors was developed to address the theological issues of natural disasters.

Leadership of the General Board of Global Ministries met with the pastors, as they engaged in Bible study, prayer, small group discussions, and theological lectures, all to come to clearer comprehension of this life-changing event for the people they served, and for themselves as pastoral leaders. God's Grace was at the core of these conversations. God was not the source of the tragic tsunami, but God was there with the hurting people as they grieved and then set about to rebuild life in the towns and villages. God was more apt to offer bread than stones for sustenance (Matthew 7:9), and turn water to wine for celebrations (John 2:1-11), than to cause death and destruction of any persons (cf. Ezekiel 18:23, and 2 Peter 3:9).

Paul Dirdak, former deputy general secretary for the United Methodist Committee on Relief, has written that while God does have a plan for our lives,

God does not have a map. Dirdak describes a map as a diagram of where some-one has been, or the known world. A plan is a diagram of what one hopes will become, or the unknown world. Natural disasters are not the plan of God, for God does not desire death and destruction. The tsunami and all other similar events are not the will of God. God does, however, have a plan for our lives, a program for love and care and support in time of need. "God's love is so great that nothing can separate us from it, so we call it grace."[4]

It is simplistic to say that we care because God cares. And yet, that is pre-cisely the essence of divine grace active in our world; grace upon grace lived out in our care for all in need, at all times and all places. Thus, our mission of physical care for the uprooted, the marginalized, and those whose lives are ravished by war or natural disaster is a spiritual issue first and foremost. Grace. Suffering is not the plan of God. That is just the map of life, of where we have been from day to day. The plan of God is grace; and we are called to be those who seek to deliver God's grace to all in need.

Concepts to Consider

1. Why do you care about others, based on the Scriptures?
2. What is your understanding of the spirituality of bread?
3. How is humanitarian aid synonymous with Christian aid?

Notes for ESSAY 8

[1] Nikolai Berdyaev, *The Origin of Russian Communism*, translated by R. M. French (London: Centenary Press, 1937), pp. 225-226.

[2] Dietrich Bonhoeffer, *Letters and Papers from Prison*, Eberhard Bethge, ed. (New York: Macmillian Co., 1971), p. 382.

[3] *The United Methodist Hymnal* (Nashville, TN: United Methodist Publishing House, 1989), #427.

[4] Paul Dirdak, *Did We Make God Angry?* (*New World Outook*, Vol. LXVI, No. 6, July/August, 2006), p. 6.

ESSAY 9

Going Into the Spokes of the Wheel:
Eliminating Barriers to the Kingdom

Scripture understood through Misson Goal 4:
To Seek Justice, Freedom, and Peace

Isaiah 40:3-5/Luke 3:1-6; Isaiah 58: 6-12:
Filling in valleys and lifting yokes of burden from oppressed persons.

Amos 5:21-24; Acts 16:16-24:
Justice flowing like waters, as leaders insert their lives to protect others.

Personal sacrifice may be needed in God's Mission to eliminate the barriers to
God's kingdom of justice, freedom, and peace, by being an inclusive Church,
seeking to break down barriers and walls, fill in the valleys, and bring down the
mountains, thus building a straight highway for our God.

Into the Spokes of the Wheel

As the Nazi party solidified its control over the German nation in the 1930s,
Dietrich Bonhoeffer was one of the strident voices calling for an end to the injustice
and prejudice of state-sponsored violence against minorities and the marginalized
in society. He spoke of the need for the Church to so advocate for justice in not
just a passive way but by active engagement in all that seeks to separate people
from each other, and build barriers to life as God has created it for all.

   Bonhoeffer was very clear about the church's obligations to fight political
injustice. The church, he wrote, must fight evil in three stages. The first stage
was to question state injustice and call the state to responsibility; the second was
to help the victims of injustice, whether they were church members or not.

   However, "the third possibility is not just to bandage the victims under the
wheel, but to personally put oneself like a stick into the spokes of the wheel."[1]
He saw the government of his day as a wheel rolling over minorities and
oppressing them under its massive weight. Christians, specifically when organized
as the Church, are called to end this injustice by throwing ourselves into the
spokes of the wheel to stop its movement of violence. By so engaging evil and
injustice, therefore, the Church becomes an agent of force in the destruction of
unjust policies and organizations of the culture, and specifically of government.

For us in the United States, with our seemingly absolute separation of church and state, this later conclusion of Bonhoeffer may seem difficult if not totally inappropriate. There is, however, a strong tradition of civil disobedience in both Christianity and in American culture to which we must give significant credence. Bonhoeffer knew that when barriers are created which destroy human life in our midst, we cannot stand idly by and let the wheels of this destruction go unmolested.

The words of the prophet Isaiah, reiterated by John the Baptizer in Luke's Gospel, sound loudly in our ears on this same tune.

> A voice cries out: "In the wilderness prepare the way of the Lord, make straight in the desert a highway for our God. Every valley shall be lifted up, and every mountain and hill be made low; the uneven ground shall become level, and the rough places a plain. Then the glory of the Lord shall be revealed, and all people shall see it together, for the mouth of the Lord has spoken" (Isaiah 40:3-5; and Luke 3:4-6).

Fill in the valleys and remove the mountains that make the travel on God's pathway to justice and restoration of peace and wholeness for all nations, to whom this glorious new life will be revealed in our active engagement. Eliminate the barriers, making the highway to God's marvelous kingdom a straight shot into our lives. Isaiah, John, Jesus, Bonhoeffer, Martin Luther King, Jr., John Wesley, and many lesser-known prophets have all shouted this call to get involved in removing all that is wrought by governments and institutions, human mechanisms all, which are barriers to justice, peace, and freedom for all of God's children.

> Heralds of Christ, who bear the King's commands,
> Immortal tidings in your mortal hands,
> Pass on and carry swift the news you bring,
> Make straight, make straight the highway of the King.[2]

When we so choose to be sticks in the spokes of the wheel of injustice, then what Isaiah goes on to to state will come to pass: "Your ancient ruins shall be rebuilt; you shall raise up the foundations of many generations; you shall be called the repairer of the breach, the restorer of streets to live in" (Isaiah 58:6-7, 12). And the words of another prophet, Amos, will come to fruition: "But let justice roll down like waters, and righteousness like an ever-flowing stream" (Amos 5:24). Our culture and all cultures of the world can live in peace with justice for all persons. The prophetic vision can be a reality, as we confront the evil forces that build the barriers, the walls that separate, and the impassable streets on which people seek to live their lives as God's people.

The whole Gospel story of Jesus' interaction with persons and the world forces illustrates this kingdom principle of inclusivity. The clear understanding is that God's coming kingdom is for all persons of all places, stations, and backgrounds. As missiologist Dave Bosch notes, "What amazes one again and again is the inclusiveness of Jesus' mission. It embraces both the poor and the rich, both the oppressed and the oppressor, both the sinners and the devout. His mission is one of dissolving alienation and breaking down walls of hostility, of crossing boundaries between individuals and groups."[3]

Keith H. Reeves, a New Testament professor at Azusa Pacific University, writing a commentary on the story of the Ethiopian official in the Acts of the Apostles, understands this story to be that of the early church's struggle with who is included in God's kingdom. He believes that Luke has woven a tapestry of a story on his broad social concern for any and all who are outcast or excluded by society and particularly the Church, and goes on to draw the importance of this truth for our day. "Are the people of God erecting barriers to the work of the Kingdom? Are they the same old barriers, such as ethnic origin or handicap, that the early church faced or are they new barriers to ministry?"[4]

Thomas Thangaraj sees this same engagement with evil in the power and authority of commercial interests and government in the story in Acts. Paul and Silas free the enslaved woman from the money-making power in fortunetelling that she possessed. Her slaveowner had Paul and Silas beaten and thrown in prison when Paul prayed to have the woman's evil spirit leave her (Acts 16:16-24).[5] Putting oneself into the spokes of the wheel of economic or political exploitation for God's Mission, and causing the breaking down of these barriers, will often result in personal sacrifice.

Not all barrier breaking requires that we are personally crushed in the spokes of the wheels of injustice, prejudice, and greed. And yet, we must enter into our call to God's Mission knowing that this is always a possibility. Most often, as you will read, this engagement with the evil barriers in the world produces inspiring results by the power of the Holy Spirit working among us.

Cultural Barriers

Beverly Moon, a United Methodist missionary, teaches world religions at Tunghai University in Taiwan, which was founded by ecumenical agencies following the expulsion of Christian educators from China. She has discovered that when

Protestant and Roman Catholic missionaries arrived, each community began to translate the Scriptures into Chinese. Working separately, they chose many different words for important theological terms and phrases. As a result, the people of Taiwan have come to believe that Protestantism and Roman Catholicism are two very separate and different faiths.

For example, there is no one word for God in Chinese, nor is there just one way to suggest that Christianity is a universal faith with variant interpretations of the Gospel. Our choice of words in mission settings can build walls that separate us from our brothers and sisters of the faith, and can speak loudly of a divided Church to the non-Christian world. Beverly's task as a missionary is to create doors through these cultural walls that will allow all people to come in and out through our Church; doors that open onto the world about us and allow us to meet our brothers and sisters.

Legal Barriers

As the son of an immigrant, Alberto Silva knows the life of struggle for a family seeking a new life in a new land. Most Americans, or their ancestors, have similarly come here with these same dreams. As a United Methodist church and community worker and an attorney assigned to the UMCOR Justice for Our Neighbors (JFON) program in Omaha, Nebraska, Alberto met a young girl who came to the legal center with her father. He reviewed the facts of their case and was able to determine that the girl was eligible for citizenship, which allowed her to remain safely in her grade school. Though a young child who spoke little English, she realized the importance of that piece of paper, which was her naturalization certificate. "After seeing the smile on her face," Alberto writes, "I know we are doing God's work, and I truly am thankful for the opportunity God has given me!"

Society, through various governmental regulations, has built many barriers and walls to keep people out, to separate God's people into humanly created categories of "legal" and "illegal." God's Mission calls us to smooth the legal road to secular acceptance for all of the children of God, by filling in the valleys and bringing down what seems to many of them to be huge mountains of legal paperwork and regulatory language. These are the sojourner in our midst, whom God has called us to love and care for (Deuteronomy 10:19; Zechariah 7:10).

Language Barriers

Sarah Harkness, as a Hispanic missioner in the Oregon-Idaho Annual Conference, tells of a Mexican family attending worship at a non-Hispanic United Methodist congregation in Oregon. While the two young children spoke English, the parents did not yet. An outgoing, mature woman of the congregation befriended the mother of the family, and while they could not easily communicate with words, they did share much over time, as they sat together at the church coffee hour, visited in each other's homes, celebrated birthdays, and when the young mother had an accident, the older woman visited her in the hospital.

The younger woman said, "I am so far away from home and my family in Mexico, and my own mother. We came here not knowing anyone. She became like my mother here in the United States, and like a grandmother to my children." "Perfect love casts out fear" (1 John 4:18-19). The grace of God reaches across language and cultural barriers and makes God's people one. Separated by these barriers, these two women knew no barrier to God's Mission in their midst.

Physical Barriers

Wilber Alvarado holds a degree in chemistry, but is active in the church, working with university youth groups and local youth in his barrio, offering an alternative to street violence, and transporting youth to events in a minivan. He also travels around Nicaragua directing a health-development program in rural communities. Missionary Belinda Forbes says that he is "a testimony to Christ's love in the world and to the hope found through faith and action."

The amazing fact is that Wilber does all this without the use of his legs, being one of Nicaragua's last victims of polio. He has overcome the physical barriers in his life with the help of crutches and God's grace. With powerful and callused hands he moves through his journey of faith with smiles and enthusiasm for God's will in his life, and his struggle for the rights of persons with disabilities, a calling which has led him all around his nation and to other Central American countries, raising awareness among organizations and governmental authorities.

With courage and a commitment to God's Mission, born of his faith in Jesus Christ, Wilber does not allow any physical barrier to keep him from using his gifts and graces to serve others and point us all toward God's glorious reign.

Economic Barriers

It is increasingly difficult for farmers in rural Appalachia to earn a living from their work with the land, and fewer and fewer young people from the farms stay in agriculture. Part of the mission of the Jubilee Project, directed by missionaries Diantha and Steve Hodges, is to enhance economic development for small family farms in Hancock County, Tennessee. By developing a large communal kitchen where farmers can process their fruits and vegetables into food products that can be transported and kept for sale elsewhere, they are overcoming the economic barriers that have kept these families in poverty. Selling fresh vegetables does not offer significant income, but by using the approved kitchen they can make jams, salsas, and soup starters, which are sold through a cooperative also organized through the Jubilee Project.

As we eliminate the economic barriers in rural America, new leadership emerges, the communities are strengthened, and God's promise of prosperity for all is beginning to be realized from the fruits of God's good earth.

Political Barriers
"Walls don't work. Fences don't make good neighbors. You have to win over your neighbors' hearts," believes Janet Lahr Lewis, a United Methodist missionary in Palestine. She is very concerned that the decades of violence in the Middle East are depleting the Christian population, as these persons leave the country. Rather than the hard and harsh stone walls of separation being built around Palestinian communities, she would like to see the living stones of God's people, who for 2,000 years have proclaimed the teachings and peaceful vision of Jesus Christ in this Holy Land.

Through her work at the Sabeel Ecumenical Liberation Theology Center in Jerusalem, Janet seeks to promote nonviolent solutions to the Israeli-Palestinian conflict. It is an educational process with prayer vigils, peace marches, media campaigns, and worship opportunities to help bring about freedom for the oppressed Palestinian people, and build a lasting and just peace, reconciliation, and healing, where there are now the barriers of ignorance, sectarian strife, and war.

As United Methodists engaged in God's Mission, we are removing all of these barriers to the fullness of life for God's people; and in so doing we are, by the power of the Spirit among us, making the highway straight in this world toward the vision of God's coming kingdom.

Concepts to Consider

1. Who fills the valleys and flattens the mountains of oppression, and how?
2. How can you see yourself intentionally being a stick in the spokes of oppressive wheels?
3. When has the Church erected barriers, or disassembled barriers?

Notes for ESSAY 9

[1] Dietrich Bonhoeffer, "The Church and the Jewish Question," in *No Rusty Swords: Letters, Lectures and Notes 1928-1936* (New York: Harper and Row, 1965), p. 226.

[2] *The United Methodist Hymnal*, (Nashville, TN: United Methodist Publishing House, 1989), #567.

[3] David J. Bosch, *Transforming Mission, Paradigm Shifts in Theology of Mission* (Maryknoll, NY: Orbis Books, 1991), p. 28.

[4] Keith H. Reeves, "The Ethiopian Eunuch," in Gallagher and Hertig, *Mission in Acts*, op. cit., p. 120.

[5] M. Thomas Thangaraj, *The Common Task* (Nashville: Abingdon, 1999), p. 106.

CHAPTER THREE

TRADITION

Tradition is the collective living history of the church through the ages, which allows us to be in the ongoing stream of God's involvement in the world. Through understanding the tradition from which we have come we have a measure of authentic Christian witness, as the Theological Task states, in essence allowing us to be in community through time in our theological study.

ESSAY 10: *From Everywhere to Everywhere: the Dimensions of Mission*

Tradition understood through Mission Goal 1:
To Make Disciples of Jesus Christ

Matthew 28:16-20: Making disciples everywhere.

Ephesians 3:16-19: The dimensions of mission.

Contextualization calls us from everywhere to go everywhere as faithful witnesses of Jesus Christ, and to make disciples through involvement in the context of people's lives through partnering *with*, rather than mission *to*. United Methodism has been organized in these responsible partnering ministries for over a century and a half.

ESSAY 11: *Organizing to Beat the Devil: The United Methodist Connection*

Tradition understood through Mission Goal 2:
To Strengthen, Develop, and Renew Christian Community

1 Corinthians 12:12-27: Be the body of Christ.

John 15:1-8: Abide in mission as the vine and branches of the living Christ.

Our life in mission is organized for us to "abide" in Christ and with one another, as the vine and branches of the living Church. Connectionalism is the biblical organizing principle of mission in the United Methodist tradition that allows us to live as the universal and global body of Christ.

ESSAY 12: *No More Children for Calamity*

Tradition understood through Mission Goal 3:
To Alleviate Human Suffering

Isaiah 65:17-25: No more children for calamity.

Mark 10:13-16: Jesus blesses little children.

Our United Methodist tradition is to care for the most vulnerable in society, who are often the children, and to receive them as Jesus did, with blessing and love, which moves us toward the vision of God's coming kingdom for all children.

ESSAY 13: *The Feet of the Messenger: Servanthood in God's Mission*

Tradition understood through Mission Goal 4:
To Seek Justice, Freedom, and Peace

Philippians 2:5-8: Jesus models servanthood.

John 21:15-19: Feed my sheep; the call to serve God's people by nourishing/feeding.

Servanthood in God's Mission is seen in the United Methodist tradition of seeking justice, freedom, and peace through service in the world, particularly among women organized for mission. Servant messengers proclaim God's kingdom, which is in our midst and available to all oppressed by greed, hate, stereotyping, and the demonic systems that steal physical and spiritual life from God's people.

ESSAY 10

From Everywhere to Everywhere: the Dimensions of Mission

Tradition understood through Mission Goal 1:
To Make Disciples of Jesus Christ

Matthew 28:16-20: Making disciples everywhere.

Ephesians 3:16-19: The dimensions of mission.

Contextualization calls us from everywhere to go everywhere as faithful witnesses of Jesus Christ, and to make disciples through involvement in the context of people's lives through partnering *with*, rather than mission *to*. United Methodism has been organized in these responsible partnering ministries for over a century and a half.

Making Disciples Everywhere

And Jesus came and said to them, "All authority in heaven and on earth has been given to me. Go therefore and make disciples of all nations, baptizing them in the name of the Father and of the Son and of the Holy Spirit, and teaching them to obey everything that I have commanded you. And remember, I am with you always, to the end of the age" (Matthew 28:18-20).

Traditionally, the end of Matthew's Gospel has been the beginning of Christian mission. Much has been written and spoken of what is commonly referred to as "The Great Commission." For Matthew, the point of the Resurrection is this culminating statement of the whole Gospel. But look again at this doxology of the faith: "Go therefore, and make disciples of all nations..." The call is to go. Go from where you are to all places in the world. Go and make others be disciples as you yourselves are disciples. Do not make disciples of individuals, but make disciples of the nations of the world—all peoples in their own cultures and ways of living. Jesus, the Risen Christ, the Son of Man, the enthroned authority of the creator God, has sent the disciples forth to call others to discipleship in the context of who they are and where they are. Christianity is not a faith for the few, but the salvation of the whole world, in the context of the world they live in. The Great Commission is the great calling to the contextualization of the good news, as we take this faith from everywhere to everywhere. The global ministries of the church are to baptize, teach, and celebrate Christ's eternal and global presence in the world in which we live.

> "Go, make of all disciples," We hear the call, O Lord,
> that comes from thee, our father, in thy eternal Word.
> Inspire our ways of learning through earnest, fervent prayer,
> And let our daily living reveal thee everywhere.[1]

What Is a Context?

Context is the whole of life that is experienced by persons. Context is the water to the fish, and all that the water means even if the fish don't understand these implications. We live so much in our own context that we often do not comprehend the full meaning of our faith in another context. The most basic issue for expanding the global ministries of the church as we live into the reign of God through the *missio Dei*, is understanding the local context of our mission partners. To, as the hymn states, "let our daily living reveal thee everywhere."

The word "context," taken from the original Latin, means to weave together, or literally, to create the texture as of a textile by weaving threads together. Responsible mission partnership is being in mission by weaving together the diverse threads of the world in which we are called to proclaim the gospel in word and deed. God's world is rich in texture, and we are called to understand the origin and current impact of these diverse and sometimes complex characteristics of the human experience. Contextualization in mission reflects this rich tapestry of the many interrelated contexts of mission and ministry, such as the environment or life situation of a person, faith community, or cultural aspects of a nation or world region. In partnership, we seek to weave the rich and diverse threads of the common work of mission together in each setting of mission.

Professor Alan Neely, writing in a work on grasping context through case studies, states: "Contextualization is an attempt to communicate the gospel in a way that is faithful to its essence, understandable by those to whom it is presented, and relevant to their lives."[2] Mission is not about taking our view of the world, both present and eternal, to another group of persons. Mission is global ministries among persons in other cultures and contexts to whom God has already offered grace and hope. Our task is to be the salt and light

(Matthew 5:13-14) that makes this grace and hope visible, understandable, and desirable to these persons.

It took a reasonably long time for the Western church to understand that much of what we thought was "Christian" was simply our cultural heritage masquerading as the practice of faith. Few persons would mistake our preference for coffee after worship as an essential aspect of koinonia—the fellowship of the faithful. However, we often presume that a building is necessary for worship on a regular basis. Not just the style of building, but having a building in the first place is a cultural bias that we need to question. As are specific modes of dress, music, liturgical practices, and so on.

The notion of "democratic" methods of church governance is also a cultural bias. How a community chooses leadership and how that leadership relates to the community are both culturally related, and not a theologically important issue. For us in the West to mandate governance policies in other lands is to demand a cultural bias over and above the necessary missional needs of that locale. This also extends to our American need to control the use of funds we make available for mission. The whole notion of the ownership of land and resources, and therefore wealth production and use, varies greatly from culture to culture. The idea that individuals determine the use of a gift as well as the amount, and that the recipient is called to be graciously thankful, is not a specifically Christian system of stewardship of resources. It may well be meaningful in one cultural context, but very disruptive in a more communal or more hierarchical social structure.

Cross-Cultural Proclamation

The inherent difficulties of bringing the Gospel across cultural boundaries is illustrated by Roman Catholic missiologist Karl Muller, using the David and Goliath story to illustrate that "the medium is the message" in cross-cultural mission:

> The missionary steps into the arena expecting that the smooth stones of the Gospel which he thinks he has at hand cannot miss their mark— and he does not understand that in actual fact he is coming along in the heavy armour of a Goliath which speaks louder and even more unintelligibly than what he actually wants to communicate. This problem of the credibility of the witness is a structural problem of all Christian proclamation. But today it hampers in a particularly acute

way the encounter of Western Christianity with people, churches, and movements in the Third World."[3]

Mission theology, as well as the mission practice based on this theology, must arise from the context in which the church lives—that is locally—understanding that all localities where God's people gather for worship, witness, and work arise from the same essential creation. Yet, the context, meaning, style, and form of the worship, witness, and work are very different from place to place. For the gospel to be heard and heeded, there must be a local "flavor" that both invites the hearer and engages the listener so that the universal message of Christ may be accepted.

Contextual Discipleship, Not Church Growth

The Great Commission is, however, not a call to make church members, and the evangelistic task of mission is not ecclesiastical number-crunching. Evangelism is one methodology of mission. However, evangelism is not the same as mission, meaning that it is not, in itself, the *missio Dei*. David Bosch, in his groundbreaking work, *Transforming Mission*, is very clear that mission is more than evangelism, and that evangelism itself is not church extension. To extend the church numerically may be a symptom, or even an effect of engaging in mission, but it clearly is not the point. "The focus in evangelism should, however, not be on the church but on the irrupting reign of God."[4] Biblically based evangelism proclaims, in word and deed, the reality of God's presence in the world, calling all persons to new life in Jesus Christ. Any motivation for evangelistic practices that comes from a desire to add numbers to any church organization will lead to disjointed and disconnected results. The more appropriate motivation comes from our life as the church together, as stated in the Book of Acts: "Day by day, as they spent much time together in the temple, they broke bread at home and ate their food with glad and generous hearts, praising God and having the goodwill of all the people. And day by day the Lord added to their number those who were being saved" (Acts 2:46-47). As we seek to "be" the church, God increases the numbers. This is the biblical evangelistic attitude in mission.

Thus, to "make disciples of all nations" is not to grow the church, though this will surely happen. To fulfill the Great Commission is to actively be present in all places, seeking God's prevenient grace—the presence already there before we are—and discover how to understand the context of mission in each place.

This is what is meant by contextualization, and being in partnership. The message of the Good News of Jesus Christ is always the same. The context—place, language, historical experience—varies all around the world, and even from neighborhood to neighborhood in some cases. Our theology of mission, drawing upon the sources of theology, needs to be communicated in ways and images which connect with each person's and community's experience.

Missions versus Mission

What are "contextualized" are the methods and strategies for engaging in the whole of God's Mission. As previously discussed, missions and mission are not the same. To be more precise, mission is the *missio Dei*, God's Mission, as revealed in the person and work of Jesus Christ. It is God's ongoing movement toward the ultimate reign of God, by God's own actions, often in and through both God's people and others. It is the very nature and activity of God in the world. Missions may be understood as the *missiones ecclesiae*, the missional programs and activities of the church in particular forms and strategies for specific times, places, and needs in fulfillment of our call to participate in the *missio Dei*. The point here is for us not to confuse the theological call to mission with the methods and pragmatic strategies for mission. David Bosch asserts that, "it is not the church which 'undertakes' mission; it is the *missio Dei* which constitutes the church."[5]

Responsible Partnership

As we seek to create and carry out the methods of mission in various contexts, we must constantly look back to our theology, as well as all around us in the world at God's ongoing actions, to renew and reconceive our missional program choices. This is the contextualization of mission: the interaction of the *missio Dei* with the *missiones ecclesiae*. Mission always comes before missions. That is, we are first in partnership *with* rather than mission *to*. As God is already in mission with the whole world, we then construct the appropriate methodologies for transmitting the gospel across cultures. Responsible partnership is cross-cultural mission respecting the contexts of each and all persons, presenting Christianity in such a way that it meets people's most deeply felt need, but also connects with their worldview, thus allowing them to follow Christ and remain within their own culture. It is the incarnation, for just as Jesus came as the Word and dwelt among us, we must do likewise as we enter another culture with the gospel. The incarnation is our model for contextualization, in every cultural context.

Mission in Context, Not Acquiescence

This does not mean that God's Mission is like water, simply flowing into the cultural bucket and fitting to the form it finds there. William Sloan Coffin wrote, "We are called on not to mirror but to challenge culture, not to sustain but to upend the status quo, and if that to some sounds overly bold, isn't it true that God is always beckoning us toward horizons we aren't sure we want to reach?"[6] It was thus for the Israelites perceiving the Promised Land as they wandered in the wilderness, or the New Jerusalem as John sat on the secure island of Patmos. God is always calling us to move forward into the new future that God is creating, toward the coming kingdom. Contextualization in mission is not the confirming of any or all cultures. Rather it is to bring the gospel to a culture from the inside, not force the gospel onto a culture from the outside. Contextualization is not making the gospel take the shape of a culture, as if tailoring a coat to fit, or worse, to think that "one size fits all." It is to be the yeast in the bread, mixing in with the very substance of the culture in order to raise the bread with a wonderful texture and flavor (Matthew 13:33).

United Methodist missiologist, and former United Methodist missionary, Dr. Darrell L. Whiteman, has identified three challenges as we seek to contextualize our work in any particular missional setting: First, the *prophetic* challenge in that contextualization changes and transforms the context itself. Second, the *hermeneutic* challenge as contextualization expands our own view of the Gospel because we now see it through a different cultural lens. And third, the *personal* challenge of contextualization enables the individual to be fully engaged in mission, because we will be changed once we have become part of the body of Christ in a context different from our own.[7]

The Dimensions of God's Mission

D.T. Niles, the noted Sri Lankan Methodist theologian and missiologist of the mid-20th century, conceived of contextual mission partnerships as having four dimensions, just as Paul noted in Ephesians 3:18, which are like the four sides of an object.[8] Length is the *eschatological* dimension, which moves mission from the beginning to the end of time. At any one time we are in the midst of a timeline of mission which literally goes from creation to the coming of God's reign, from Genesis to Revelation, in a sense. Breadth is the *ecclesiastical* dimension, concerned with the relationships of all church structures and organizations around the world in both their unity and separation. To understand mission is to appreciate that all churches are as much involved in God's Mission as any other. Height is the *Christological* dimension, of the vertical reference to Him who is Lord of all and constantly at work among us; the incarnation. Depth, the *secular* dimension, is the Christian responsibility to penetrate into the life of the world and face all the reality, of good, and evil that we find there.

Paul seemed to recognize that God's Mission has these physical dimensions, when he wrote to the church in Ephesus, "I pray that you may have the power to comprehend, with all the saints, what is the breadth and length and height and depth, and to know the love of Christ that surpasses knowledge, so that you may be filled with all the fullness of God" (Ephesians 3:18-19). To comprehend the fullness of God's grace, of God's Mission in and for the world, is a gift of the Holy Spirit. Partnership in God's Mission brings the various communities of the body of Christ into relationship with each other, not as one-way, or even two-way relationships, but fully dimensional relationships in all the complexity, as well as joy and excitement, of the whole people of God in all places.

Missionaries from Africa to Africa

Partnering through the Connection has enabled The United Methodist Church in the Democratic Republic of Congo to engage in evangelistic work in Tanzania. The Rev. Mutwale Ntambo and The Rev. Umba Kalangwa are both United Methodist missionaries serving as pastors and district superintendents of the Tanganyika Annual Conference. Their work in frontier evangelism, enabled by their missionary status, as well as organizational assistance from the whole Church in Africa and the United States and Europe, has witnessed to the growth of United Methodism with 25 local pastors serving over 60 congregations and refugee ministries. "We offer new hope to weary, burdened refugees, widows, orphans, and others who long for spiritual renewal," writes Mutwale. Umba says that, "The presence of a missionary is a sign of hope" to the people living through drought and famine. They both have gone from home in the North Katanga Annual Conference of the DRC Congo to Tanzania, because of the universal connectional mission of our denomination. Rev. Ntambo goes on to affirm, "We are not created to stay in one place. Jesus told his followers to make disciples of all nations."

Making Disciples in a New Context

Helen Sheperd is a United Methodist missionary seeking to make disciples through the Global Ministries Mission Initiative in Mongolia. Learning to live and work in this new cultural context, Helen says that even as the persons they share the gospel with are very poor economically, she learns hospitality from them in her new home. She is developing a mission center for educational and youth activities, and a medical clinic has been established in partnership with the Korean Methodist Church.

Emmanuel Barte is a United Methodist missionary making disciples using his skills as an auto mechanic in the Mission Initiative in Cambodia. in Phnom Penh, Emmanuel and his wife Beverly are using their skills to witness to their faith in Jesus Christ, to youth in educational and vocational classes offered by the growing Methodist churches there.

Partnership Makes Disciples in Their New Context
As the only Laotian United Methodist congregation in the United States, Johnson City Laotian UMC has been carrying out faithful ministries serving the Laotian community in the greater Binghamton area of New York state since 2002. The Wyoming Annual Conference has a very strong commitment to support and nurture this ministry, in partnership with Global Ministries. In the context of an immigrant community in a small metropolitan region, Johnson City Laotian UMC offers ministries that include English as a Second Language, computer skills training, citizenship classes, translation services, and legal counseling for new immigrants. Through these ministries, the congregation has become a true example of how a church should serve people as a worshiping community for persons in a new life context.

> Lord, you bless with words assuring: "I am with you to the end."
> Faith and hope and love restoring, may we serve as you intend
> And, amid the cares that claim us, hold in mind eternity.
> With the Spirit's gifts empower us for the work of ministry.[9]

Words: Jeffery Rowthorn

Concepts to Consider

1. What is your tradition of making disciples?
2. How does your missional context define your faith?
3. Who are you in partnership, within the four dimensions of God's Mission?

Notes for ESSAY 10

1 *The United Methodist Hymnal* (Nashville, TN: United Methodist Publishing House, 1989), #571.

2 Alan Neely, *Christian Mission: A Case Study Approach* (Maryknoll, NY: Orbis Books, 1995), p. 9.

3 Karl Muller, *Mission Theology: An Introduction* (Nettetal, Germany: Steyler Verlag – Wort und Werk, 1987, distributed in US by Divine Word Seminary, Techny, IL), p. 23.

4 David J. Bosch, *Transforming Mission, Paradigm Shifts in Theology of Mission* (Maryknoll, NY: Orbis Books 1991), p. 415.

5 Ibid., p. 519.

6 William Sloan Coffin, *Credo* (Louisville, KY: Westminster John Knox Press, 2004), p. 146.

7 Darrell Whiteman, "Contextualization: The Theory, the Gap, the Challenge" (New Haven, CT: *International Bulletin of Missionary Research*, January 1997).

8 Daniel T. Niles, *The Message and Its Messengers* (Nashville: Abingdon Press, 1966) p. 34ff.

9 *The United Methodist Hymnal* (Nashville, TN: United Methodist Publishing House, 1989), #584.

ESSAY 11

Organizing To Beat the Devil:
The United Methodist Connection

Tradition understood through Mission Goal 2: To Strengthen, Develop, and Renew Christian Community

1 Corinthians 12:12-27: Be the body of Christ.

John 15:1-8: Abide in mission as the vine and branches of the living Christ.

Our life in mission is organized for us to "abide" in Christ and with one another, as the vine and branches of the living Church. Connectionalism is the biblical organizing principle of mission in the United Methodist tradition that allows us to live as the universal and global body of Christ.

Connecting the Connection

> For just as the body is one and has many members, and all the members of the body, though many, are one body, so it is with Christ (1 Corinthians 12:12).

Organizing into relationships in order to accomplish a task, or even to survive, grow, and develop, is a creational principle of life itself. Throughout the universe organizations and connections are being made all the time. As the scientist and organizational expert Margaret Wheatley states in her book, *A Simpler Way*, life seeks organization:

> There is an innate striving in all forms of matter to organize into relationships. There is a great seeking for connections, a desire to organize into more complex systems that include more relationships, more variety. This desire is evident everywhere in the cosmos, at all levels of scale.[1]

Even Paul, in pre-scientific times, understood this basic fact of life. While our bodies have many different parts that all function in different ways, look different, and feel different, we are still one whole body. Each member of the body is absolutely important and significant, and the body is able to grow, thrive, and totally be alive because of the many and varied relationships among the various parts. The human body is organized, and is connectional. And so it is with Christ and the church, says Paul.

Paul, in this first letter to the church in Corinth, is not so much admonishing the Corinthians, and all Christians, to strive to become members of the body of Christ. He is stating the fact that as baptized Christians they, and we, are already fully members of the body. "For in the one Spirit we were all baptized into one body—Jews or Greeks, slaves or free—and we were all made to drink of one Spirit" (1 Corinthians 12:13). We *are* the body. We do not need to become such an organized structure of relationships. It is more a matter of knowing this, and living out our life of faith with this understanding. The connectional principle is of the very innate nature of the church, just as it is of the innate nature of the cosmos.

If there is a problem for the church in this, it is that modern civilization tends to move people away from the natural process of relationship and connectionalism. Emil Brunner, in *The Word and The World*, wrote concerning the nature of the Church:

> There is no such thing as Christian faith without the Christian Church.... Christians cannot exist outside of the Body of Christ....Individual private Christianity is a self-contradiction, like iron made of wood."[2]

And later on he says of the dilemma we face:

> The theological problem as well as the Church problem is this—to deliver modern man and the modernized Church and theology from the illegitimate self-sufficiency of reason and the spirit of autonomy....This moreover is the one central social problem. The disease of our time is that fundamental individualism which makes community impossible."[3]

To be the church, the body of Christ, as well as to be participants in the *missio Dei*, we must seek the natural relationships that enable us to be both visible as Christ's body in the world, and to engage the world with the Gospel. Connectionalism is being the body of Christ, Christ's visible body in the world. Paul speaks of the various gifts for service and the unity of the body of Christ. This describes the essential connections of the whole church, which celebrate individual vocation and corporate action. Mission and ministry are only possible for each of us and all of us, together, as we are structured in such a way that we are connected. Our denominational polity is such a system of conferences (i.e., local, district, annual, jurisdictional and central, and general) through which we are connected, each having its own basic responsibilities, yet intricately connected with the other conference levels, as well as laterally connected with collegial conferences.

The Essential Nature of the Connection

The Connection is the ecclesiastical organizing principle that has allowed Methodism to grow and develop during the past four centuries. An interesting historical book written in 1971 by Charles Ferguson, a former Methodist clergyman and journalist in the 1970s, characterized the Wesleyan movement in America as one that was, in the words of the book title, "Organizing To Beat the Devil."[4] The devil, as the chaotic force of evil that seeks to separate and destroy creation, is a reality we continue to face each day. The Wesleyan understanding is that through organic organization we can literally beat the devil. It would seem that we United Methodists are certainly organized, when you consider *The Book of Discipline*, *The Book of Resolutions*, *The Book of Worship*, even that little black book, the *Daily Suggester*, made available each year to clergy by Cokesbury, so that they can remember all those meetings (not to mention the liturgical calendar). All these speak to the reality that Mr. Ferguson's somewhat whimsical title succinctly illustrates.

John Wesley (1703-1791) was a Renaissance man of the Enlightenment in 18th-century England, a time of great advancement in Western thought, but also a time of the culturally devastating Industrial Revolution; wars across Europe and the newly emerging United States of America; and economic upheaval, creating a middle class between the poor working class and elite wealthy class. In response to all of this, John and Charles Wesley called together a few fellow Oxford scholars to live out Christianity in a "methodical" way. Some would suggest that, if they were diagnosed by a 21st-century psychologist, the Wesley brothers might be considered as having an obsessive compulsive disorder. However, this obsession with creative order has worked, and worked well, ever since the Wesleys' time. United Methodism does reflect the Wesleys' passion for bringing order, organization, and attention to detail to all of life, and to ecclesiastical activities in particular. We are organizing to beat the devil, as our basic principle of missiology.

Connectionalism is not merely a form of polity that is optional for the church. It is the biblical model for the church to be organized for its task of witnessing in all the world (Cf. Acts 1:8). The church in its very nature is connectional, a people connected to one another by faith and grace. As Jesus stated the nature of his mission and presence in the world in relation to God the Creator, in John 15, he described it as a vine and branches. Branches are of necessity connected to the vine, and therefore to each other. To be disconnected is to be literally useless. The nourishment of the whole plant moves through each branch and the trunk of the vine. All of this is how we are connected. Our church structures and relationships can be no less than this. The branches of a vine are virtually impossible to distinguish from one another. The unity of the church is found in the interrelationships of the constituent members. Just as the different parts of a body cannot exist, much less function, separated from each other, the branches are not independent outgrowths of the center vine, but are intimately networked with each other.

Our life in mission is organized for us to "abide" in Christ and one another, as the vine and branches of the living church, which means not just to live into or with, but more a stance of being fully present, patiently and acceptingly waiting on one another for the movement of the Spirit, or as Wesley would say, to conference together to understand God's Word and will for us in our day. This is to abide with Jesus, as when he states:

> Abide in me as I abide in you. Just as the branch cannot bear fruit by itself unless it abides in the vine, neither can you unless you abide in me. I am the vine, you are the branches. Those who abide in me and I in them bear much fruit, because apart from me you can do nothing (John 15:4-5).

He is saying that as we abide in him we will bear fruit, be productive, and be the living visible witness to the presence of God in the world. Connectionalism is this biblical organizing principle of mission in the United Methodist tradition that allows us to abide as the universal and global body of Christ. As we abide in Christ's love, living together in mission, the vine and branches of the church keep us connected with all persons in all nations, races, and faiths.

The Gospel Rings of United Methodism

United Methodism, as an organizational community, is structured much differently from either a hierarchical corporate entity, or from a loose federation of groups. We are connectional. This means that while there is no one person or group that guides and directs the work of the whole organization, neither are all of our units independent from one another. We are connected by our faith and heritage, but more so by our common mission. That is, our common faith in the Triune God, and living out our common heritage of the past several centuries, into the present and yet-to-come reign of God.

This connectional system enables The United Methodist Church to embody the mandate Jesus gave to all disciples, as recorded in the Book of Acts, chapter 1, verse 8: "But you will receive power when the Holy Spirit has come upon you; and you will be my witnesses in Jerusalem, in all Judea and Samaria, and to the ends of the Earth." We are called to be witnesses to Jesus Christ in all places all at the same time. How can we do this? Because we, as a connected body of Christ, are literally everywhere all at once.

The structure that allows this is our system of conferences. Christian conferencing is perhaps John Wesley's most significant contribution to Christian spirituality. By this the church makes decisions, sets goals, creates accountability, and in general pays attention to the will of God throughout our structure. We listen and speak to each other knowing that no one individual or group can speak God's whole will, but that each has some aspect of it. Together, in conference, we discern that which God is calling us to be and do.

We have five distinct forms of conferences in The United Methodist Church: General, Jurisdictional (and Central), Annual, District, and Charge (or Local). Each form of conference refers both to the actual meeting—the conference session itself—and to a more or less geographic area from which the members of the conference session come, and from whom representatives are selected for the next level of conferences.

The General Conference is the whole denomination from all over the world, which meets once every four years. The Jurisdictional Conferences also meet every four years, a few months after the General Conference, and each encompasses a broad geographical area of the United States. Outside of the US, this form of conference is called a Central Conference and is also a region of the world. Because of the different needs of the church around the world, Central Conferences function the same as Jurisdictional Conferences, but with variant rules of order to meet these needs.

The Annual Conferences meet every year and encompass a state, part of a state, or several states, in the US. Outside the US, the Annual Conferences represent a comparably sized area, though usually with fewer constituent local churches than in the US. District Conferences are a smaller unit of the Annual Conferences, also meeting every year. The Charge Conference is a local church, or several local churches working together, served by an appointed pastor.

We can envision these five categories of conferences graphically like the Olympic Games symbol of five interconnected rings. Each ring is one of the types of conference. They are all interconnected, yet there is no top or bottom, no exact flow chart of power and authority. Each conference has its own particular responsibilities, as defined in *The Book of Discipline*. Using the Olympic rings to portray our form of church structure emphasizes that our policy and decision-making process is not a "top down" or "bottom up" type of organization. We are not hierarchical, nor "grassroots." Rather we comprise a network of interrelated and interactive Christian conferences. Each one of the forms of conferencing has its own responsibilities, integrity of membership, and accountability. Each one relates to the others in the structure, though not all relate to each other equally. The Annual Conference is the center and most basic unit of our denomination, the body that relates to every other level of the church. The Annual Conference elects members of the General and Jurisdictional/Central Conferences, but it is also from the Annual Conference that local churches are formed, and from which pastors are appointed to these churches. The Charge Conference works closely with the District and Annual Conferences, but much less so with the Jurisdictional and General Conferences. And so on. Thus, the linkages of the ring system keep United Methodists tied together (that is, United, not Untied!), and working together in God's Mission.

Connectional Blessings

Because God's Mission is being implemented via the Connection, Church and Community Worker Gary Locklear, who serves the Native-American community in North Carolina, tells of a Volunteer-In-Mission team from Georgia installing a new roof on "Larry's" house. He was in failing health with very limited resources. Gary writes of the blessing available by blessing others. Larry was blessed with the much-needed roof, and the VIM team was equally blessed by having the opportunity to serve Christ from the housetops! "Sun and salvation do wonderful things to the soul," Gary reports.

After witnessing the murder of her husband during a time of civil conflict, Marceline had escaped the Democratic Republic of Congo (DRC), and was now in the United States, walking the streets of Philadelphia. She was familiar with the United Methodist church in the DRC and asked passersby, "Do you know where the Methodist church is?" With the help of Frankford Group Ministry, a United Methodist Community of Shalom sponsored by the Eastern Pennsylvania Annual Conference and Global Ministries, Marceline began a new life, and was even able to bring her children to the United States to live with her. The Connection works worldwide, to bring blessings to a sojourner in our land.

The Rev. Denise Honeycutt and her husband, Pat Watkins, served as United Methodist missionaries in Nigeria. Now, as the Virginia Annual Conference Director of Mission, Denise sees the connection of mission working every day. She remembers the support they received while in Nigeria, and is now able to encourage and enable this same support for other missionaries through the Covenant Relationship program. She writes, "We have people all over the world who have heard God's call in their life. We are so blessed as United Methodists to be part of this wonderful connectional system that offers each of us the opportunity to grow and learn from each other."

In the mission of the church, the *missio ecclesia*, our connectional system that rings the world allows us to be the body of Christ, because we are intimately connected to one another through the conference rings. As we organize to be in mission, we will find the resources and persons in each of the conferences through which we are linked, that assists each unit to share the good news of God's wonderful grace with the least and the last of this hurting world. Take the time to read about the specifics of our United Methodist system in *The Book of Discipline*, and see the interactions and connections of the United Methodist gospel rings.

Jesus' call to be faithful witnesses, here, there, and everywhere in the world in Acts 1, means that we as the church must be everywhere at once. We are to be everywhere, and to go from everywhere to everywhere, all at the same time. Because of the organic organizing principle of the body of Christ, which we refer to as the Connection, we can be everywhere at once. We are intimately connected with all believers around the world, as well as across the street, so that we can fulfill the Lord's clarion call to be witnesses, here, there, and everywhere. The Connection is not a mechanical imposition of a utilitarian business principle, it is rather the organic relationships of "all who follow Jesus all around the world, yes, we're the Church together."[5]

Concepts to Consider

1. Why is individual Christianity a self-contradiction, like iron made of wood?
2. How do you abide—live in and with—other faithful witnesses?
3. When have you seen the organic connection of United Methodism in your congregation?

Notes for ESSAY 11

[1] Margaret J. Wheatley and Myron Kellner-Rodgers, *A Simpler Way* (San Francisco: Berrett-Koehler, 1996), p. 30.

[2] Emil Brunner, *The Word and the World* (New York: Charles Scribner's Sons, 1931) pp. 106-107.

[3] Ibid., p. 126.

[4] Charles W. Ferguson, *Organizing to Beat the Devil* (Garden City, NY: Doubleday, 1971).

[5] From the song, *We Are the Church*, by Richard K. Avery and Donald S. Marsh, 1972.

ESSAY 12

No More Children for Calamity

Tradition understood through Mission Goal 3:
To Alleviate Human Suffering

Isaiah 65:17-25: No more children for calamity.

Mark 10.13-16: Jesus blesses little children.

Our United Methodist tradition is to care for the most vulnerable in society, who are often the children, and to receive them as Jesus did, with blessing and love, which moves us toward the vision of God's coming kingdom for all children.

Innocent Faith in a Chicken Seed

While making a routine check on the children napping at the Methodist Day Care Center in Rocinha, Rio de Janeiro's largest *favela* (Portuguese for shanty town), Nancy, the child-care worker, realized that a three-year-old girl had been put down to nap without washing her hands. Still greasy from the chicken eaten at lunch, she clutched her little fist securely, as though holding something very valuable.

Nancy woke the child before the others in order to have her wash her hands before playing. She discovered that this child had the bone from her piece of chicken in her hand and wasn't about to give it up. Asked why, she said it was the chicken seed, which she was taking home to plant. Her dream was to have a chicken tree burst forth from that seed planted in the tiny yard of her small family home. Why? "So my mommy and sisters and brothers can all have meat to eat like I do here!"

A small group of street children in São Paulo, Brazil, took Methodist pastor The Rev. Zeny de Lima Soares, well known in Brazil for her leadership in specialized ministries to street children, to see how they stayed warm on a freezing cold day. They led her into a shelter made from cardboard boxes, with a hole in the "roof" in the middle of the space where they had a small fire. Off to one corner was a large bucket of shoemaker's glue. The children sat around that fire sniffing glue from small plastic containers they salvaged from the garbage cans. They told Zeny, "The glue keeps us from feeling cold or hungry. It really works, pastora."

Children are in danger in our world because of war—when food production is stopped and food shipments are prevented from going to the hungry children because of the political differences of their fathers; when children die of contaminated or no water, disease, shrapnel, and Napalm.

Children are in danger in our world because of poverty, when a few government and corporate leaders decide how much the food is worth and will let it rot before they drop the price, or allow medical centers to be destroyed or abandoned as resources are used for weapons, or are hoarded by a few wealthy individuals.

Children are in danger in our world because they are too sick and too weak to eat, dying of dehydration as the result of poor water and ignorance of hygiene and public health measures; or because they have not been immunized against preventable, yet fatal diseases.

Children are in danger in our world because they are the least and the last, the dispensable and the despised; because all too often children are seen as the root of the problem, rather than the fruit of our generation.

And we do remember that this is not only an issue of the care of children across the seas. According to the Children's Defense Fund, every day in America four children are killed by abuse or neglect, five children or teens commit suicide, eight children or teens are killed by firearms, and 2,411 babies are born into poverty. Eighteen percent of all American children live below the poverty level.

It does not have to be this way—here or anywhere. Our Creator God has given us a vision of a glorious new creation that awaits fulfillment. The prophet Isaiah proclaims:

> For I am about to create new heavens and a new earth; the former things shall not be remembered or come to mind....No more shall there be in it an infant that lives but a few days....They shall not labor in vain, or bear children for calamity; for they shall be offspring blessed by the Lord... (selected verses from Isaiah 65:17-23).

God intends a far different life for the world's children than most now experience. This vision of God's coming kingdom is in our midst, within our reach, literally "at hand" as Jesus told us (Matthew 4:17). It is a very realistic vision. No more children born into calamity. No more children suffering, forsaken, lost, and alone. And so this is the agenda of the church as we engage in God's Mission. One of our most important goals is to be about God's business of caring for children as we respond to their cries for food, housing, and simple decency and respect—to love and care for our innocent offspring who desperately need our concern. That's what United Methodist mission with children is essentially about—blessing children, as Jesus accepted and blessed the children.

People were bringing little children to him in order that he might touch them; and the disciples spoke sternly to them. But when Jesus saw this, he was indignant and said to them, "Let the little children come to me; do not stop them; for it is to such as these that the kingdom of God belongs. Truly I tell you, whoever does not receive the kingdom of God as a little child will never enter it." And he took them up in his arms, laid his hands on them, and blessed them (Mark 10:13-16).

John Wesley has been credited with a clear call to all Christians, to: "Do all the good you can, by all the means you can, in all the ways you can, in all the places you can, at all the times you can, to all the people you can, as long as ever you can...."[1] The Church as it cares for all, in all ways, is the essential unity and wholeness of God's Word of salvation and grace, and this is God's call to care for the least and last in our theology and practice. When accused by an Irish government official of taking from the poor rather than serving them, Wesley emphatically replied:

You affirm, sixthly, that I "rob and plunder the poor, so as to leave them neither bread to eat nor raiment to put on." A heavy charge, but without all color of truth—yea, just the reverse is true. Abundance of those in Cork, Bandon, Limerick, Dublin, as well as in all parts of England, who a few years ago, either through sloth or profuseness, had not bread to eat or raiment to put on, have now, by means of the preachers called Methodists, a sufficiency of both.[2]

Methodism has always had a strong tradition of reaching out to the least, the last, the marginalized, who often are the children of all societies, to affect the suffering of the world's children. We continue in this mission with all the ways we are simply blessing children following in the footsteps of Jesus through the global ministries of serving these children and their families. Let the children come to Christ, do not hinder them but respect them for the important people they are to Jesus' ministry, and therefore to our continuing mission in the Way of Christ.

Blessing Children in Africa

United Methodist missionary Jerri Savuto tells of meeting Priscilla, a seven-year-old AIDS orphan in Kenya. She lives with her grandmother and two bothers, and when Jerri first met her, she and her family were severely malnourished, and could not attend school, as their grandmother had no income. Across Africa orphans of the AIDS pandemic live with their grandmothers, but without parents who previously supported both the grandmothers and the children, they have no land, no food, no resources for education. At the Maua Methodist Hospital in rural Kenya the AIDS Orphan Program has since 2001 been able to share food, education, faith, hope, and God's love. Priscilla and her brothers came to the orphan program and are now attending school, well fed, joyful, and full of hope. The program is supported by gifts to the Advance for Christ and His Church from across the United States.

Blessing Children in America

Mark and Rebecca Smallwood teach at the Red Bird School, a mission of the Red Bird Missionary Conference in the poverty-encased hills of southeastern Kentucky. Through the mission school they seek to assist children to move forward in life. Mark says of their ministry, "Kids are so special. They're real. They'll tell you what they're thinking. You just get to be yourself and to encourage them to see what they can become, to see their potential."

Betsy and Chuck Jack are also missionaries at Red Bird. Betsy works with the Early Childhood Development (ECD) program. Visitors go to the homes of three- and four-year-olds to get them ready for the school. It is a time to share their lives as they listen to stories, sing, and learn basic skills needed to succeed in the academic world of the school, along with the love of Christ expressed for these often isolated rural children. The school and the ECD program are a real blessing in this community.

Blessing Children in Asia

Clara Biswas is a General Board of Global Ministries missionary serving in Phnom Penh, Cambodia. Upon seeing the horrible situation of some of the children there, whose families pick through the garbage dumps to earn enough money to survive, she began the Light at the Dumpsites program. Clara shares, "All desire a better economic present and a hopeful future, but trying circumstances bring all to what seems a forsaken place." The Light at the Dumpsites program provides Christian education through a Sunday school program in addition to scholarship and nutritional support for around 25 children. As Christmas was celebrated at the dumpsite, the children joyously presented the Christmas drama with an even deeper understanding of what it means to have the gift of "Light" and hope in a seemingly very dark and hopeless place.

Blessing Children in Europe

Nikola is a high school student who lives in a village in Macedonia, southeastern Europe. His home village has a primary school, but he must go into the city for high school, and the cost of transportation, books, and supplies is just too much for his farm family's meager income. The United Methodist Church in that nation, with whom Carol Partridge serves as a missionary in Christian Education programming, sponsors Nikola to go to school. When, on a cold and damp winter morning Nikola came to the church for his money for the van, he told Carol about the recent flooding in his village, and showed her his water-soaked shoes, his only shoes.

Carol had been given some men's clothing to give away, and had just one pair of boots left. "What size are your feet?" she asked Nikola, and of course they matched the boots perfectly. She said to herself, "They had been waiting for the right person, someone who really needed them." Carol is there for the children of Macedonia, in a growing United Methodist presence, with innovative Saturday Bible schools and other programs that bless the children, whose feet can be set on a warm, dry journey of faith.

Blessing Children in Latin America and the Caribbean

At La Mar Methodista (The Methodist Home) in Santa Maria, the state of Rio Grande du Sul, in southern Brazil, former street children live in group cottages with house parents, attending school on site with academic disciplines as well as vocational training to help them into the future. They live together as a community, learning, praying, and laughing. When living on the streets of Rio de Janeiro, they did not laugh much, for most survived an existence of fear and anger. At this country home on a hillside, children play soccer together, learn to live in peace with one another, and experience a sense of love and family not possible in their former lives.

In Puerto Rico the Methodist Church operates Centro Met, a six-day-a-week day-care center and seven-day-a-week church and sanctuary, in the fullest sense of the term, that is a place of rest and respite from a cruel world, particularly for a three- or four- or five-year-old. The center is housed in an old school building in a low-income section of Santurce, an inner suburb of San Juan. Throughout the week there, the dirt and macadam playground is filled with laughter and giggles and life "in all its fullness." It is so different from the quiet desperation of grinding poverty in the surrounding streets.

Their Name Is "Today"

In the name and spirit of Jesus we are reaching out to bless, care for, and love children across the continents through our connectional church, meeting real needs of the suffering world. Again and again Jesus speaks to us in this day and says, "Whoever welcomes one such child in my name welcomes me" (Matthew 18:5). This is not an issue for us to take up sometime, for children will not wait. The Chilean poet and educator Gabriela Mistral[3] wrote: "Many things can wait, the children cannot. Right now is the time their bones are being formed, their senses are being developed. To them we cannot answer tomorrow. Their name is today."

Concepts to Consider

1. What is God's vision for children?
2. Who is carrying on the tradition of care and concern for children in your community?
3. Why is "today" the name of all children of the world?

Notes for ESSAY 12

[1] Wesley likely did not use this phrase as such, but it is a compilation of this sentiment which he wrote in several letters and sermons, and it is widely attributed to him in this fashion.

[2] "A Letter to the Reverend Mr. Bally of Cork" (referencing a letter to the Mayor of Cork, Ireland, May 27, 1750), from *The Complete Works of John Wesley* (Baker Publishing Group; 4th edition, 1996).

[3] Pseudonym of Lucila Godoy Alcayaga, a Chilean poet and educator, 1889-1957, who was awarded the Nobel Prize for Literature in 1945.

ESSAY 13

The Feet of the Messenger:
Servanthood in God's Mission

Tradition understood through Mission Goal 4:
To Seek Justice, Freedom, and Peace

Philippians 2:5-8: Jesus models servanthood.

John 21:15-19: Feed my sheep, the call to serve God's people
by nourishing/feeding.

Servanthood in God's Mission is seen in the United Methodist tradition of seeking justice, freedom, and peace through service in the world, particularly among women organized for mission. Servant messengers proclaim God's kingdom, which is in our midst and available to all oppressed by greed, hate, stereotyping, and the demonic systems that steal physical and spiritual life from God's people.

The Entangled Feet of the Messenger

> How beautiful upon the mountains are the feet of the messenger who announces peace, who brings good news, who announces salvation, who says to Zion, "Your God reigns" (Isaiah 52:7).

The Managua dumpsite, what we might refer to as a landfill, is called a *basurero* in Spanish. It lies just outside of the city, along the shores of Lake Managua. The relentless sun shines down in 100-degree heat on the hard-packed, light brown dirt that rises in large puffs of dust as the garbage trucks roll through the gates. To keep the dust out we closed the windows of the van we rode in, which also lessened the oppressive odors that rose up out of the land. As we drove past the handful of shacks that lined the entranceway, we passed by the makeshift "recycling market" where the kids bring their treasures to trade for cash. We came to visit these children and youth of the *basurero*, who dig out a living from the waste of society.

When we stopped after driving a short way into the center of the dumpsite, a trio of male teens came over and, through our interpreter, told us about their "profession"—the tattered shoes to protect their feet, the hoe for digging, and the large plastic bag with a shoulder strap for collecting the valuables. "Do you ever go to school?" we asked. "Well, I used to," reported one of the trio. "I guess

I'd like to go back...but I need to be here when the trucks arrive. If I'm not here, I miss the best stuff."

While we talked with the teens there was a bit of a rustling noise behind us. There, rolling in the dirt, was a small bag-of-a-boy, covered head to toe in caked-on dirt. He wore cut-off pants and a pair of sneakers that would fit him better in four or five years than they did on that day. He was giggling and laughing as he rolled in the dirt, and we thought at first he was just playing at some game, but as we watched closely we noticed that wrapped around his feet, and those huge sneakers, was a coiled length of barbed wire. As he struggled to free himself from the entanglement he continued to laugh and giggle until he suddenly jumped to his feet, and freed of the wire, he scampered off.

As I reflected on the lad, I realized that he *is* Nicaragua: young, full of life, happy with life as God has created it, yet continually tripped up by the barbed wire of North American greed. We have figuratively buried barbed wire all over this beautiful land of lakes and volcanoes, in the form of a century of military occupation, inhuman sweatshops to make our jeans, and unrealistic expectations for economic development from the International Monetary Fund. Our nation's corporate and governmental policies are like barbed wire entangling the feet of this young country's people. Yet they do not so much cry out of the injustice as they sing and dance and celebrate life. They are very aware of the afflictions we have placed upon them, much more than we North Americans are aware of their plight, but on the whole they are a welcoming and forgiving people who simply want the economic freedom that will allow them to put their feet on firm ground and walk proudly into the future.

A Missionary Response to North-South Injustice

United Methodist missionary Paul Jeffrey, who works globally to interpret to our Church the realities of God's Mission today, has written of these observations, "I often write about what Christians are doing to empower people at the margins to live the abundant life that's promised to them in the Gospel. I focus on why they're doing that and what the consequences of that work may be for ordinary women and men in the pews," says Paul. "When I do that well, people in the global north begin to understand how we are intrinsically linked to our sisters and brothers in the global south, not just because they share the same Gospel, but also because we share an international economic system that manufactures poverty and injustice for the majority."

The message of peace involves justice, more than simply well-being and ease from conflict. A young boy's feet, entangled in barbed wire, can show us this important pathway as we seek to follow in the footsteps of the Master. How beautiful upon the mountains of trash are the feel of the young messenger of peace. He reminds us that God reigns, now and forever. It is from these servants of peace, servants of God's love, that we can learn to be disciples seeking justice, freedom, and peace.

Jesus The Servant

The model for our servanthood in God's Mission is directly from Jesus' life of service. As Paul reminded the church in Philippi of this ancient hymn:

> Let the same mind be in you that was in Christ Jesus,
>> who, though he was in the form of God,
>>> did not regard equality with God
>>> as something to be exploited,
>> but emptied himself,
>>> taking the form of a slave,
>>> being born in human likeness.
>> And being found in human form,
>>> he humbled himself
>>> and became obedient to the point of death—
>>> even death on a cross (Philippians 2:5-8).

Jesus modeled mission servanthood and partnership in the kingdom by emptying himself of divine rank, taking the form of a servant, and assuming the trials and risks of servanthood. To be in mission with others as Jesus was present in the world is the Christology of God's Mission; taking the form of a servant, not using his divine status to be placed above humanity, but becoming one with humanity. It is the incarnational nature of *missio Dei*, as previously discussed. David Bosch, in analyzing the several biblical scenes of Jesus calling the disciples, notes that this call was not the same as becoming students of one of the many wandering prophetic rabbis of the day. Rather, Jesus' call is to servanthood.[1] Even in this Jesus himself was not so much a master as a servant also, for as is stated in Mark's Gospel, "For the Son of Man also came not to be served but to serve and to give his life as a ransom for many" (Mark 10:45). Disciples are called to mission as a life statement of our faith, all belonging to Christ and to each other in community. Discipleship is servanthood, just as Jesus is the servant of the world. We are called not only to be with Jesus, but also to be like Jesus.

Servanthood of Methodist Women Organized for Mission

The history of Methodist mission is filled with the servanthood discipleship of women organized in and for God's Mission. Dr. Dana Robert, United Methodist missiologist and mission historian, wrote in the introduction to a significant work on the history of women in mission, "Outnumbering men by two to one on the mission field during much of the [20th] century, women's own distinctive contributions to mission practice and theory have been ignored by scholars until fairly recently."[2] Beginning in the late 19th century, Methodist women organized mission societies because the male leadership of the day would not hear of the cries for justice and bread of women and children around the world. With the pennies, nickels, and dimes they gathered through local unit meetings, the women worked tirelessly in God's mission, sending missionaries; building mission centers and educational institutions in the United States and around the world; and advocating for the just rights of women, children, and youth, most often the marginalized in all societies. Humble servants of the Lord, they sought little recognition in the seats of ecclesiastical or governmental power, but fervently spoke truth to these powers on behalf of the oppressed of the world.

In the mid-19th century, Methodist women saw the realities of the world about them, and with their biblical understandings of the call of God to teach, heal, and comfort, they began to organize to bring this faith into the lives of the needs of this hurting, especially among women and children.

> They wanted to do something about it. Missionary leaders of the church failed to share their enthusiasm or catch their insights, so the women simply formed their own "missionary societies." This did not happen easily, for few women were accustomed to public speaking and working outside their homes. Husbands and fathers, as well as other church leaders, had decided opinions about the role and place of women. They belonged at home![3]

But they did not stay home, rather they went into all the world. From very humble yet enthusiastic beginnings, the various women's missionary societies grew in number, resources, and influence into the 20th century. They sent missionaries across the United States and around the world. Local units of women met to pray, study, and raise financial support for these efforts. They learned about leadership from their work, and trained others from what they had experienced in this practical education. They were bound together in their faith and commitment to the common cause of God's Mission. Over time the individual societies came together in a national organization, and as the denomination went through structural mergers so did the women, resulting first in the formation of the Woman's Society of Christian Service in 1939, and the United Methodist Women in 1972.

Women organized for mission over all this time have made real Jesus' admonishment to Peter to: "Feed my lamps...Tend my sheep...Feed my sheep" out of love for Christ (John 21:15-19). This call to serve God's people by nourishing and feeding them is a foundational understanding of the work of the Women's Division of the General Board of Global Ministries, and of all United Methodist Women in local units and district and annual conference organizations. Servanthood discipleship is service to all the world, beginning at home and moving toward the ends of the earth (Acts 1:8).

Learning Servanthood as Volunteers

During a recent summer, Lyndsey Beutin served as a Global Justice Volunteer (GJV) through Global Ministries, a Mission Volunteers program for young adults. Lyndsey and two other young adults volunteered in Nicaragua with Acción Medica Cristiana (Christian Medical Action), a Global Ministries partner. As they arrived in Nicaragua, their host explained to them the challenges that the community faced, with a list that included lack of employment opportunities, lack of health-care facilities, lack of clean water, violence, and poor roads. Lyndsey and the other volunteers soon learned that despite the many hardships, people of faith in this rural community in Nicaragua had hope and strength, and worked in a variety of ways to address these problems in service with one another. They held educational seminars on clean water, led discussions on violence, established a medical brigade, and much more. As servants through the GJV program, Lyndsey and her teammates had the opportunity to learn from and be served by the work of her Christian brothers and sisters in this community.

When she returned to her campus ministry in North Carolina, a drop fell into a pond and a ripple has followed. Through Lyndsey, other students have learned about the struggles of people in Nicaragua, as well as the ways these brothers and sisters are powerfully working as servants of all to transform the community in which they live. Inspired by the Nicaraguans' faithfulness and action, these young people are seeking ways to work to address challenges that people continue to face, both in Nicaragua and in their own community. As students in Lyndsey's campus ministry explore how to live as faithful Christians, a small community of believers is growing closer to each other and to the world beyond their campus. As more relationships are established and partnerships are created between brothers and sisters around the world, all are building God's beloved community of servant disciples.

Vehicles of Servanthood

Diane Wimberly, a United Methodist missionary to Bolivia, writes of the pastors of that country who, without autos, bicycles, or even roads, walk many miles in pastoral ministry. They make home visits, carrying medicines to sick church members, or the wool yarn to artisans upon which their livelihood depends. Diane sees the sandals the pastors wear as holy icons of mission. The feet of the messengers of God's good news—in word and deed—travel on these holy sandals of grace. They are the vehicles of servanthood. The feet of the messengers of peace and good news are beautiful along those mountain roads. These servants of all make visible to us salvation and God's reign.

> Consecrate me now to thy service, Lord, by the power of grace divine;
> Let my soul look up with a steadfast hope, and my will be lost in thine.[4]

Concepts to Consider

1. Why is servanthood a lifestyle of faithful witnesses in the 21st century?
2. What is the tradition of United Methodist Women that moves them into God's Mission?
3. How can you engage in offering freedom and peace in the world as a servant?

Notes for ESSAY 13

[1] David J. Bosch, *Transforming Mission, Paradigm Shifts in Theology of Mission* (Maryknoll, NY: Orbis Books, 1991), p. 38.

[2] Dana Lee Robert, ed. *Gospel Bearers, Gender Barriers: Missionary Women in the Twentieth Century* (American Society of Missiology Series), p. ix.

[3] Barbara E. Campbell, *In the Middle of Tomorrow* (New York: Women's Division, General Board of Global Ministries, 1975), p. 2.

[4] *The United Methodist Hymnal* (Nashville, TN: United Methodist Publishing House, 1989), #419.

CHAPTER FOUR

EXPERIENCE

Through the understanding of our own experience in life, our personal witness as well as the struggles of being God's people, we bring theological analysis into a contemporary perspective. It is these experiences of the whole body of Christ in all places and cultures that most effectively informs our missiological study.

ESSAY 14: *Equipping the Body for Mission Through Mission Education*

Experience understood through Mission Goal 1:
To Make Disciples of Jesus Christ

Romans 12:4-8: Functions in the body of Christ.

Matthew 20:1-16: Focus on the tasks of mission.

Ephesians 4:1-16: Equip the saints for the work of mission.

Functional Connectionalism is the experience of the church through a variety of programs that enable us to be the body of Christ in mission, and allow us to make disciples by building up the whole church through the activities of mission education. We use every function of the body to facilitate the usefulness of the whole body together.

ESSAY 15: *Paddling The Canoe Together: The Experience of Partnership*

Experience understood through Mission Goal 2:
To Strengthen, Develop, and Renew Christian Community

John 15:8-17: Mission is love that bears fruit by friends of God.

John 17:20-21: "That they may all be one."

To experience mission partnership is the full expression of what it is to be ecumenical, which is to involve all of the inhabited world. This means working across denominational boundaries with governmental and other secular agencies worldwide. When mission partners are joined together in interdependence with mutual trust, they respect the integrity of their common confession of God revealed in Jesus Christ.

ESSAY 16: *Coming Home to Abundant Life*

Experience understood through Mission Goal 3:
To Alleviate Human Suffering

John 10:1-18: Abundant life for all.

Hope and wholeness for all of God's people is the invitation from Jesus Christ, the Good Shepherd who leads us home toward God's coming kingdom. Working on behalf of those in need is our experience of the reality of this abundant life here and now, as we reach out toward the future.

ESSAY 17: *Justice is "Done" by Loving Kindness and Walking Humbly*

Experience understood through Mission Goal 4:
To Seek Justice, Freedom, and Peace

Micah 6:6-8: Doing justice is to love kindness and walk humbly with God.

Luke 4:16-21/Isaiah 61:1-4: The Spirit of the Lord brings freedom
and justice.

Doing justice by being Christ in the world is the experience of doing justice by loving kindness and walking humbly. Ministries of justice, freedom, and peace are not so much about setting an agenda for action, while this may well happen. They begin with a relational understanding of whose lives we are seeking to impact, and with whom we walk about on the face of the earth.

ESSAY 14

Equipping the Body for Mission Through Mission Education

Experience understood through Mission Goal 1:
To Make Disciples of Jesus Christ

Romans 12:4-8: Functions in the body of Christ.

Matthew 20:1-16: Focus on the tasks of mission.

Ephesians 4:1-16: Equip the saints for the work of mission.

Functional Connectionalism is the experience of the church through a variety of programs which enable us to be the body of Christ in mission, and allow us to make disciples by building up the whole church through the activities of mission education. We use every function of the body to facilitate the usefulness of the whole body together.

Functional Connectionalism

> For as in one body we have many members, and not all the members have the same function, so we, who are many, are one body in Christ, and individually we are members one of another (Romans 12:4-5).

While to "make disciples of Jesus Christ," both as the Disciplinary mission statement of The United Methodist Church,[1] and as the first of the Four Program Goals of the General Board of Global Ministries, is not a manufacturing enterprise, it does require a certain amount of forming, shaping, and preparing, all with specific tasks involved. Disciples are "made" through the faithful communal actions of the church. Paul understood this nature of the church very well, stating that not everyone has the same function in the body of Christ. We are all of the same body, but just as the parts of the body function differently, so do the various parts of the church. We are many, but all members of one another, and together our ministry is to make other disciples. So, to make disciples requires what could be called "Functional Connectionalism." This involves specific programs, which together make disciples out of mere participants. It is a pattern of growth exercises designed to enable the whole church—local, regional, national, and international—to function as a whole body in mission as we move toward God's coming reign.

The Connection, described earlier, is not simply a good theological and biblically based understanding of how to organize the church, though that it surely is. The Connection exists to serve the *missio Dei*, not the reverse. The Connection functions on behalf of God's Mission because the members of the Connection so function. As Paul continues, "We have gifts that differ according to the grace given to us: prophecy, in proportion to faith; ministry, in ministering; the teacher, in teaching; the exhorter, in exhortation; the giver, in generosity; the leader, in diligence; the compassionate, in cheerfulness" (Romans 4:6-8). The gifts we are given by God serve God's Mission with various functions, all of which are carried out in relation to other disciples. The thrust of all this activity, however, is not just to exist as the church, but to *be* the body of Christ in the world, to engage in God's Mission.

Get the Grapes Harvested!

In an address to the Global Ministries directors several years ago, the Rev. R. Randy Day, former general secretary of the General Board of Global Ministries, offered a new look at Jesus' parable of the workers in the vineyard (Matthew 20:1-16).[2] Traditionally, most preachers and biblical interpreters regard this story of day laborers being paid the same regardless of time worked as one that emphasizes the importance of all persons, regardless of background, or more specifically, seniority. It was spoken to the religious leadership of Jesus' day that tended to look at their ethnic or religious heritage as a sign of salvation. Rev. Day sees the point of the parable as the need to harvest the grapes—nothing is more important! The focus is not about compensation for work completed; rather, getting the grapes harvested is the most important issue. Get the job done. Get on with the task at hand. Call in more workers and resource them as they need, not based on some external formula for compensation and assistance. The fields are ripe for harvest, but the laborers seem to be few (Matthew 9:37-38; Luke 10:2). And for him and our denominational mission agency this means that we need to be about the work of God's Mission, using all available persons to "harvest the grapes." In contemporary cultural slang...*just do it!*

Rev. Day went on to emphasize that the parable also called for the inclusion of all persons in the work of mission as the only way to get the work done. The *missio Dei* is inclusive of all races, ages, genders, nationalities, abilities, and disabilities. No one is excluded from God's work in the world that is global ministries. We must look for any and all available persons who can carry out the *missio Dei*, making resources available to them for the tasks at hand. This means that while all persons are to be included in the workforce for mission, training in mission is crucial.

To go back to the parable, ripping the grapes off the vine will damage the vine, or rough treatment will damage the grapes. In order to have the workers know how to appropriately care for the grapes and the vines, it is necessary to train supervisors to train the workers. As Paul wrote so well to the church in Ephesus, there are a variety of skills and tasks which are needed, and are given by God, in order to get the work done (Ephesians 4:11-16). Naiveté is one sin of the church. We must use gifted persons and all knowledge to "speak the truth in love," while we are joined together in the connection as the body of Christ, with the ligaments helping all parts to work by making the connections. Global ministries requires connecting ligaments, the workers and trainers and supervisors: "The gifts he gave were that some would be apostles, some prophets, some evangelists, some pastors and teachers, to equip the saints for the work of ministry, for building up the body of Christ" (Ephesians 4:11-12). The point of the training is not to make persons feel valuable, as wonderful as this may feel, but to equip everyone to get on with the tasks of God's Mission, to build up the body of Christ because the harvest is there before us.

Paul began this passage with a kind of doxological call for unity and peace in the church as a sign of our very nature, because: "There is one body and one Spirit, just as you were called to the one hope of your calling, one Lord, one faith, one baptism, one God and Father of all, who is above all and through all and in all" (Ephesians 4:4-6). This unity comes from the gifts God gives to carry out the various tasks for mission and ministry, that he goes on to list, which are what keeps the whole body working as we are constantly becoming more like Christ: "But speaking the truth in love, we must grow up in every way into him who is the head, into Christ, from whom the whole body, joined and knit together by every ligament with which it is equipped, as each part is working properly, promotes the body's growth in building itself up in love" (Ephesians 4:15-16).

This is Functional Connectionalism. All parts of the body of Christ—the church visible in the world—being equipped for mission, joined and connected together as a human body is connected by ligaments and muscle, skin and bone, all a whole being. The church in mission is this whole being, in unity and peace, seeking to harvest the grapes. Connectionalism works because it is pragmatic and task-oriented, while at its best exhibiting what it means to be a whole being as the body of Christ. A significant aspect of the *missio Dei*, then, is equipping the saints for mission, and this comes under the broad heading of mission education.

Gathering Around the Fire of Mission Education

Education is not the filling of a pail, but the lighting of a fire.

—William Butler Yeats

To expand once more on that well-known quote from Emil Brunner, that: "The church exists by mission as a fire exists by burning," we find here a helpful image for the ways we need to equip the church for transmitting the gospel across cultures, which are the global ministries of the church. It is as if we are sitting around that campfire or home hearth, experiencing the warmth and light, and telling the stories of how it was built and why, and all the people whose lives have been changed by that fire.

Although this may be a bit of a stretch in analogies, it does fit what mission education is. While mission education may not seem to be mission work itself, it is in reality as crucial to carrying out mission programming as the direct missional methods of a missionary or partner church. To be in mission one must understand what mission is and how it is organized and implemented. To interest many church members in mission programs often necessitates telling the stories of the changed lives, the scope of the partnership, and the diversity of what is done in mission work. It is as if we were watching the fire, explaining what the fire is about and how the fire affects others. That essentially is mission education.

This is a primary function in the connection of a local congregation, for it is out of that local church that mission becomes alive in the world. That means it is the place where the first spark of the fire is spread, and this fire continues to burn throughout the whole connection. All of God's Mission is in essence local, for it occurs and is spread from one locality in the world to another, yet through a vast network of interconnected entities, all of which are local. It is important to understand this local/global nature of all missional enterprises, and the related necessity for each local church to become connected with all other local churches in mission. Each local congregation is a member of the body of Christ, as much as individual persons are, and each congregation has a function to fulfill in the *missio Dei*. The saints in every place must be equipped for mission, lest the vines are ruined or the grapes damaged by inappropriate understandings of the harvest.

Equipping Saints Through Education

The Evangelical Church in the Dominican Republic (a United Church with a United Methodist background) is giving special attention to Christian education for children, through Sunday schools, camping programs, and extended Bible schools. This initiative is being supported in part by a grant from Global Ministries, as a means of evangelization to make disciples throughout the country. God has led this church to become more intentional with Christian education, equipping leaders to bring a better life for the children and youth of the church, but also the wider community.

In the new United Methodist Mission Initiative in the African nation of Cameroon, United Methodist missionary Leah Magruder reports of a cooperative ecumenical effort with German Presbyterian missionaries, which brings Sunday school curriculum in the French language to villages. The "Vien et Vios!" (translated as "Come and See!") packets took many years to develop. The missionaries train local persons to use the material with many hours of workshops, and are very thorough in the biblical material which is covered. As "Amos" was passing by the new church in Yaounde, he noticed the group of children that had gathered to join in vibrant singing, storytelling, and discussion, and he sat down to listen. "Amos" was moved by this experience and he too joined in, learning what it means to be a disciple of Jesus Christ and to set about his own personal journey with God. Through the open invitation to "come and see," every week new disciples in a new church are being made.

Connecting Congregations, Saving Ourselves

"We can save ourselves by helping those most in need," says Stanley Campbell, executive director of the Rockford, Illinois, Urban Ministries 7th Street Shalom program. This United Methodist-based program engages 25 local congregations in its work. Using the Shalom Zone model developed through Global Ministries, these partners have rehabilitated neighborhood homes, opened a Fair Trade store, and educated community members on HIV prevention through the Total Health Awareness Team. In seeking the wholeness of the community, Rockford Urban Ministries 7th Street Shalom recognizes the strengths in its neighbors and the resources that are available in neighborhood homes and local businesses. While predominately United Methodist churches participate in this Shalom project, there are Episcopal, Unitarian-Universalist, and United Church of Christ partners, also. By becoming missional congregations, these churches are strengthening for all of ministry. They are equipping persons, but also whole congregations, for mission, and in the process are becoming more healthy bodies. Their missional outreach into the community is like an exercise regimen for an individual, getting rid of excess weight and growing strong muscles and ligaments of Connectionalism.

On Good Friday, participants in the Shalom program processed through downtown Rockford, stopping at "stations of the cross," which included places that help heal the city's wounds or need attention. Each "station," which included stops at Allen Chapel's soup kitchen and the state office building, represented a part of the biblical story of Jesus' crucifixion. In a real way, the people of "Shalom" were able to experience how the cross relates to everyday life by recognizing the hurts and needs right around us that Christ can heal through His people who respond to serve the *missio Dei*.

In Dorchester, Massachusetts, Greenwood Shalom's education programs focus on the importance of parental involvement and low teacher-student ratios. "My daughter has been enrolled in the program since 2000," said Magnolia Gonzales. "When I first started the program I was very skeptical and didn't know what to expect, but the staff has helped me and my daughter work together as a team in all aspects to improve social academic barriers that will present themselves." Greenwood Shalom is located in a very diverse neighborhood with many youth and children. Greenwood Shalom works with these young community members and their families in order to guide children in achieving their potential.

In similar fashion, the Wood Institute in Mathison, Mississippi, offers resource and leadership development opportunities to small membership churches in this rural area. The Wood Institute is the new expression of mission on the campus of what was Wood College, a United Methodist school dating from 1886. It is a mission in cooperation with The Women's Division of Global Ministries and the Mississippi Annual Conference. The college closed in 2003, but the facilities now serve as the base for a variety of ministries serving communities and churches. As many of these congregations have been very insular in the past, living only for and unto themselves, Wood is challenging them to be mission-oriented and to reach out to the community. This is expected to spark new life and growth in their congregations.

Global Ministries Mission Seminars

The Global Ministries Mission Seminar program is an opportunity for United Methodists to experience the magnitude and diversity of our denomination's missional involvement. Groups come to the offices of Global Ministries in New York City to meet with staff and learn about the many areas of global ministries in which the church is engaged. They may consist of a confirmation class, a college choir on tour, or a seminary class. One pastor noted that teens from her church were able to understand that "It's more than just our church back home, we're a much larger group of churches altogether. They learned church is more than just our four walls—it extends out into the world. We're many gifts and talents combined to help the church function."[3] The Central Pennsylvania Annual Conference has organized an annual Global Ministries seminar for over 30 consecutive years, averaging 50 people each year. These active United Methodists are the core of mission promoters all across that conference. The Virginia Annual Conference has begun a similar annual seminar, with equally similar success and enthusiasm for the promotion of the global ministries of the church.

For the first time many seminar participants feel proud to be United Methodists because they see the ongoing reality of their churches' total commitment to God's mission, and understand that they're not just one local congregation, but are in connection with the global church, a universal body of Christ with many members around the world all focused on that *missio Dei*.

Mission Education Emphases

There are many other ways to equip the saints of any local congregation for involvement in God's Mission. Here are five mission activities that every church can strive to achieve:

1. Form a Covenant Relationship with a United Methodist missionary, supporting that missionary with prayer, encouragement, and financial gifts through the Advance for Christ and His Church of the General Board of Global Ministries.

2. Promote financial support for other Advance projects, such as a Sunday school class, or adult fellowship choosing a year-long program of support for a school or church building or scholarship, while learning about the project. There are several thousand Advance projects from which to choose, and remember that through this "second-mile" giving program, 100 percent of the donation goes to support the missionary or other project designated by the giver.

3. Sponsor an annual Mission Sunday, or other event for the congregation that celebrates all aspects of mission in the church, including volunteer work; food pantry and shelter contributions; United Methodist Women's educational and program work; and mission committee planning functions, all funds that undergird mission.

4. Encourage mission education by working toward broad participation in the Annual Conference Schools of Christian Mission and the use of the annual mission studies in various settings in your congregational programming.

5. Promote the United Methodist Special Sundays and educate the congregation about their purpose and goals, and how these express God's Mission.

As your congregation engages in these educational and interpretive programs, they will be more and more equipped to understand the fullness of the *missio Dei*, and their part in upholding, supporting, and participating with the whole body of Christ in mission.[4]

Concepts to Consider

1. How do you see functional Connectionalism in your church life?
2. Who has lit fires of mission education in your life?
3. When is mission education lived out in your congregation's mission program?

Notes for ESSAY 14

[1] *The Book of Discipline of The United Methodist Church* (Nashville, TN: The United Methodist Publishing House, 2004) ¶ 120, 87.

[2] From an unpublished speech by R. Randy Day, at Stamford, CT, October 12, 2005.

[3] In a letter from The Reverend Diane Prentice, Wyalusing and Springhill (PA) United Methodist Churches, Wyoming Annual Conference, April 2006.

[4] For much more on specific mission education programming ideas, see John Edward Nuessle, *Mission: Reaching The World*, Guidelines for Leading Your Congregation series (Nashville, TN: Cokesbury, 2004). A new edition for 2009-2012 is available in early 2009.

ESSAY 15

Paddling The Canoe Together:
The Experience of Partnership

Experience understood through Mission Goal 2:
To Strengthen, Develop, and Renew Christian Community

John 15:8-17: Mission is love that bears fruit by friends of God.

John 17:20-21: "That they may all be one."

To experience mission partnership is the full expression of what it is to be ecumenical, which is to involve all of the inhabited world. This means working across denominational boundaries as well as with governmental and other secular agencies worldwide. When mission partners are joined together in interdependence with mutual trust, they respect the integrity of their common confession of God revealed in Jesus Christ.

Partnership Is Paddling Together

"Partnership is paddling the canoe together so that all of us arrive at the destination at the same time," according to Bishop Philemon Riti of the United Church of Solomon Islands, speaking at a Pacific Islands Regional Gathering of ecumenical mission partners sponsored by Global Ministries in the year 2000. Using the imagery of the South Pacific, Bishop Riti expressed hope and excitement that the national churches scattered across the vast Pacific Ocean could paddle together toward a new era in mission and ministry.

All the churches are in the same canoe rather than separate entities, and they could all paddle together and arrive at the common goals of God's kingdom. This is a full expression of mission partnership.

As a result of the gathering, everyone learned of the missional concerns of the Pacific Island churches and of its leaders. Yes, some of the women and youth at this conference did rock the canoe, encouraged by each other and partners from the United States. Many of these issues, like the bias against women in leadership, the alienation of young people, and ethnic tension, were issues within Pacific Islands societies that churches there are facing together. But environmental pollution, nuclear testing, and the economic bondage that accompanies globalization are all signs of the region's encounter with the world beyond its palm-tree-lined beaches. They are not isolated communities from one another, nor from the rest of the world. They are one neighborhood in the global village.

The experience of mission is a journey of faith with our mission partners of all nations and of all communions. Christian communities are strengthened by this act of partnering. It is work that bears good fruit from the connectional vines and branches spread throughout the earth.

Bearing Fruit Together

> My Father is glorified by this, that you bear much fruit and become my disciples. As the Father has loved me, so I have loved you; abide in my love….You did not choose me but I chose you. And I appointed you to go and bear fruit, fruit that will last, so that the Father will give you whatever you ask him in my name. I am giving you these commands so that you may love one another (John 15:8-9, 16-17).

As previously noted in the description of the biblical nature of Connectionalism from this chapter of John's Gospel, the Church is the network of God's vines and branches throughout the world. Jesus makes the obvious point that the purpose of the vine and branches is to bear fruit. Of what use is a vine with no grapes? To bear fruit is to make the love with which God has loved the world in Jesus Christ visibly manifest. It is the tangible sign of being disciples. As expressed by Jesus in this passage, bearing fruit is the corporate act of faithfulness. We cannot bear fruit alone, either as individuals or as separated congregations or denominations. We are the community called out of the world to bear much fruit together, fruit which lasts because of this communal faithfulness to God's everlasting love of the whole world.

Ecumenical Involves the Whole Inhabited "House"

The term ecumenical generally is used to describe both the stance and the activities of various Christian groups—denominations and other organizations—working together in mutual respect and cooperation. To take a broader view, however, we can note that the word ecumenical is derived from the Greek, οικουμενη (oikoumene), which means "the inhabited world," and was historically used with specific reference to the Roman Empire. Its roots are in the word *oikein*, meaning "to inhabit," and *oikos*, meaning "a house,"—specifically a house surrounded by other houses, where people live in a village. The term ecumenical relates to all who inhabit the whole world, as if the world was a village, a global village, composed of many neighborhoods.

In this broadest meaning then, ecumenism refers to initiatives aimed at worldwide unity. In a narrower sense (and the only true meaning according to some), it refers to the movement toward unity among Christians, based on the idea that there should be a single Christian church, a single Christian faith. But as the original Greek did not refer to a religious organization or even a faith stance, but rather to where people live together in a village in peace and harmony, it could be suggested that this broader understanding is the movement toward the inclusive and worldwide kingdom of God in our midst.

To be in partnership in God's Mission involves joint efforts with all people and organizations toward the goal of the coming kingdom. Just as God used people of faith as well as secular authorities to accomplish this movement throughout biblical history (cf. Cyrus and the Israelites return from Exile in Ezra 1:1ff), so too is this now our call to inclusive and worldwide partnership through the *missio Dei*.

We Are One as God Is One

Partnership in mission, in its truest form, expresses a relationship among churches and groups of persons, based on mutual respect, reciprocal activities, and a sincere and pragmatic sharing of the power in decision making and use of resources. It expresses the biblical call of Christ that we all be one, as in fact God, Christ, and the Spirit are one. The body of Christ, the contemporary visible witness to God revealed in Jesus Christ, is a whole unit, and when living in the world needs to be seen as unified as well as acting in unity in reality. In mission practice, however, mission partnership is often fraught with conflict and misunderstandings, leading to division. As with the whole understanding of mission as the *missio Dei*, partnership is not so much what we *do* as the church in mission as it is who we *are* as the church in mission. There is "one Lord, one faith, one baptism, one God and Father of us all" (Ephesians 4:4-5). And as Jesus so sincerely prayed before his trial and execution:

> I ask not only on behalf of these, but also on behalf of those who will believe in me through their word, that they may all be one. As you, Father, are in me and I am in you, may they also be in us, so that the world may believe that you have sent me (John 17:20-21).

The body of Christ, the church, is one organism, one organization, one fellowship (*koinonia*), and in our participation in the *missio Dei* we must strive to be in unity with partnership as the basic experience of mission. "Partnership is therefore not a nice slogan that some clever committee has dreamt up; it is the expression of one, indivisible, common life in Jesus Christ."[1]

The most significant obstacle to mission partnership, whether among churches, with secular or governmental agencies in the United States, or around the world, is the unequal distribution of material resources. J. Andrew Kirk, in a profound analysis of partnership in his book, *What is Mission?* states:

> As long as economic relationships are not changed, dependency rather than full interdependence is built in the situation. There can be no genuine partnership. To be able to exercise responsibility, people must have the freedom to make decisions. This means owning resources so that decisions can be fully acknowledged and not imposed. Both money and the personal gift of one's life can only be shared when two groups of Christians have a genuine (not conditional) say in the activities they engage in. The ideal would be for resources to be pooled and mutual decisions taken about how they are used. There are a number of substantial difficulties in the way.[2]

Professor Kirk goes on to list these difficulties of partnership: Needs outstripping supply of resources requiring discrimination in their use, past guilt concerning former patterns of resource use, differing perceptions of the goals of mission, and the lack of recognition of mission insights and intellectual resources.

Partnership requires a great deal of effort toward sharing not just our funds, but more importantly the responsibility for the use of these funds and the power to make decisions on all aspects of mission. One significant methodology for moving our mission efforts in this direction is to ensure that persons from all mission partners are involved at all levels of decision making and program implementation. To put it bluntly, just because someone gives money does not give them the right nor the ultimate responsibility to determine how that money is to be used in God's Mission. Movement of ideas, decisions, personnel, and the financial resources themselves must not be unidirectional; rather all these must be on a two-way, or even a three- or four-way, or multidirectional street. Such partnership, while difficult and requiring significant study, discussion, and more than all else prayer, is possible, as we can seek to paddle the canoe of mission together.

Partnering in Spirituality
United Methodist missionaries Kristin and David Markay tell of a large international gathering of youth in Milan, Italy where they serve, for a week-long

Taize-type event. Fifty thousand young people from all across Europe came together for prayer, song, and discussion at the small Methodist congregation, where the Markays' pastor hosted some of the participants during the event. They all discovered the "Christ of communion present in fullness in that mystery of communion which is his Body, the Church," in the words of Taize founder, Brother Roger. The Markays wrote of the event, "As strangers communicated with smiles and hand signals, as songs were sung in dozens of different accents, as small-group discussions revealed hidden commonalities, people 'who were once far off' from each other (Orthodox, Protestant, Catholic) felt 'brought near' in Christ. As one person commented after one meeting, 'I liked the way the church looked today.'"[3]

Now that the crowds have returned home, members of a local Roman Catholic church and the Methodist congregation are moving forward to continue this ecumenical spirituality with a small neighborhood feeding ministry, after gathering in weekly prayer in each other's buildings.

Partnering for Children's Health

The Evangelical Methodist Church in Nicaragua is working in collaboration with Acción Medica Cristiana (Christian Medical Action) and Global Ministries to provide medicines at a minimal cost for the children of the Hialeah community in Managua. This area of the city is engulfed in poverty and challenged by many social problems, such as a high crime rate, lack of education, and the lack of health-care services. Through the local Methodist congregation, programs have been developed for children, youth, and women to respond to the health needs of the community in particular. The Good Samaritan Medicine Program obtains and distributes the medicines through a volunteer local physician who makes the diagnosis and the prescriptions. This is partnering together for the ongoing health of God's children.

Partnering in Pioneer Evangelism

Cambodia represents a special pioneer-evangelism mission situation, because of the partnership forged by five branches of Methodism that are involved. Those branches are The United Methodist Church in the United States, the United Methodist Church in Switzerland and France, the Methodist Church in Singapore, the World Federation of Chinese Methodist Churches, and the Korean Methodist Church. This international cooperation among Methodists is proving fruitful for the kingdom. In 1989, Cambodia had three local Methodist churches. Today, the Methodist Church in Cambodia has been formalized, with more than 150 local congregations served by over 20 Methodist and United Methodist missionaries, 10 ordained deacons, and 100 lay leaders. One of the main objectives is to empower the Christian-youth movement through employment, leadership, and Bible study. These Methodists in partnership evangelism also help eradicate landmines, combat malnourishment, assist people to find employment, and teach literacy.

Emmanuel and Beverly Barte, United Methodist missionaries to Cambodia, write (in a missionary letter) concerning the fruits of this interchurch, evangelistic partnership:

> In our ministries, we had new adventures. In the Faith Engine Ministry, we offered the very first mechanics training for young women. We believe this is not just new for the Methodist Mission in Cambodia (MMC), but in the kingdom of Cambodia. This is one opportunity of empowering our women to gain skills and find jobs that only used to be offered to the men. We also included basic English conversation and computer skills. Foremost, we continue to share with them God's love.

In addition, the Christian Education Ministry gathers Sunday school teachers from the whole of the Methodist Church in Cambodia, offering training in basic skills of teaching, and organization of children's ministries. Local pastors have been trained to become curriculum writers for their own congregations, with the creation of a one-year Sunday school curriculum written by Khmer pastors.

Partnering With Food and Hope

Through the East Sub-district of United Methodist Churches in Fayette County, Tennessee (Memphis Annual Conference), God has moved the hearts and hands of United Methodists to be in partnership with several Christian Methodist Episcopal churches in the area, in joint outreach ministries.

The South Lebanon Community of Shalom, in Lebanon, Indiana, strengthens multicultural relationships through their weekly free lunches. Guests include seniors, teenagers, and families from a variety of ethnic and cultural backgrounds. Some volunteers from several congregations and the community at large prepare the meal, while others bring food to share. One of the goals of the South Lebanon Community of Shalom is to grow into a community that is characterized by what they share rather than what they have. "The Community of Shalom is what the church is about," said Danny Walker, pastor of Otterbein UMC. "It is exactly what discipleship means; letting the vision and reality of God take on flesh and become real within our lives and communities."

They share not just what they have materially, but who they are as God's people together. They are being formed into a community of faith through these partnership activities. As diverse local communities "paddle their canoe together" in God's Mission, we will all reach the destination of God's kingdom all at the same time, that is...in God's time.

Concepts to Consider

1. When have you experienced paddling the canoe together in mission?
2. How do you experience full ecumenical life (global Christianity) in your congregation?
3. Why do economic resource differences impact missional partnerships?

Notes for ESSAY 15

[1] J. Andrew Kirk, *What Is Mission?* (Minneapolis: Fortress Press, 2000), p. 187.

[2] Ibid., p. 192.

[3] Kristin and David Markay, *Penne & Ink*, February 2006, a missionary newsletter available from the Global Ministries Mission Personnel unit.

ESSAY 16

Coming Home to Abundant Life

Experience understood through Mission Goal 3:
To Alleviate Human Suffering

John 10:1-18: Abundant life for all.

Hope and wholeness for all of God's people is the invitation from Jesus Christ, the Good Shepherd who leads us home toward God's coming kingdom. Working on behalf of those in need is our experience of the reality of this abundant life here and now, as we reach out toward the future.

Hope Brings Wholeness in Life

"What oxygen is for the lungs, such is hope for the meaning of human life....As the fate of the human organism is dependent on the supply of oxygen, so the fate of humanity is dependent on its supply of hope," begins the Swiss theologian Emil Brunner in his book, *Eternal Hope.*[1] Hope is how we are able to live as human beings. In our efforts to alleviate human suffering, making hope real and assisting in bringing wholeness to human life, particularly after natural disasters or human-made crises, we are engaging in God's Mission of loving the world. Hope enlivens persons' lives, just as a refreshing breath of oxygen brings life to our bodies. Without meaning, as Brunner would say, life does not seem worth living. Aiding in material ways, as well as being present in time of need, are hopeful signposts for people facing tragedy and seemingly hopeless futures.

The missiologist and former general secretary of the World Council of Churches, Philip Potter, writing in his collection of speeches and essays, *Life in All Its Fullness*, observes, "Being human means having anxiety—the anxiety that we are finite and must die, that our lives make no sense, that we have failed to live up to what is demanded of us as responsible persons."[2] This is the situation all people find themselves in, if not constantly then particularly in times of distress and danger. Dr. Potter goes on to state the answer God brings to us through truth of the gospel, that Christ came to "break through the straitjacket of death by taking death on himself and bringing us the endless life of the resurrection." And thus, as recorded in the 10th chapter of John's Gospel: abundant life, or life in all its fullness, is available to all.

The abundant life Christ offers all—sheep of this fold and other folds—has all the characteristics of this caring life of the shepherd and the sheep. As Christ offers life for all, we as the body of Christ exist to make this abundant life of hope and wholeness real in the lives of persons the world over. Abundant life is Jesus' wish for all people, those we know in our own sheepfold, and those others for whom Christ died everywhere.

Dr. Potter in this essay identifies four aspects of this caring, abundant life.[3] First there is safety. "I am the gate. Whoever enters by me will be saved, and will come in and go out and find pasture" (John 10:9). The sheep are free to go in and out and find good pasture. Abundant life requires the safety to secure food, shelter, health care, and in general to have a sense of security from danger. If one does not feel safe from imminent danger it is difficult to go about one's daily life. God does not simply supply us with the means for life, but the safety and security to obtain these resources in the world. Abundant life is the ability to live as God has created us to live in the world.

Second, a factor in being safe is to be living in community. "I am the good shepherd. I know my own and my own know me, just as the Father knows me and I know the Father. And I lay down my life for the sheep" (John 10:14-15). The sheep know the shepherd's voice and together they live and move and have their being. Being known is a mark of community. Safety and security are found in being known within a caring community. Christ offers all he is—his life—for the sake of this community. Third, Christ offers this abundant life for all. It is universal, rather than an exclusive community. "I have other sheep that do not belong to this fold. I must bring them also, and they will listen to my voice. So there will be one flock, one shepherd" (John 10:16). None are excluded from the safe and secure abundant life. We are all in this one flock together, even when we don't necessarily acknowledge this. God does.

And last, God is the source and power for Christ's offer of abundant life. "No one takes it from me, but I lay it down of my own accord. I have power to lay it down, and I have power to take it up again. I have received this command from my Father" (John 10:18). It does not come from our own striving and seeking for security. We do not offer safety and security, rather Christ does. We are the community of faith, entering through the gate which is Christ, and into which all persons are invited to share in this abundant life. There are obstacles and threats to our safety (cf. John 10:8, 10, 12-13), but as we listen to Christ's voice and remain in community, we will have life in all its fullness as a present reality pointing us toward the coming kingdom.

A Haven of Hope

"I knew it was bad, but I could not believe my eyes when I arrived in town. I still can't believe it." Ozel Martin returned to his hometown in Florida to see it leveled by Hurricane Charley. "It brought tears to my eyes to see the houses that were completely devastated," reported The Rev. David Harris, pastor of Trinity United Methodist Church in Arcadia, Florida.

Trinity United Methodist Church of Arcadia is near where Hurricane Charley made landfall, unleashing torrential rain and 130-mph winds. The church began serving the community before the hurricane even arrived by offering its facility as a shelter for 80 people. Within half an hour after Charley left, Trinity's pastor, The Rev. David Harris, drove out to assess the damage and formulate a plan for long-term disaster response. The church has since been a haven of hope for the local community, serving hot meals, distributing necessities and organizing volunteers who helped with cleanup efforts and continue with long-term repairs and reconstruction. "I'm just thankful to be able to come here and get some help," said one resident who received assistance from Trinity.

Trinity and other United Methodist churches in areas affected by the multiple hurricanes that caused damage in 15 states during 2004 and 2005, were equipped to reach out because of the United Methodist Committee on Relief's (UMCOR's) disaster-response program. Rev. Harris, as the Florida Conference's disaster response coordinator, receives training on what to do when disaster strikes. Through networks and training, United Methodists can mobilize to respond following a disaster. Long after other aid agencies have left, UMCOR is still there providing a haven of hope.

Long Distance Community of Hope

Many have called Saint Mark's Community Center in New Orleans, Louisiana, an anchor for the children in the community. In the aftermath of Hurricane Katrina this again has proven to be true. Almost all of the staff, board members, and children served by the organization were dispersed to other areas of the country. However, during these months, James Rogers, the program director of the Awesome Girls Mentoring Program, made contact with all of the girls in the program. He was still mentoring long distance. Mr. Rogers received a grant to continue the program and is now continuing to serve the girls as they return to the community. Needing assurance and stability, one young woman called Mr. Rogers and said, "I just needed to hear your voice."

Rebuilding a Community of Shalom

Despite the devastation of Hurricanes Katrina and Rita, First Street Community of Shalom in New Orleans continues to be in ministry with neighbors who are slowly returning and rebuilding. The neighborhood seeks "shalom"—peace and justice—as never before. One local volunteer, Doris Brown, was baptized as a child at First Street Church. She later moved to the Gentilly neighborhood of New Orleans, where she was when Hurricane Katrina struck. She found shelter in the Superdome, where she weathered another storm of confusion and fear, broken water pipes, and uncertainty. She was able to keep her family of uncles, aunts, and cousins together, and eventually they were evacuated to Baytown, Texas.

She returned to New Orleans to find that her house had been flooded and many of her belongings destroyed. A group of volunteers at the First Street Relief Center came and removed the debris. Another group will gut the house so new construction can begin. Ms. Brown became a volunteer at First Street Church. "I came back to First Street to work and to thank God," she explained. She thinks of her effort as part of the healing process needed in the city. She feels good as she distributes health and school kits from UMCOR and other donated goods. "It's good to know that United Methodists care from all over," says Doris Brown, opening yet another box. United Methodists, who before the tragedy offered Christ's hope and wholeness in this poverty-ridden area, are continuing this mission as abundant life is returning, albeit very slowly, to the lives of persons in this rebuilt community.

Hope Is Dignity and Full Life

"We have felt alone and without help. Through UMCOR, now we see hope," said a tsunami survivor in Sri Lanka. Sunil (not his real name) is a member of a fishing society in Batticaloa, Sri Lanka. On the day the tsunami struck, Sunil and his fellow fisher folk watched their livelihoods wash out with the tides. Their nets, boats, homes, even the beach itself, disappeared in the churning water. On this unseasonably cool rainy day Sunil is working with members of his fishing society and other societies in a project sponsored by UMCOR and the Methodist Church of Sri Lanka (MCSL). They are clearing the beach of debris that could easily tear their nets when they resume fishing. UMCOR and MCSL paid the now-unemployed fisher folk for their work to help them earn an income. Sunil is happy to help. "Today I have something to eat," he says. "Today I have money." UMCOR and MCSL are assisting people like Sunil by providing nets, boats, oars, and advocacy to help them regain their livelihoods and an abundant life with dignity.

United Methodist missionaries Gordon and Teca Greathouse direct and coordinate the São Gabriel Community Center in Belo Horizonte, Brazil, which offers hope and full life to many without either. For three decades, with their Brazilian colleagues in the center, they have worked with children, youth, older adults, women, and families together to help them gain self-esteem and self-sufficiency—to go in and out of life and find good pasture—through the love of Jesus. Their programs assist with access to food, housing, and education, with which these persons with very few opportunities can develop their God-given talents as well as grow spiritually. Gordon believes, "When people feel that they have dignity and hope and that they can help, they really feel they are made in God's image." Many teachers at the center came there as children with few if any opportunities for a full life. Now they are making a difference in the lives of others.

Hope Is Finding Good Pasture

United Methodist missionaries in several nations are assisting with programs that enable persons to "find good pasture," that is to grow and raise food for themselves, their families, and their communities. Mozart Adevu works with the Liberia Annual Conference, developing agriculture for rural communities, particularly in use of the Moringa Tree, the miracle tree which is a source of nutrition and energy, and with regular consumption helps to strengthen persons' immune systems. Through the "Give Ye Them To Eat" program in Mexico, Muriel and Terry Henderson provide training in agricultural, community, and livestock development, along with community-based primary health care, and church and faith development. Larry and Jane Kies are teaching agriculture through the living laboratory farm at the Africa University in Zimbabwe. Larry says, "Helping people to eat isn't just a matter of sending surplus food from the United States to other countries. Rather, it is working with indigenous people to develop their technology and skill to grow their own food."

Hope in the AIDS Pandemic

Elmira Sellu, as a United Methodist regional missionary related to the Women's Division and United Methodist Women, seeks to facilitate support and caring community for women infected with the HIV/AIDS virus in East Africa. As she organizes workshops and seminars through the Leadership Development for Women programs of the East Africa Annual Conference, Elmira hears the stories of women who are deliberately infected with the virus by their infected husbands, and then, as their hopes and dreams for the future are shattered, come asking the question, "Was that love?" The church community of these women offers hope and wholeness in the midst of this tragedy of the AIDS pandemic, as they seek together to live positively with the disease.

United Methodist missionary Maria Humbane works similarly with the orphans of AIDS-devastated families in both Harare and Mutare, Zimbabwe. Through aid for tuition and books for school, tutoring, Bible study, and two meals each day for the children, she works with the Zimbabwe United Methodist Annual Conference to keep the children focused on positive goals and future plans for a full life, while educating them about the sources of HIV/AIDS. The United Methodist Global AIDS Fund is offering support for education, prevention, care, and treatment programs for people living with HIV/AIDS. This critical work is starting with the next generation: infants infected by HIV at birth. Pregnant women have a one-in-three chance of transmitting HIV to their infants. United Methodists are working to provide a life-preserving drug, Nevirapine, which prevents the transmission of HIV from mother to child in Zimbabwe and seven other countries.

Coming Home to the Kingdom

Jesus the Good Shepherd is the gate to abundant life, the hope of a hurting world. He welcomes all of God's people home to the sheepfold. Our wholeness as the church of Jesus Christ comes as we see both the needs of individuals and of the entire world together, for all of whom Christ died and was raised to new life by the power of God's Holy Spirit.

The preacher, novelist, and theologian Frederick Buechner states in his book, *The Longing for Home*, that, "To be whole, I think, means among other things that you see the whole world."[4] The abundant life God offers each of us through Christ is a matter of living in, of, and for the whole world, an expansive understanding of the unity of all of God's people, and a foundation of all mission. The kingdom is not so much a reality for you or I, but for us, all of "us" in the world. This vision is a mark of wholeness, of our salvation through Christ that makes us whole with all others, and this is the holiness of our life in faith. As Buechner has come to understand, abundant life is found as we journey toward God's coming kingdom, meaning we are coming "home":

I cannot claim that I have found the home I long for every day of my life, not by a long shot, but I believe that in my heart I have found, and have maybe always known, the way that leads to it. I believe that [The Rev. George] Buttrick was right and that the home we long for and belong to is finally where Christ is. I believe that home is Christ's kingdom, which exists both within us and among us as we wend our prodigal ways through the world in search of it.[5]

God's Mission is found as we together seek hope and wholeness, abundant life in the safety of God's community through Jesus Christ, the good shepherd. The *missio Dei* is found as we journey together toward God's ultimate reign over all that is, both present and yet to be. It is a matter of seeing both the individual trees and the forest as a whole. In God's Mission these are one and the same, inseparable. We see the glimpses of this new life in Christ all about us, as in the experience of God's people witnessed to us in these stories of hope and wholeness.

Concepts to Consider

1. What does it mean to you to have hope of abundant life?

2. How has the church offered a way home to God's sheepfold?

3. Who needs the gift of hope in your community?

Notes for ESSAY 16

[1] Emil Brunner, *Eternal Hope* (London: Lutterworth Press, 1954), p. 7, US printing, translated by Harold Knight, (Philadelphia: Westminster Press, 1954).

[2] Philip Potter, *Life in All Its Fullness* (Grand Rapids, MI: William B. Eerdmans, 1982), p. 21.

[3] Ibid., pp. 26-27.

[4] Frederick Buechner, *The Longing for Home* (New York: HarperCollins, 1996), p. 108.

[5] Ibid., p. 28.

ESSAY 17

Justice is "Done" by Loving Kindness and Walking Humbly

Experience understood through Mission Goal 4:
To Seek Justice, Freedom, and Peace

Micah 6:6-8: Doing justice is to love kindness and walk humbly with God.

Luke 4:16-21/Isaiah 61:1-4: The Spirit of the Lord brings freedom and justice.

Doing justice by being Christ in the world is the experience of doing justice by loving kindness and walking humbly. Ministries of justice, freedom, and peace are not so much about setting an agenda for action, while this may well happen. They begin with a relational understanding of whose lives we are seeking to impact, and with whom we walk about on the face of the earth.

Loving Kindness Is to Love Being Kind

[God] has told you, O mortal, what is good; and what does the LORD require of you but to do justice, and to love kindness, and to walk humbly with your God? (Micah 6:8).

As we have often heard Micah's prophetic call of what the Lord requires of us in life, we understand that to do justice is an action of the faithful life. Just do it. And to walk humbly with God is an action of the spiritual life. Again, we just do it. But to love kindness in Hebrew is *hesed* or *checed,* which means loving mercy and gentle acceptance of others; being good, kind, and faithful; loving kindness. This is a being, a presence. Micah proclaims that God is not so much interested in uninvolved sacrifice of material goods—not a matter of what has come to be called charity in American culture—but rather we are called not just to be kind, but to *love* being kind and merciful. It is the opposite of road rage and ethnic cleansing and fear of terrorists. We wholly desire to live a life that leads to justice, kindness, and humble presence with God. Justice is a matter of lifelong and whole-life presence that respects the lives of all persons, and thus results in justice for all. To do justice and walk humbly with God one must also "love kindness." While it is nice and polite to be kind or to act in a kindly manner, the *missio Dei* is about actively loving the idea of kindness, wholly desiring the notion of "being" kind, not just acting kind, in and with your life. North Americans are well known around the world for doing things; getting the job done. Micah is suggesting that doing justice is based on loving kindness and thereby walking humbly with God, concepts that are not well understood or practiced among Americans in general, or the American church.

Thus, to "do" justice is a relational activity among God's people, meaning that it requires us to engage in actions both of commission and omission, which bring about just interaction among people, individually and collectively. Justice is brought about by our intentionally planned actions that exhibit respect for all persons. We make justice happen with our whole lives. To "love" kindness is more than a nice feeling in this context. We must love the very activity of kindness, as in the biblical phrase, "loving kindness." It is the agape love of God for the world (cf. John 3:16); it is what God is. God is love. Not an attitude, but a presence. To love kindness is a lifestyle of looking out for the welfare of all by how we spend our lives. Our love of kindness is reflected in the presence we live daily. Therefore, to "walk" humbly is to get up and move out in specific directions, even when you do not necessarily know where you are going. Walking humbly with God is recognizing our daily need to be in God's loving presence, and to bring just relations into the world, not to meet our own needs but humbly living for others.

Compassion is thus the prerequisite to justice. Compassion is to have "passion" with others. "Com" is from the Latin word *compati*, meaning to bear suffering with another. Compassion is empathy with a passionate desire to both be involved in and to take action on behalf of those in need. Justice requires this lifestyle of passionate care, which connects our lives with the lives of others, particularly those in situations of despair or oppression.

In her compellingly clear book, *The Compassionate Community*, about creating caring, just, and successful mission programming for dealing with human need, Sr. Catherine Harmer writes, "Compassion involves the ability to imagine the reality and situation of the other."[1] She goes on to state that, "The call to be just is not a matter of choice but rather of responsibility."[2] Reaching out to those in physical and emotional need cannot be based upon our emotional needs, but must emanate from a lifestyle of entering into the lives of those in need as if there is not separation from ourselves. It is to create community among all of God's people. It is to be Christ to all, which is doing justice by actively loving kindness with a humbling walk through life.

A Christology of Mission Through Relational Actions

The Spirit of the Lord is upon me,
because he has anointed me
to bring good news to the poor.
He has sent me to proclaim release to the captives
and recovery of sight to the blind,
to let the oppressed go free,
to proclaim the year of the Lord's favor (Luke 4:18-19).

All this active presence of justice, kindness, and humility is reflective of our Christology in mission. As Jesus began his mission, he sat with the community in Capernaum and reflected with them on the call in Isaiah to bring good news to persons oppressed by outside forces; to bind up those overwhelmed by this despair; to proclaim freedom (liberty and release) and peace (the year of the Lord's favor); to comfort those mourning loss, with celebratory elements and encouragement so that they might build a new future. The people there in the synagogue in Capernaum were oppressed by an occupying foreign army, with their lives ruled and controlled from Rome. Just as Peter was portrayed in the next chapter (Luke 5:1-10), they were mere fish of the sea, being exploited for the vast commercial gluttony of the Roman empire, and their Hebrew leaders were also so browbeaten that they could only capitulate and acquiesce to the seemingly overwhelming power of Rome. Jesus came not just with words of encouragement, but a lifestyle of resistance with God's love and grace. He did not seek to "fight fire with fire," but to do justice, love kindness, and walk humbly with God, and with these he actively lived out the faithfulness to which God calls all persons of faith. Seeking justice, freedom, and peace are the active signs of the church being the body of Christ, and being Christ to, with, and for the hurting world. This surely does involve caring for persons in need, but even more it involves creating a just and ethical world where such caring is a matter of course, and in many cases unnecessary due to the nature of this just world. We will be in Christly relationship to all persons, and thus needs are automatically met. Clearly this is a vision of the coming kingdom, and not a current reality in our experience. The church can, however, be the signpost of this just reality of the coming kingdom with our missional lifestyle as we advocate on behalf of people the world over.

Loving Kindness in the Midst of Despair

"When will there be an end to the flow of refugees at the Buduburam Refugee Camp?" laments United Methodist missionary Priscilla Jaiah. It is located in the West African nation of Ghana, and serves hundreds of Liberian refugees, mostly women and children, who have fled the ongoing fighting in their homeland. While the United Nations High Commissioner for Refugees and the Liberian government have repatriated thousands of persons, still more arrive, some from Sierra Leone and the Ivory Coast, because of rebel and government fighting there. They lack housing and food. Some are not granted refugee status because of international regulations, yet they have no homes to return to and no means of support if they did.

Priscilla is a calm presence in a fearful setting, nurturing a United Methodist congregation in the camp, offering education and vocational training to prepare the women, youth, and children for an uncertain future, as well as counseling in the high-risk situation of substance and domestic abuse. She is loving kindness incarnate in these desperate places. She is creating a compassionate community of love and justice, where these values are often derided and ignored. In this she asserts that, "One aspect of my work I have come to love most is being able to empower and to be an advocate. I admire the refugees' high level of spirituality, joyful attitude, and strong hope and trust in God." Priscilla is a Christly relational presence, a signpost of the kingdom of God.

Leadership Development for Loving Kindness

The Methodist Church of Uruguay has long sought to impact the whole society in that Latin American nation, and now experiences a new sense of urgency in its prophetic role, denouncing injustice while calling other social and governmental institutions to new methods in meeting the needs of all people. The Institute of Pedagogical and Pastoral Studies, with assistance from The United Methodist Church through the General Board of Global Ministries, has a program of formation for leaders to work with the marginalized of society in diverse areas of social and church life, through theological reflection and debate for social change. It also created a communication network for this work. This organized educational work seeks to promote the love of kindness in a harsh world for society's most needy persons.

Loving Kindness Brings Hope

Haitian-born United Methodist missionary Charline Galbeau Pierre, a church and community worker serving in Miami, Florida, is a Christly presence of loving kindness in that Haitian neighborhood awash in sadness, resignation, and discouragement. She sees broken windows and doors, worn-out and discarded appliances and furniture, damaged and rundown buildings. She seeks to support the three or four residents who refuse to give up and give in. While the resources are meager, and the results are very slow, it is God's good news that strengthens and renews them for the next day and the one after that. Charline sees her missionary role as nurturing her sisters and brothers through the challenges they face, the struggles to overcome the obstacles of life, and the attempt to reclaim their cultural heritage in support of one another. She knows her presence, loving the very acts of kindness she lives, does make a difference, showing people the pathway to healing and hope through Jesus Christ.

Loving Kindness Brings Life to the Land
Several years ago, Ted Warnock, a United Methodist missionary working with UMCOR, walked across a cleared minefield in Mozambique. It is now the location of a school where a thousand students learn skills such as welding, plumbing, and electronics. People in the surrounding communities have new opportunities for success in life, because our church has made a commitment to remove landmines from this area. Ted stopped along the road to speak with a woman living near this school. She was clearing the land to prepare to plant a crop, her first in years. Her little girl at her side had never seen her mother work the land before, and now life would be growing out of this previously "dead" ground. Now there are children playing in the schoolyards, and crops growing in the fields, houses being built and rebuilt, all in areas untouched for years because of the landmines placed during the civil war in Mozambique. This is justice through loving kindness in a land ravaged by war for years after the fighting stopped, because of the landmines left behind.

Loving Kindness Is Justice for Our Neighbors
Wei Li Chin (not her real name), a woman from Hong Kong, waited four years to be with her family while her immigration case made no progress. She went to Justice for Our Neighbors (JFON), a program of the United Methodist Committee on Relief, for help. There she met T. J. Mills, an immigration attorney who helped her through the process. Due to his persistence, Ms. Chin was reunited with her husband and son shortly after their meeting. She is grateful for the help she received. "Without Mr. Mills' hard work, his efficiency, without your program...my family could never be in reunion."

There are between 10 and 11 million undocumented immigrants in the United States. The majority of them fill essential low-paying jobs, often in the service industry. They pay taxes, receive no benefits, and are productive and law-abiding members of their communities. Yet our national immigration law is growing increasingly complex in our post-9/11 world. JFON provides a pathway through the maze of rules and regulations in the US immigration system. Through administrative means, JFON is justice-seeking loving kindness for sojourners in our midst. These sojourners live in fear, in the midst of exploitive work and housing situations. Participating congregations operate volunteer-based immigration clinics with the help of JFON-trained staff and attorneys. These clinics provide a compassionate community that offers a safe haven to vulnerable people.

> What does the Lord require for praise and offering?
> What sacrifice, desire, or tribute bid you bring?
> Do justly; love mercy; walk humbly with your God.[3]

Text: Albert F. Bayly (1901-1984)
© Oxford University Press. Used by permission. All rights reserved.

Concepts to Consider

1. When have you experienced loving kindness?
2. Who, in your congregation, expresses the passion of sharing suffering with others?
3. How can you organize loving kindness in a mission program?

Notes for ESSAY 17

[1] Catherine M. Harmer, *The Compassionate Community* (Maryknoll, NY: Orbis Books, 1998), p. 3.

[2] Ibid., p. 4.

[3] *The United Methodist Hymnal* (Nashville, TN: United Methodist Publishing House, 1989), #441.

CHAPTER FIVE

REASON

R eason is our common God-given gift that allows us to bring our study of Scripture, tradition, and experience into a usable whole theology, rather than scattered, disconnected ideas. We reason together as we seek to live into the totality of God's Mission, looking for the ways we can be most faithful and effective in our witness.

ESSAY 18: *God Is Doing a New Thing:*
Missionaries From Everywhere, To Everywhere

Reason understood through Mission Goal 1:
To Make Disciples of Jesus Christ

Isaiah 43:16-21: God is doing a new thing.

Matthew 9:16-17: New wineskins.

Luke 9:1-6; 10:1-12; 17-20: Sending the 12 and the 70.

We use contemporary missionary methods for making disciples through the sending of personnel for discipling. Missionaries now go from everywhere to everywhere in God's Mission, as God is doing a new thing in our midst with new wineskins.

ESSAY 19: *The Bread of Life, Food for the Journey*

Reason understood through Mission Goal 2:
To Strengthen, Develop, and Renew Christian Community

Colossians 3:16-17: Be the body, with prayer, worship, and service.

Matthew 5:1-7, 13:33: The elements of the Bread of Life.

1 Corinthians 10:16-17: Eucharist as mission in the body of Christ.

Worship, prayer, and study are the foundations of a missional congregation. Creating Christian congregations as missional communities requires preparing and sharing food for the journey; for the Eucharist is the celebration of God's Mission.

ESSAY 20: *Being the "Glocal" Church in the 21st Century:*
The World is Our Parish

Reason understood through Mission Goal 3:
To Alleviate Human Suffering

Luke 9:11-17: Jesus cares for human need, by healing and feeding.

Isaiah 65:17-18: New heavens and a new earth.

All mission is local mission carried out on a global scale, and this is the concept of global ministries: to think and act "glocally." We are able to care for all by caring for the specific needs of some; a biblical concept through which Jesus understood the universal needs of all by understanding a particular person's needs.

ESSAY 21: *No Canning Jars in the Kingdom:*
Stewardship Is the Bread of Heaven Meant for All

Reason understood through Mission Goal 4:
To Seek Justice, Freedom, and Peace

Exodus 16:11-21: Manna—The God who leads us also feeds us daily what we need.

2 Corinthians 8: 1-7, 13-15: The response of the Macedonian churches in stewardship.

Philippians 4:10-20: Paul's principles for mission giving.

The stewardship of financial resources for mission, or how we use the manna of God, is a matter of living into God's vision of bringing together the whole world into the kingdom with justice, freedom, and peace for all persons. This requires the appropriate faithful offerings of all the resources that God has provided for us.

ESSAY 18

God Is Doing a New Thing: Missionaries From Everywhere, To Everywhere

Reason understood through Mission Goal 1:
To Make Disciples of Jesus Christ

Isaiah 43:16-21: God is doing a new thing.

Matthew 9:16-17: New wineskins.

Luke 9:1-6; 10:1-12; 17-20: Sending the 12 and the 70.

We use contemporary missionary methods for making disciples through the sending of personnel for discipling. Missionaries now go from everywhere to everywhere in God's Mission, as God is doing a new thing in our midst with new wineskins.

Missionaries Are in New Wineskins

Remember not the former things, nor consider the things of old. Behold, I am doing a new thing; now it springs forth, do you not perceive it? I will make a way in the wilderness and rivers in the desert (Isaiah 43:16-21).

No one sews a piece of unshrunk cloth on an old cloak, for the patch pulls away from the cloak, and a worse tear is made. Neither is new wine put into old wineskins; otherwise, the skins burst, and the wine is spilled, and the skins are destroyed; but new wine is put into fresh wineskins, and so both are preserved (Matthew 9:16-17).

At the Crandon Primary and Secondary School, Miguel Arenas-Herrera is a United Methodist missionary who is sharing his faith, and his life, with children from around the northern Uruguayan city of Salto, close to the Argentinean border. It is an English immersion school, with classes taught in English for half the day and in Spanish the other half, with Portuguese, computers, physical education, and Christian education along the way. Miguel serves as the chaplain of the school, and helps in many of these classes with all ages of youngsters, teaching some violin lessons and a bit of cooking classes in addition. Is he from the United States? No. He is an English teacher from the Methodist Church of

Chile, having crossed over the towering Andes and the plains of Argentina to serve Christ and the church there among the Methodists of Uruguay.

God is doing a new thing in missionary service. Do we perceive it? It is springing forth as a resounding call to mission service that goes out to all believers, everywhere. As a global denomination, our missionaries come out of all nations to make disciples in all nations. Our missionary community has expanded its geographic calling in the past few years. The percentage of non-US-based missionaries serving in the United States and internationally, through the United Methodist Board of Global Ministries, is at its highest level and growing. Approximately one-third of all standard support missionaries come from countries other than the United States. We now have faithful servants of Christ going from everywhere to be in mission everywhere, just as Miguel has.

What does he say about his work in Uruguay? Miguel writes, "I would like to start by saying 'Thanks God.' He has been taking care of me since I arrived here (in Uruguay) from Chile. And I have been learning more and more about this country, about its people, and about my mission here. Every day, when I am in the school with the kids, trying to understand the way they are, the way they work, and the way they behave, I am learning that patience and love are the main tools in this journey of faith."

God is, just as the prophet Isaiah proclaimed, doing a new thing! Do we not perceive it? He is making a way in the wilderness and rivers in the desert. This means that by God's grace we are participants in the mission outreach that brings the whole world together in faith. For mission, and the work of missionaries, is about finding ways through the wilderness of poverty and poor education, of hunger, disease, and injustice, and bringing the cooling waters of the free-flowing river to people trapped in the desert. We have persons from all over the world who, with ready skills and steadfast faith, are showing us a new thing in mission.

Joshua and Emelia Kyeremeh find the Danish winters to be bitter cold and very changeable in comparison to their native Ghana in Africa. "We do not know what tomorrow will bring," Joshua writes. But he does know the warmth and love of Christ, which he and Emelia are bringing to the International Congregation of The United Methodist Church of Copenhagen, as a constant reality.

Immigrants and asylum seekers from several African nations come together under the Kyeremeh's leadership to worship and celebrate their faith, sing praise to God through a youth choir, organize prayer groups, and also to learn Danish and support one another in this place so different from their native roots. The numbers at the church are growing, even as their faith warms their shared lives.

As Filipinos, Lamberto and Angelita Valino believed that becoming a seafarer meant a life with a bright and prosperous future, traveling the world in a secure job. Yet after moving from the Philippines to Yokohama, Japan, to serve in the port chaplaincy for the Seaman's Mission there, they realized that their perceptions were very wrong. Lamberto writes, "[The seafarers] are routinely denied the rights and protection given to workers ashore." The Valinos are in a pastoral ministry on the cutting edge of justice and welfare for these international sailors. Lamberto and Angelita visit and counsel hundreds of seafarers each year, who face illness, long separation from family, life about the ship in a very diverse community, abuse and ill treatment by some officers, unpaid wages, and potential unemployment far from home. The Valinos try to offer them a "home away from home" in the port of Yokohama, being good listeners and advocates, and even helping with small errands and needs during the sailors' short stays in port.

As the Valinos have traveled far from home to be in mission to those "that go down to the sea in ships," so all these faithful missionaries of The United Methodist Church go from everywhere to everywhere to proclaim the Gospel of Jesus Christ on our behalf. We are called by God in Scripture to reflect on leaving behind old habits and ideas, and allowing God to give us a new start in whatever is happening in our lives, whether it is emotional, spiritual, or physical.

So, also, we are called to reflect on our notions and ideas of what God's Mission is about, and how to faithfully respond to this vital call. God is doing a new thing in our midst, as the world becomes more and more of a global village. Missionaries are not just persons from the US going across salt water to share the gospel with non-believers. Missionaries come from everywhere in the world and go to everywhere in the world, even here to the US! Brazilian pastors, such as the Rev. Juarez Goncalves, who serves in the New England Annual Conference in the Brazilian Portuguese Language Ministry, has been joined by several others who have come to Massachusetts and New Jersey to minister among Portuguese-speaking immigrants from both Brazil and Portuguese Africa.

And, as with all these persons, our United Methodist mission efforts for almost two centuries have resulted in faithful Christians who are now bringing God's love and care to people all around the world. We are an international movement of caring Christians, a global denomination with a global reach. The mission methods of Methodism have clearly been very successful. Mission breeds mission. God is doing a new thing, by calling Christians to go from everywhere to everywhere, as our movement has always done.

Our Methodist Missionary Heritage

Methodism began with John Wesley's renewal of the church of his day, by cross-ing boundaries of ecclesiastical propriety with field-preaching and lay-led small group ministries. Wesley knew that the fresh new wine of the gospel, for people in the cultural transitions of the industrial revolution of the 18th century, required new wineskins in the church to carry the good news into the places where the transplanted people lived. These were the missionary methodologies needed in response to God's Mission for all persons in Wesley's day.

American Methodist mission began in 1816, when John Stewart, of African and Native-American descent, felt called to minister to the Wyandotte tribe in Upper Sandusky, Ohio. Stewart had been converted at a camp meeting in Marietta, Ohio, and went to the reservation in Ohio, where he met Jonathan Pointer, a black man taken prisoner in his youth by the Wyandotte. Pointer knew their language, so he interpreted for Stewart, whose work prompted the formation of the Methodist Episcopal Missionary Society in 1819.

The first Methodist missionary to serve outside the US was The Rev. Melville Beveridge Cox of Maine and Baltimore. He received an appointment as the first foreign missionary of the Methodist Episcopal Missionary Society, and was sent to the colony of Liberia. He arrived at his field of labor on March 8, 1833, established a Sunday school, summoned conferences, and organized the Methodist Episcopal Church in Africa under the supervision of our General Conference. Unfortunately, he became the first missionary martyr, as in less than five months after his arrival in Liberia he fell victim to an African fever.

Jesus understood the new life that God is bringing into our midst. I believe he was telling the disciples that we must bring his presence to a hurting world, using whatever methods are useful and appropriate, not just what we've always done. John Wesley was living out this new thing when he admonished Francis Asbury as he set sail for America in the 18th century to "Offer them Christ." And this is what we do. Mission work will never be fully and finally accom-plished in advance of the kingdom. The gospel must be proclaimed anew in each day and year, in every age. But now, through our faithful efforts, we have a whole world of people ready, willing, and able to join this great work with us. And so, God has done this new thing among us, to show us a new way to continue our advancement toward the kingdom.

Renowned missiologist Dr. Philip Potter asserts that, "The God of the Bible is a missionary God, a God who sends."[1] He reminds us that God sent

Abraham and Sarah, as well as Moses and Miriam. God sent Jesus and the Holy Spirit, and sent the Apostles through the power of the Son and the Spirit. "God did not send the Son into the world to condemn the world, but in order that the world might be saved through him," is the missionary affirmation of John 3:17. God has sent persons to be in mission throughout the biblical witness.

The Sending of the 70

One such significant witness is the sending of the 70 by Jesus (Luke 10:1-12, 17-20). "The harvest is plentiful, but the laborers are few," Jesus proclaims. The needs of the world and the opportunities for proclaiming and living out the gospel are very real because of God's prevenient missionary presence in the world. The missionary task is in reality a missionary lifestyle, which Jesus explains to the "70 others" he calls and sends with the instructions here for missionary methods for making disciples and the sending of personnel for discipling.

First, they were sent "like lambs into the midst of wolves" (v. 3). The world will not easily welcome or even accept the missionary proclamation of the good news. Yet, we must approach this dangerous world with innocence, rather than either fear or aggression. We are not sent by our own authority or resources, but by God in God's Mission. Therefore, the lifestyle Jesus commends is the following.

Take only what you need for the journey (that is *de jour*—of the day), and stay where you are welcome, not wandering around (vv. 4-7). Live in the community and sink roots. Be among and of those whom you are offering the gospel, rather than separate from them. Establish lasting relationships on a personal level, and not as a task or activity to be accomplished and moved on from. Receive your support as a laborer is paid for work done, for this is significant work in building the kingdom.

That work is first to cure the sick (v. 9), to bring healing to hurting persons, whatever is ailing them, with the proclamation of the reality of the kingdom which is here, not some other place or time; to point toward God's reign in life. It's all about the kingdom. Lastly, if you are not welcomed, move on (vv. 10-11). This seems an obvious statement, yet the church through the ages, and well into present times, has gone where it is not welcome, and stayed longer than was productive. Still, as the 70 discovered, when they did as Jesus instructed (vv. 17-20), even the demons, the evil of the world, submit to God's authority when it is presented. There is great joy in this missionary life. It must be an essential methodology of the church.

Former missiology professor at the School of Mission and World Christianity at the Selly Oak Colleges, Birmingham, England, Dr. J. Andrew Kirk, states, "The Church is by nature missionary to the extent that, if it ceases to be missionary, it has not just failed in one of its tasks, it has ceased being Church."[2] The church must always have persons going forth as the incarnation of the Gospel, moving with God's Mission in every place and every human situation. Christians everywhere are being called by God to be in missionary service. Yet we still must remember that as David Bosch asserts, missionary efforts are not mission in and of themselves.[3] Mission is the *missio Dei*. To be a missionary is only one, albeit important, method through which we are engaged in God's Mission. As a method of mission, missionary service is constantly changing, evolving, molding to the new contexts of the world's cultures.

As John Stewart went into frontier evangelism in Ohio, and Melville Cox to begin the church in Liberia, so now our missionaries go from their homes on all continents, to be the faithful witnesses to God's coming reign on all continents. From everywhere to everywhere the United Methodist missionary presence continues to be the historic "new thing" that God is doing in our midst.

Concepts to Consider

1. What qualities are necessary to respond to God's call to be sent?
2. Who have you known to be sent by God into service as a full-time missionary?
3. How do missionaries incarnate the Gospel in our day?

Notes for ESSAY 18

[1] Philip Potter, *Life in All Its Fullness* (Grand Rapids, MI: William B. Eerdmans, 1982), p. 71.

[2] J. Andrew Kirk, *What Is Mission?* (Minneapolis: Fortress Press, 2000), p. 30.

[3] David J. Bosch, *Transforming Mission, Paradigm Shifts in Theology of Mission* (Maryknoll, NY: Orbis Books, 1991), p. 494.

ESSAY 19

The Bread of Life, Food for the Journey

Reason understood through Mission Goal 2:
To Strengthen, Develop, and Renew Christian Community

Colossians 3:16-17: Be the body, with prayer, worship, and service.

Matthew 5:1-7, 13:33: The elements of the Bread of Life.

1 Corinthians 10:16-17: Eucharist as mission in the body of Christ.

Worship, prayer, and study are the foundations of a missional congregation. Creating Christian congregations as missional communities requires preparing and sharing food for the journey; for the Eucharist is the celebration of God's Mission.

The Bread of Life

For the bread which you have broken, for the wine which you
have poured,
For the words which you have spoken, now we give you thanks, O Lord.
In your service, Lord, defend us, in our hearts keep watch and ward;
In the world where you have sent us, let our kingdom come, O Lord.[1]

There is an old Russian folktale that tells of a tired and destitute man knocking at the door of an old widow. He told her of his plight and asked for just a crust of bread and some water to drink. The woman welcomed him into her small home, saying that she herself did not have much to live on, but that she was about to bake some bread and would share this with him. As she kneaded out the dough, she thought to herself how little she had and that she had better not offer too much to the beggar, lest she find herself in his position. So she cut out only a small bit to bake into a loaf for him. But each time she cut off a piece from the dough, it grew larger and larger. So she cut off a small part of that which had grown, and it too grew larger and larger. Finally she just put the loaf into a pan and placed it in the oven. Each time she checked on it, the loaf had grown even larger still.

When it was fully baked she took the loaf out of the oven and began to slice the warm bread, and as she did, thinking that she should save this magically growing bread for her own needs, the small slice she prepared for the beggar grew ever larger right before her eyes. She gave the now loaf-sized slice to the beggar, whose very presence began to glow and shine, until it was very obvious that he was no ordinary beggar, but a vision of Christ. He spoke to the woman, saying, "This is the living bread that came down from heaven. Whoever eats of this bread will live forever."

One definition of something that is alive, in biological terms, is that which is always growing and changing; to be alive means that you are not the same today as you were yesterday. You have grown in some fashion. That Christ is the living bread of heaven means that this powerful presence is with us today, working changes and growth within us; moving us to respond to God's call to discipleship that comes to each and every Christian believer.

The bread that we share in Holy Communion is not a static, historical commodity. It is alive as we decide to share Jesus with the world. It lives and grows within each of us; causing us to be different than we have been; to seek out new ways to proclaim the good news of Jesus Christ; new directions to move toward God's coming kingdom. As we carry out this work as disciples the bread grows and grows ever larger, never fading away.

> Let the word of Christ dwell in you richly; teach and admonish one another in all wisdom; and with gratitude in your hearts sing psalms, hymns, and spiritual songs to God. And whatever you do, in word or deed, do everything in the name of the Lord Jesus, giving thanks to God the Father through him (Colossians 3:16-17).

The bread that we break is living bread because we allow The Word of God to live in us. It just looks like ordinary bread, and that's just what it is. The sacrament is holy because we are chosen for service and are nourished for this by God's Word and share that Word with the world. Holy means that which is set apart for God's purposes. This sacrament is holy because we, together, are the holy body of Christ, each one of us saying yes to God, as together we are in mission. In communing with each other and all Christians the world over, we all become holy—set apart for service as faithful witnesses—living and working for the salvation of the world through Jesus Christ our Lord.

Food for the Journey

Renowned Methodist missiologist D. T. Niles believes that the foundation of mission for the church is to be the people of God, the body of Christ visible in the world. To be this people in the world is to be everywhere in the world, which requires that we are also a pilgrim people, a people constantly on the move, on a journey from here to there, bearing the good news of Jesus Christ. "A Church at rest is no Church,"[2] he states, going on to observe that being a pilgrim people means that we will not act or behave as a more settled community:

> A pilgrim people is bound to have a set of values which are different from those held by people who have settled down. It will tend to accumulate less luggage, it will tend to be over concerned with creature comforts, it will enjoy its food provided for the journey....The sacraments of the Church, the worship of the congregation, the study of God's word, the practices of religion in the home and in one's personal life—all these are food for the journey. So many neglect them because they do not need them. Theirs is a sedentary life, and all this food is unnecessary."[3]

The *missio Dei* requires that we are constantly on the move as God's people, just as God is constantly on the move in this world. Methodism was originally a movement, rather than a settled church, being known by its itinerant circuit riders, who spent more time on horseback than in the office, and now we must recover that sense of movement and "pilgrimness" through our life in God's mission. As Dr. Niles so well states, this means that our value system will be different from that of a sedentary community. We have quite of bit of luggage (perhaps we should call it baggage?) hanging around our congregations. Our ability to get up and go is often hindered by our need for extra stuff, which we don't need for the mission on the road, and this keeps us from getting up and getting going in the first place.

Our food for the journey is simple yet very nourishing. The Bread of Life and the Cup of Salvation; the Word of God for the pilgrim people of God: worship, sacraments, Bible study, prayer (listening to God for God's witness to us as we gather in Christian conference); these are all the elements of our take-out menu. This food is very portable and durable and it tends not to spoil. A settled community does not need this portable food, as Dr. Niles states, but is content with growing and accumulating resources for itself. A missional pilgrim people must have food it can carry with it, living off the land with all that God provides for us on the journey of faith.

The Ingredients of Life

Bread is a simple combination of flour, water, salt, and yeast, mixed together with time and heat. This is an apt description of how to create a missional community committed to the global ministries of the church. It is to prepare food for the journey. Salt and yeast are the hidden ingredients for the bread, but without them it will not work.

Jesus gave us what we call the Beatitudes (Matthew 5:1-12) as the basic materials for making bread—the flour and water. Blessed, honored, and life-giving are those who are humble, who seek what is right connected with God (righteousness), who are merciful and who make peace. Be these, and you are the pilgrim people of God.

But then he goes on to to remind us what else is necessary to make this into useful, eatable bread. We are the salt of the earth (Matthew 5:13), for salt brings out the flavor of the basic ingredients of life; we are the light of the world (Matthew 5:14-16), for light and heat are needed to bind all the ingredients together; and the kingdom of heaven is like yeast (Matthew 13:33)—a people raising up the flatness of the flour into a wonderfully delightful texture that is delicious to the palate. Salt, light, and yeast make the food for the journey the Bread of Life for the world. We are being fed and feeding others with our very being, growing and becoming more visible and useful for the kingdom of God, just as the bread made in Christ's presence for the old woman in the fable grew and transformed into food for all.

David Bosch describes this as the church in mission being both a sacrament and a sign in and for the world.[4] It is sacrament as a mediating entity, representing God and God's presence to the world, anticipating the coming kingdom. It is a sign that points toward the reality of this kingdom. At the same time we are both called out of the world and sent into the world through our communal, connectional, and missional life. As we ourselves are fed along the journey by the Bread of Life in worship, prayer, study, and community, we are at the same time proclaiming the reign of God to the world beyond the church. These activities, which often are seen only as internal and even exclusive to believers, are in fact missional activities for the sake of the world for whom God sent his very visible presence in Christ (cf. John 3:16).

> The cup of blessing that we bless, is it not a sharing in the blood of Christ? The bread that we break, is it not a sharing in the body of Christ?

Because there is one bread, we who are many are one body, for we all partake of the one bread (1 Corinthians 10:16-17).

To act in God's mission is to *be* a different kind of presence in the world—feeding the world with the Bread of Life as the visible body of Christ. What is the salt and light and yeast of the church? It is the diversity and "tasty" spice of the global community of faith, lived out within your local community. It is to be present with all who seek new life in Christ. "Companion" means "one who eats bread with another"; i.e., *com* (with) *-pan* (bread) *-ion*. To accompany each other along the journey of mission is to eat bread together, sharing our resources and life-giving sustenance.

We need to bring the whole of God's world into our worship experiences. "Bread for the world, in mercy broken, wine for the soul in mercy shed." We can accompany others around the world on this journey of faith, by insuring that we include prayer concerns from the four corners of God's earth, by remembering the needs of persons we will never meet in our offertory prayers, by having visible symbols of other places and other cultures adorn our chancel spaces. Different forms of bread representative of the world's cultures may be used for the celebration of Holy Communion, not just on Worldwide Communion Sunday in October, as important as this is, but on every occasion of the Eucharist, and even on every Sunday. The essentially global nature of our faith is a cause for celebration and observance whenever and wherever God's people meet to sing, pray, and worship God, who loves the world so much, the whole world.

Making and Sharing Bread

Church school leaders from several new United Methodist Mission Initiatives in Eastern Europe (Lithuania, Latvia, Estonia, and Russia) came together recently to learn and share the joys and challenges of their mutual task, that of developing Christian education: the lack of resources for teaching, the church buildings being reclaimed or newly built very slowly, and the numbers of persons coming to be fed by God's Word far outnumbering the resources for Christian education of their limited missional structures.

Yet, one teacher offered a model of teaching the children in Lithuania about the importance of bread in Christian life, both in worship and in service, by baking bread and then taking it into their community in the city of Kaunas, to persons who have very little to eat. As the children are fed by the Word, they are feeding others with the bread made with their own hands, growing in so many ways in this new mission of the church.

Food for Body and Food for Soul

Deaconess Shay Blackwell, who serves as a church and community worker in the Missouri Annual Conference, recalls a time when she knew that God was moving through the family center and child advocacy ministry to which she has been called: "It was a Tuesday morning and I was in the middle of an anger management class, when our door bell rang. A homeless man asked if we could give him a piece of bread or a few crackers, maybe a glass of water, no money, just something to eat. When he left, he took with him a bottle of soda, some fruit, and a sandwich filled with meats and cheese. He left knowing someone cared enough to feed him, willingly and with a smile. Not a big deal by most standards, but it was for him and for us. He came to our door with an empty stomach; he left with food for his body and some food for his soul. We were left with a warm feeling that we could help, even a little, and with a reminder of blessings we can be in people's lives. Thanks be to God for these happenings."

Will There Be Enough Bread?

A young boy wandered into a Methodist Church in Rio de Janeiro, Brazil, just as the congregation was celebrating Holy Communion one Sunday. The lad sat down at a seat in the back, next to a regular parishioner. He intently watched as the pastor prayed over the bread and cup, and then began distributing the elements to worshipers as they came forward. The boy asked that person in the pew if he might go forward also and be fed, to which the answer was, of course, "Yes, if you want to." The boy's face beamed in delight, until he watched as more and more of the loaf was given away. As he became increasingly worried and upset, he leaned over again and asked, "Will there be enough left for me?"

There is always enough of the living bread of Christ for everyone who comes to the table by faith, for this is our food for the journey, which both feeds us and feeds the world. It is very portable and preserved. But will we continue to break off pieces for all who come and those afraid to come? The loaf made in Christ's presence will grow and grow to feed the world, as we reach out beyond ourselves and become a pilgrim people of faith. Will we share the loaf that is made up of the resources from God, which we have abundantly at our disposal? Take this bread, and let the seemingly small piece grow within you as you share your life with all who have not heard nor heeded the Word of God.

> O food to pilgrims given, O bread of life from heaven,
>   O manna from on high!
> We hunger; Lord, supply us, nor thy delights deny us,
>   whose hearts to thee draw nigh.[5]

Concepts to Consider

1. What is missional in the sacrament of Holy Communion?
2. When have you experienced the *com–pan–ion–ship* journey in sharing sacramental bread?
3. How would you create a global setting for worship every Sunday?

Notes for ESSAY 19

[1] *The United Methodist Hymnal* (Nashville, TN: United Methodist Publishing House, 1989), #614.

[2] D. T. Niles, *Upon the Earth: Foundations of the Christian Mission, Studies in the Gospel and the World* (New York: McGraw-Hill Book Co., 1962), p. 76.

[3] Ibid.

[4] David J. Bosch, *Transforming Mission, Paradigm Shifts in Theology of Mission* (Maryknoll, NY: Orbis Books, 1991) p. 11.

[5] *The United Methodist Hymnal* (Nashville, TN: United Methodist Publishing House, 1989), #631.

ESSAY 20

Being the "Glocal" Church in the 21st Century: The World is Our Parish

Reason understood through Mission Goal 3:
To Alleviate Human Suffering

Luke 9:11-17: Jesus cares for human need, by healing and feeding.

Isaiah 65:17-18: New heavens and a new earth.

All mission is local mission carried out on a global scale, and this is the concept of global ministries: to think and act "glocally." We are able to care for all by caring for the specific needs of some; a biblical concept through which Jesus understood the universal needs of all by understanding a particular person's needs.

The World Is Our Parish

In his journal for June 11, 1739, John Wesley refers to a quote from a letter to the Rev. James Hervey (a former student of his), discussing Wesley's preaching in London at Fetter Lane Chapel. Wesley wrote on his "many thoughts concerning the unusual manner of my ministering among them," meaning the parishioners of that congregation to which another pastor was assigned and for whom, in the Anglican polity of the day, Wesley had no ecclesiastical authority or responsibility.

> You accordingly ask, "How is it that I assemble Christians, who are none of my charge, to sing psalm, and pray, and hear the Scriptures expounded?" and think it hard to justify doing this in other men's parishes, upon catholic principles. Suffer me now to tell you my principles in this matter. **I look upon all the world as my parish**; thus far I mean, that, in whatever part of it I am, I judge it meet, right, and my bounden duty to declare unto all that are willing to hear the glad tidings of salvation....His servant I am, and, as such am employed according to the plain direction of His word: "as I have opportunity, doing good unto all men."[1]

The world as our parish is that ringing mantra of Methodism with which we have understood our movement into the world for lo, these past three centuries.

It is a forceful and dynamic image for a global church with far-reaching missional enterprises. Wesley here states his principle that wherever he is, that is the place where God would have him proclaim the good news of Jesus Christ; to whoever will listen, or not listen in some cases! He was often derided and physically attacked for his preaching. Yet, as he states, as much as he has opportunity, he would be about doing good unto all.

The corollary to this profound truth, however, is that "my" parish must never become the whole world to me. It is very easy for church leaders to become so meaningfully busy with the personal and organizational affairs of the local congregations they serve, either as lay leaders or pastors, that they forget there is a wide world out there for whom Christ died (John 3:16-17). "God so loved the world," means that God loves the whole world all at once, not piece-meal. The world is our parish, not the parish is our world! And yet, we must acknowledge the inherent tension between local concerns and global issues. The term we United Methodists use, "global ministries," is a call to be engaged in God's Mission locally, on a global scale.

Global and Local Experience

The Methodist "Connexion" as envisioned by Wesley in 1738, and continuing on down the ages to our present United Methodist Connection in the 21st century, is founded upon the model of Christian conferencing as a spiritual discipline coming from Wesley. That is, we engage in missional decision-making, through the gathered community of believers for any particular setting, geographically or thematically, most often using a representative convening process. This process is simultaneously global and local. It derives from our theological understanding that church membership begins with our baptism and confirmation as Christians, and then moves us toward commitment to The United Methodist Church as a denominational tradition, and only lastly with placement in a particular congregation. This is a theological movement of membership that goes from the global to the local.

Theology, the divinely revealed truth known to us through the sources of theology described previously, originates from the universal and moves toward the particular. Energy and workforce, however, flow from the particular to the universal. That is the 20th-century saying: "Think Globally, Act Locally"; but it is now necessary to move beyond that to: "Understand Locally, Witness Globally." It is a "yin-yang" type of movement for mission, expanding our understanding of the local and global realities of the world for which God sent his only Son, as the specific realities of God's call to reach out beyond ourselves. Missiology, as a theological discipline, begins with global understandings and universal teachings, with the work energy moving from the local activity back toward meeting the universal need.

Bishop Lesslie Newbigin, writing of the present and future of the ecumenical movement, and of the World Council of Churches in the context of God's Mission, puts this global/local ecclesiastical issue this way: "I would plead that the focus must be this: to help the whole Church to bring the whole gospel to the whole world by helping each local Eucharistic community to be faithful to that gospel."[2]

Centripetal and Centrifugal Forces for Mission

Missiologists Robert Gallagher and Paul Hertig identify a specific set of forces at work in the Book of Acts, that created the missional church as it moved both globally and locally. These are the centripetal and centrifugal forces for mission. It begins with the gathering of the community to receive the power of the Holy Spirit, and then moves outward in mission with this power. "The church begins in Jerusalem with a centripetal mission, attracting people lovingly into its dynamic community, and then expands to Judea and Samaria with a centrifugal mission that boldly ventures into the Gentile world."[3] These same forces can be the power that moves our contemporary church into global ministries, from a local base of empowering support by the Holy Spirit within the community of faith, and on toward increasingly outward movements to the ends of the earth.

For this to happen, Bishop Newbigin sees us not as the actors of salvation, but as the messengers of salvation. The local congregation is not a private club for a personal religion, just concerning itself with the centripetal forces inward, to care for each other. Rather, every local Christian church is a universal fellowship that exists for the people who are not yet in the fellowship.[4] The centripetal forces give the impetus for the centrifugal force outward into the world. The parish is not our world; rather, the world is our parish.

The account of the feeding of the 5,000 (Luke 9:11-17) is the only miracle of Jesus that is recorded in all four Gospels, and is the quintessential statement of the nature of God's Mission that is understood as a global life lived out locally. As Luke records it, Jesus welcomes the crowd of people who seek him out, and then teaches them larger theological truths about the kingdom, as well as healing those in distress (Luke 9:11). As evening approaches, Jesus recognizes their simple need for sustenance. The disciples urged him to send the crowd away to fend for themselves, but Jesus connects the global kingdom teachings with the local need for food, calling the disciples to feed the people with the five loaves and two fish which they had on hand.

Jesus teaches us that by meeting local needs we are living into the reality of the universally global reign of God, the coming kingdom. By relating to some we will be relating to all, for all people have the same needs and basic life situations. The world is our parish. Wherever we happen to be in the world is the site for our mission and ministry, as John Wesley stated, and is where we must be working to alleviate human suffering and bring the experience of new life to God's people. This arises out of the twin missional forces of thinking globally as we act locally, while we understand locally through witnessing globally. In this inward and outward movement, the centripetal and centrifugal forces for mission, we live into the coming kingdom which Jesus announced.[5]

A Global and Local Church Is "Glocal"

Dr. Robert J. Harman, as a former deputy general secretary of the General Board of Global Ministries, wrote and spoke about the realities of mission in the 21st century, out of his significant experiences of the late 20th century, and brought to our attention a new term to describe the global/local truth of Christian mission. To be both global and local at the same time is to be a "glocal" church. It may be a bit of word play, but the term does closely identify what it means to be truly global and truly local.

Dr. Harman states clearly that this is not just economic globalization, as found in the corporate business world:

> To be "global" is the objective of every enterprise in today's growing market economy. Showing signs of a "global" awareness by making experimental forays into less familiar regions of the world is one thing. Making a contribution to a lasting difference in the development of a truly global and fully human community is quite another....Not just globalization but "glocalization", a term some religious thinkers use to express cultural sensitivity, should be the aim of world mission for The United Methodist Church in this period. To create a variation of the familiar slogan, we must "think globally, but remember to pray locally," recognizing that people who pray anywhere these days must have the whole world in their thoughts.[6]

Glocalization is a secular term, coming out of 1980s Japanese business practices, and was first popularized in the English-speaking world by the British sociologist Roland Robertson in the 1990s, a sociologist and theorist of globalization. For Robertson, the most interesting movement of our globalized, post-modern world is the way in which a global consciousness has evolved for people from around the world. "Glocalization" is a historical process whereby localities develop direct economic and cultural relationships to global systems through information technologies, bypassing and subverting traditional power hierarchies such as national governments and corporate markets. To be glocal is to develop diverse and overlapping global-local linkages. This, in essence, describes the United Methodist connectional structures.

In contrast, globalization is the historical processes that encourage only one-way relationships between the global world, controlled by multinational corporations and the Western-dominated news/entertainment industry, and a dominated local world, where the identity-affirming sense of place and locality barely survive against the global onslaughts of corporate capitalism and media. Thus, instead of furthering globalization, the church is called and created in mission to engage in glocalization, where the global and the local are in creative tension and beneficial mutuality.

Glocal Is Church as a Community in Communion

Professor Andrew Kirk also identifies this tension of the global and the local as a crucial ecclesiastical understanding for the church in mission. It is necessary to have an operative balance in order to guard against improper and destructive inculturation of the gospel that is so tied to one cultural reality that it has no meaning elsewhere, or worse, encourages oppressive and unjust mission practices. To be fully global and local would tend to mitigate these tendencies.

> The church is a local community. As such it possesses a mission mandate for its own particular situation. It has to identify with the people in whose midst it is set, called to meet their needs and bear their burdens.

> The church also belongs to a communion of churches, with both great benefits and responsibilities. Somehow the local community has to commit itself to national, regional, and international structures which make it accountable to the wider communions of which it is in a sense a representative. In this way it lives the permanent tension between the particular and the universal inherent in being Church.[7]

Professor Kirk accurately describes the stance of a glocal congregation, a community within a larger communion, which itself is most often within a still larger communion. Being glocal is a creative tension for the church as much as incarnation is a tension, and the Trinity is a tension. It defines us as the unique faith structure that we are. It is in this tension that we are connecting the church with all it's constituent parts as well as the whole world, faithfully witnessing to God's coming reign.

The Kingdom Is Not Economic Globalization

This glocal lifestyle of the church, however, must also guard against being too closely tied to the rapid globalization process of the corporate economic structures of the contemporary world. Dr. Dana Robert, a preeminent United Methodist missiologist from the Boston School of Theology, in a presentation at the "Consultation on the Great Commission," held at Emory University in Atlanta, Georgia, in 2002, as she noted that the content of mission is in a globalized mission, said, "We should break the connections between globalization in an economic sense and the theological vision of the kingdom of God."[8]

Dr. Robert was calling our church to a more thorough and deeply understood theology of mission, rather than simply moving about the world with our money and technology, seeking to do some good for God. She reminds us of Paul's confessional statement that, "we do not proclaim ourselves; we proclaim Jesus Christ as Lord and ourselves as your slaves for Jesus' sake" (2 Corinthians 4:5). "In an age in which the church has finally spread all over the world, it behooves Western Christians to focus more on what it means to be faithful to the God of Jesus Christ."[9] We need to have those centripetal and centrifugal forces for mission to be alive in our lives as Christians. Neither one way nor the other will do. It is the movement of the Spirit in the process of mission that ensures we are a whole people, living in and for the sake of the whole world, which God so deeply loves in Christ Jesus.

Local Needs, Global Changes

Nan McCurdy and her husband Miguel Mairena are United Methodist missionaries in Nicaragua, who seek to connect the global realities of unjust economic systems with the local daily lives of the poor of that developing Central American nation. Nan and Miguel operate a revolving loan fund, which assists farm women in buying cows to help establish themselves and their families in a more secure future. It is as if it were a small business loan. It is necessary because of the immense burden placed on the Nicaraguan economy by the International Monetary Fund, which forces countries like Nicaragua to spend its resources on high-interest debt payments for decades-old loans to a previously corrupt government, rather than on development for their own peoples' welfare. Nan and Miguel also work in solidarity with an ecumenical group, which seeks to make public the illegal and unethical harassment of poor families, to remove them from the land for the benefit of wealthy business interests, with the encouragement of North American corporate powers.

The local needs of simple people attempting to lead quiet, humble lives are devastated by powerful global economic forces. Nan expresses what it is to be a glocal church, writing, "I don't believe in charity alone. I don't believe it does anything to make fundamental long-term changes. Our charity that springs from our love for our neighbor can be more effective when combined with work for structural change. I do believe in organizing and in working for systematic changes."[10]

Health and School Kits as Glocal Gifts of Hope

Uprooted by war and ethnic tensions, living far from the place they once called home, and knowing they may never return, a family in Azerbaijan struggles to survive alongside other displaced families living in a former hostel. Several people live in each room, sharing a communal bathroom and kitchen. UMCOR is able to present them with gifts of hope in the form of health and school kits. The children excitedly look into the school bags to find scissors, pencils, a ruler, and other supplies of their very own. The parents gratefully receive large storage bags filled with things to help them keep their families healthy: soap, toothbrushes, bandages, washcloths, and other items.

Several hundred thousand health kits were sent to the former Soviet republics in recent years, to individuals and families in similar situations. A nurse who worked in a refugee camp there watched as children opened their health kits. "I couldn't recall ever before having seen children so intrigued with some of health's most basic necessities," she said. These kits start with the loving concern of United Methodists in their home communities and travel thousands of miles to be a tangible symbol of love to strangers in need. These are physical examples of being glocal. As Paul admonished Rome, "Contribute to the needs of the saints; extend hospitality to strangers" (Romans 12:13). Care for your own and care for all others. In the process we understand that to care for some is to care for all, and all are our responsibility as a glocal church.

How to Be a Glocal Church

Thus, we are called to be *glocal* communities of believers in God's Mission, using the divine gift of reason in church life. That is, to organize and plan our responsibilities, or "response-ability," using our God-given abilities to respond to God's call to be sent into the world, which God so loves (John 3:16). What is our lifelong journey of response to all the understandings of *missio Dei*? It is to organize for God's Mission through:

Our Presence: leadership in mission.

Our Prayer: spirituality in mission.

Our Purse: financial stewardship in mission.

We bring leadership to God's Mission, through our active presence in the life of the church, in all arenas of church activity; lifting up the needs of God's Mission in worship, decision making, program planning, and implementation. We bring spirituality to God's Mission as we actively engage in prayer for missionaries and our partners in mission around the world and throughout the United States, and remind others in the church to pray for these persons. We bring the resource of our purse to God's Mission, as we intentionally decide on the use of the financial resources God has provided us with for the advancement of this mission.

A glocal congregation is one that will have an ongoing mission-education plan for all ages. This would include use of the United Methodist mission studies each year, for adults, youth, and children. There is a geographic study on one country, or group of countries, every other year, as well as a thematic study on an issue of current importance for missional understanding. The United Methodist Children's Fund for Christian Mission is an educational tool for use within the Sunday school, or in a vacation Bible school, which brings information and a planned curriculum dealing with four or five children's mission projects each year. Your presence in mission leadership would include being aware of the local impact of global, economic, and political decisions being made by governments, multinational corporations, and international bodies, such as the United Nations, the World Bank, and the International Monetary Fund. A glocal church will have information on such actions available to congregants.

Connecting our prayer lives with those of God's people, around our nation and other nations, will broaden our faith vision and deepen our spiritual presence. Who we remember in prayer, during worship, in prayer circles and small-group ministries, and in all public printed or electronic media, will say much about our global spirituality in our local context. To remember in prayer our missionaries, our partner churches in over 100 nations, our national mission institutions in the US, is to be a blessing and to be blessed by these spiritual connections.

A glocal church's budget will reflect all these areas of mission, as the use of our financial resources makes a profound statement of our connectedness with all of God's world. Where and how we choose to use the income and accumulated wealth of a congregation, all members of the congregation, will proclaim to the world our understanding of ourselves as either global citizens of faith, or a locally limited religious organization. Our budget will also say much about our belief in the future of God's reign in our midst. It is a profound act of faithful witness.

We live out our glocal perspective on God's world through our presence, our prayers, and our purse, all to the glory of God.

The Ultimate Global and Local Vision

As we seek to live in the world as our parish, we are reminded by the prophet Isaiah of God's vision for the coming kingdom: "For I am about to create new heavens and a new earth; the former things shall not be remembered or come to mind. But be glad and rejoice forever in what I am creating; for I am about to create Jerusalem as a joy, and its people as a delight" (Isaiah 65:17-18). The global new heavens and new earth are created out of all the local Jerusalems, which is where the church is gathering, in Wesley's words, "to sing psalms, and pray, and hear the Scriptures expounded." From there we go forth into global ministries which heal, feed, nurture, care for, and empower the people of the whole world for new life.

Concepts to Consider

1. How have you observed local/global interaction in a congregational setting?
2. Who is bringing the global realities of the 21st century into your local community?
3. What is needed to open the way toward a glocal vision in any congregation?

Notes for ESSAY 20

[1] Nehaemiah Churnock, ed., *The Journal of the Rev. John Wesley*, A.M. Standard Edition (London: The Epworth Press, 1939), Vol. II, pp. 216-218.

[2] Lesslie Newbigin, *A Word in Season* (Grand Rapids, MI: William B. Eerdmans, 1994), p. 200.

[3] Robert L. Gallagher and Paul Hertig, eds., *Mission in Acts: Ancient Narratives in Contemporary Context* (Maryknoll, NY: Orbis Books, American Society of Missiology Series, 2004), p. 9.

[4] Lesslie Newbigin, *The Open Secret*, op. cit., pp. 16-17.

[5] For an inspiring sermon on this topic, see Frederick Buechner's, "The News of the Day" in *Secrets in the Dark* (San Francisco: HarperCollins, 2006), pp. 245-250.

[6] Robert J. Harman, "Challenges of Mission in the Post-Cold War Context," in *Mission and Transformation in a Changing World* (New York: General Board of Global Ministries, 1998). Excerpted in Rena Yocom, ed., *New Wineskins* (New York: General Board of Global Ministries, 1999), p. 104.

[7] J. Andrew Kirk, *What Is Mission?* (Minneapolis: Fortress Press, 2000), p. 94.

[8] W. Stephen Gunter and Elaine A. Robinson, eds., *Considering the Great Commission* (Nashville: Abingdon Press, 2005), p. 35.

[9] Ibid., p. 36.

[10] "Nicaragua Mission Letter," from Nan Mccurdy and Miguel Mairena, February 2006. A missionary newsletter available from the Global Ministries Mission Personnel unit.

ESSAY 21

No Canning Jars in the Kingdom: Stewardship Is the Bread of Heaven Meant for All

Reason understood through Mission Goal 4:
To Seek Justice, Freedom, and Peace

Exodus 16:11-21: Manna—The God who leads us also feeds us, daily for what we need.

2 Corinthians 8: 1-7, 13-15: The response of the Macedonian churches in stewardship.

Philippians 4:10-20: Paul's principles for mission giving.

The stewardship of financial resources for mission, or how we use the manna from God, is a matter of living into God's vision of bringing together the whole world into the kingdom with justice, freedom, and peace for all persons. This requires the appropriate faithful offerings of all the resources that God has provided for us.

No Canning Jars in the Kingdom

Guide me, O thou great Jehovah, pilgrim through this barren land.
I am weak, but thou art mighty; hold me with thy powerful hand.
Bread of heaven, bread of heaven, feed me till I want no more;
Feed me till I want no more.[1]

You have heard that good old saying of American virtue that you should save for a rainy day. Faith is the knowledge that, "this is the day that the Lord has made; let us rejoice and be glad in it" (Psalm 118:24). And while that other old American saying may be true, that "today is the tomorrow you worried about yesterday," the truth is that there will be a tomorrow, but it can only be lived as a today. God has said to us that what are rained from heaven are the heavenly blessings we need to make it through today. "Bread of heaven, bread of heaven, feed me till I want no more, feed me till I want no more." Jesus said that he is the Bread of Life that came down from heaven (John 6:33-35). As we are fed by Christ in all things, so too we are the body of Christ that will feed the world by our missional giving.

United Methodist Bishop Judith Craig, preaching at several annual conferences in June 2006, used the illustration that there are "no canning jars in the kingdom." Bishop Craig grew up, as many of us have in this nation, with jars and jars of produce "canned up" in the summer and early autumn. Now, as sensible as this practice is for the fruit of a garden, it is not the biblical story of stewardship. God gives us all we need for each and every day. Grace cannot be stored up for future use. God is the Lord of today, and it is in today that we are called to live, and be fully alive in God's presence. Bishop Craig went on to tell the story of the manna for the Israelites in the wilderness of Sinai.

Bread of Heaven, Meant for All

In the 16th chapter of Exodus, we find the account of God providing bread for the Israelite people, as they were wandering through the desert of Sinai on the way from Egypt to the Promised Land. They called this bread manna, which really means nothing in Hebrew but is a takeoff on the question in Hebrew, "*man hu,*" or "What is it?" for they simply did not know what was there on the ground. This bread is also referred to as the "bread from heaven" in this passage (Exodus 16:4). The "it" in the question refers to all the material needs we have that God supplies. God always provides for our needs, and too often we do not recognize these as gifts. It is as if we were saying, "What is this?" It is manna. Manna is the accumulation of all the physical material God has created and blessed us with in this life. The question for us is not so much how it all came to be, or why God so "blesses" us, but rather, what shall we do with all this stuff? What shall we do with the manna we have? There is plenty to go around on this planet if we learn to share, and to equitably distribute the resources God has provided for all through Creation.

As the Israelites faced survival issues in the wilderness, they quickly forgot how abusive and oppressive their life was in Egypt. They only remembered that there was a chicken in every pot and bread on the table. When we face a crisis, we also tend to forget the other crises we have endured. The immediate overtakes our ability to remember ("do this," as Jesus said, "in remembrance of me" in Luke 22:19), and faith takes a backseat to raw emotion and human anxiety. God always hears us and knows our need. Recall the lilies of the field and how they grow (Matthew 6:28-33). Yet in the wildernesses of life, in the place of crisis, we tend not see the nurturing resources for our life, just as the Israelites did not.

There were really only two requirements of God's gracious gift of bread. First, that you don't take more than you need, so that everyone has enough to eat today (Exodus 16:17-18); and second, that you don't save any for tomorrow, or the next day, but know that God will always provide (Exodus 16:19). The first requirement is a matter of the distribution network of the resources from God. We are called to justly distribute the bread, as we have been justly blessed by the Lord. The second is a matter of our faithful knowledge that God is the Lord of each and every day, and will always care for today's needs today.

Some good people, however, don't believe in God's unfailing grace, then or now. The scriptures state that a few of the Israelites got greedy and self-serving, taking more than they needed and keeping it until morning, for they did not trust that God would continue to care for their continuing needs. The manna became rotten with worms (Exodus 16:20). There are no canning jars in the kingdom. They had tried to take advantage of God's blessings, and lost. They desired independence and self-sufficiency. They refused to be vulnerable in this equitable distribution system that God has created. Rather, they would try to return to the greedy and selfish practices they learned in Egypt, of hoarding and caring for me and mine, no one else, as also expressed in the ungraceful grace prayer of that old farmer on the prairie: "O Lord, bless me and my wife, my son John and his wife, we four and no more." This may be good old American independence and self-sufficiency, but it is the direct opposite of God's Word. Independence and taking care of "our own" has no place in Christian theology, and just like with the experience of the greedy Israelites, this attitude and understanding of life will cause our lives to become foul!

The truth for us here is that God has always provided for our needs, not lavishly nor indiscriminately, but there is always enough to go around—manna for everyone—unless someone takes too much. The Israelites were charged to gather enough manna each morning for that day's need in their family. Those who needed much gathered much, and those who needed little gathered little, and so everyone was well fed. The stewardship of worldwide resources can be a just distribution system, and recognizing that what we have comes from the Lord, each and every day, is an attitude of stewardship necessary to God's Mission.

Stewardship Is a Matter of Justice

Our faithful calling to God's Mission as Christians is to follow the contrasting example of the Macedonian churches, which Paul lifts up in 2 Corinthians 8:1-15. Though not wealthy, their joy in the faith leads to a generous offering for the relief of the Christians in Jerusalem.

First, Paul says, they gave themselves to the Lord. Once you've done this, you understand how much God has provided for your life, spiritually and physically, and then you are able to understand the right decisions to make your resources available for God's work. It's a matter of equality and justice (2 Corinthians 8:13-15). All will be cared for, if all care for each other. We are all in this world together; all of God's children are our family, whether you live in the US, Latin America, Africa, Europe, or Asia; we are all one people, traveling through this wilderness of life. God provides the manna—bread from heaven—for us to share among ourselves.

God's Mission calls us to radical discipleship as we are stewards of the manna—the gracious gifts of God that care for all needs. Mission is giving, for as John Wesley stated: "While you have the time, do all the good you can unto all men (sic)."[2]

Wesley also admonished all believers, in a sermon entitled "The Use of Money," to gain all you can, save all you can, and give all you can. He clearly makes the point that, while Paul says to Timothy, "for the love of money is a root of all kinds of evil, and in their meagerness to be rich some have wandered away from the faith and pierced themselves with many pains" (1 Timothy 6:10), Wesley understands this to mean that Christian stewardship of money is a matter of how we use the riches we have, in addition to acquiring them in a moral and disciplined manner.[3]

Mission Dollars and Sense!

How we handle the money we have is perhaps the most difficult issue for contemporary American Christians. It can also be the most freeing and liberating experience of Christian discipleship we will ever experience, as we engage in the faithful stewardship of our financial resources. Jesus' instructions to the disciples as he sent them off in mission were not to take any extra resources for the journey. God will provide. How? "For laborers deserve their food. Whatever town or village you enter, find out who in it is worthy, and stay there until you leave" (Matthew 10:9-11). In other words, mission giving: workers in the vineyard of the Lord are cared for by God through the faithful response of those of us who provide for their needs. Making the financial resources that God has given you available for those actively engaged in programs of God's Mission is, in itself, also mission, for each of these activities comes under the *missio Dei*. It makes sense that how we use our dollars and cents is how God is working in mission through us. We have significant financial resources in this nation, which God is calling us to use in the *missio Dei*, both around the world and within the more needful segments of our country. Mission giving is mission.

Paul has given us a set of guiding principles by which we can organize such a faithful life of mission stewardship. He wrote to the church in Philippi concerning their generous financial support of his mission and ministry (Philippians 4:10-20), and in so doing gives us a rich commentary on how to faithfully support God's Mission with our financial giving, for we have in this short passage Paul's instructions for mission support through four principles for giving.

First, mission support should be organized from a local community, not just from individuals (v. 10), as Paul directs his comments to the whole church there. Christianity is defined by its communal nature, and so mission support should also be an expression of the community of believers as a whole.

Second, mission support should be faithfully consistent, not just an occasional outburst of emotional awareness (vv. 15-16), for as Paul commends the Philippian church: "no church shared with me in the matter of giving and receiving, except you alone. For even when I was in Thessalonica, you sent me help for my needs more than once." Just as God cares for our needs daily, regularly, no matter what our needs are, so also must our missional giving be regular, no matter what the perceived need.

Third, mission support should be channeled through responsible agents, not sent directly (v. 18), for Paul received the gifts from an acknowledged agent, noting the accountability in the process. Administrative accountability through a responsible agency ensures that everyone, givers and recipients, has a clear understanding of the use of the funds. This does not mean that the givers always direct their use, but a fully disclosed allocation unites giver and receiver in the common mission.

Fourth, and perhaps most importantly, mission support is always a voluntary response to the gospel call, a spiritual investment in God's Mission (vv. 17, 18: "Not that I seek the gift, but I seek the profit that accumulates to your account," and "my God will fully satisfy every need of yours according to his riches in glory in Christ Jesus"). Mission giving is not so much about where your funds go, or to whom they are given, but is your faithful response to God's call in your life to be engaged in the *missio Dei*. It is our spiritual investment that connects our lives with the lives of all who share in the gospel work of proclaiming the reality of God's ultimate reign, as we pray together, "Your kingdom come. Your will be done, on earth as it is in heaven" (Matthew 6:10).

Sharing Our Lunch

What amount of financial giving is needed and necessary? Whatever you have and are faithfully willing to make available to God is the answer. In the Gospel of John we have the witness of one small boy sharing his meager lunch of bread and fish (John 6:9). How much did he give? What percentage of his income or assets did he offer to Jesus? You see, the percentage or amount is not the issue. That we give all we can for the care of the whole world, for whom God has offered God's only Son is the faithful stewardship answer. From that simple act of faithful generosity, 5,000 people were fed, by the Grace of God in Christ Jesus. Just that one small boy's action of gracious giving produced a miracle in Jesus' hands. And missional miracles still happen that way.

At the Ginghamsburg (Ohio) United Methodist Church, Pastor Mike Slaughter issued a Christmas challenge several years ago, a Macedonian-type stewardship call to this large membership congregation, to be in partnership with UMCOR in reaching displaced persons in Sudan. They have raised half a million dollars each year for several years in a holistic mission approach for Darfurian families, supporting sustainable agricultural programs, education, and child protection training in this violent and volatile situation.

Giving financially to advance the *missio Dei* is not a matter of how much you have to give, or some formula for tithing. If you have a lunch, and thousands are hungry, God will produce a miracle from your faithful offering for the benefit of all. Do not give "until it hurts," or even because "it feels good." Give simply because you have something in your hands to give. Share your lunch at the table of the Lord, and God will feed thousands with your faith. By grace we live and move and have our being. By grace we are present to the realities of God's Mission, throughout the world and next door to our home. By grace we are called to be in mission just as God is in the world, for the sake of the whole world itself. There are no canning jars in God's kingdom, and the bread and fish and all that we have is a graceful gift of a grace-filled God. Missional miracles await the offering of our lunch.

> Bless thou the gifts our hands have brought;
> Bless thou the work our hearts have planned.
> Ours is the faith, the will, the thought;
> The rest, O God, is in thy hand.[4]

Concepts to Consider

1. What canning jars of resources can you identify in your congregation?

2. How does it change our financial behaviors to see stewardship as a justice issue?

3. Why did only one small boy offer his lunch to Jesus? Why!

Notes for ESSAY 21

[1] *The United Methodist Hymnal* (Nashville, TN: United Methodist Publishing House, 1989), #127.

[2] John Wesley, Sermon 139, "On Love," February 20, 1736, point 4.

[3] Albert C. Outler, ed., *John Wesley* (New York: Oxford University Press, 1964), pp. 238-250.

[4] *The United Methodist Hymnal* (Nashville, TN: United Methodist Publishing House, 1989), #587.

RESOURCES
FOR THE JOURNEY INTO
THE *MISSIO DEI*
AND GLOBAL MINISTRIES

A Bibliography for Further and Deeper Study

Beals, Art, *When the Saints Go Marching Out!: Mobilizing the Church for Mission*, Geneva Press, Louisville, Ky., 2001.

Bevans, Stephen B. and Roger P. Schroeder, *Constants in Context: A Theology of Mission for Today*, Orbis Books, Maryknoll, N.Y., 2004.

Bolioli, Oscar L., ed., *Hope and Justice for All in the Americas: Discerning God's Mission*, Friendship Press, New York, 1998.

Bosch, David J., *Believing in the Future: Toward a Missiology of Western Culture*, Christian Mission and Modern Culture Series, Trinity Press International, Harrisburg, Pa., 1995.

———. *Transforming Mission: Paradigm Shifts in Theology of Mission*, Orbis Books, Maryknoll, N.Y., 1991.

Brunner, Emil, *The Word and the World*, Charles Scribner's Sons, New York, 1931.

Bühlmann, Walbert, *The Coming of the Third Church: An Analysis of the Present and Future of the Church*, St Paul Publications, Slough, England, 1976. Also published under same title by Orbis Books, Maryknoll, N.Y., 1978.

Campbell, Barbara E., *In the Middle of Tomorrow*, Women's Division, General Board of Global Ministries, New York, 1975.

Cardoza-Orlandi, Carlos, *Mission: An Essential Guide*, Abingdon Press, Nashville, 2002.

Dharmaraj, Glory E., *Concepts of Mission*, Women's Division, General Board of Global Ministries, New York, 1999.

Dharmaraj, Glory E. and Jacob S. Dharmaraj, *Mutuality in Mission: A Theological Principle for the 21st Century*, General Board of Global Ministries, New York, 2001.

Escobar, Samuel, *The New Global Mission: The Gospel from Everywhere to Everyone*, InterVarsity Press, Doner's Grove, Ill., 2003.

Gallagher, Robert L. and Paul Hertig, eds., *Mission in Acts: Ancient Narratives in Contemporary Context*, American Society of Missiology Series, Orbis Books, Maryknoll, N.Y., 2004.

Goodall, Norman, ed., *Missions Under the Cross*, Edinburgh House Press, London, 1953.

Guder, Darrell L. and Lois Barrett, eds., *Missional Church: A Vision for the Sending of the Church in North America*, The Gospel and Our Culture Series, William B. Eerdmans, Grand Rapids, Mich., 1998.

Gunter, W. Stephen and Elaine A. Robinson, eds., *Considering the Great Commission: Evangelism and Mission in the Wesleyan Spirit*, Abingdon Press, Nashville, 2005.

Harmer, Catherine M., *The Compassionate Community: Strategies That Work for the Third Millennium*, Orbis Books, Maryknoll, N.Y., 1998.

Glasser, Arthur F., et al., *Announcing the Kingdom: The Story of God's Mission in the Bible*, Baker Academic, Grand Rapids, Mich., 2003.

Kaiser, Walter C., Jr., *Mission in the Old Testament: Israel as a Light to the Nations*, Baker Academic, Grand Rapids, Mich., Reprint edition, 2000.

Kimbrough, S T, Jr., *Resistless Love: Christian Witness in the New Millennium: A Wesleyan Perspective*, General Board of Global Ministries, New York, 2001.

Kirk, J. Andrew, *Mission Under Scrutiny: Confronting Contemporary Challenges*, Fortress Press, Minneapolis, 2006.

———. *What Is Mission?: Theological Explorations*, Fortress Press, Minneapolis, 2000. First published by Darton, Longman and Todd Ltd, London, 1999.

Lloyd-Sidle, Patricia and Bonnie-Sue Lewis, eds., *Teaching Mission in a Global Context*, Geneva Press, Louisville, Ky., 2001.

Messer, Donald E., *A Conspiracy of Goodness: Contemporary Images of Christian Mission*, Abingdon Press, Nashville, Tenn., 1992.

Müller, Karl, *Mission Theology: An Introduction*, Steyler Verlag – Wort und Werk, Nettetal, Germany, 1987. Distributed in USA by Divine Word Seminary, Techny, Ill. 60082, ISBN# 3805001916.

Newbigin, Lesslie, *A Word in Season: Perspectives on Christian World Missions*, William B. Eerdmans, Grand Rapids, Mich., 1994.

——. *Mission in Christ's Way: A Gift, a Command, an Assurance*, Friendship Press, New York, 1987.

——. *The Open Secret: An Introduction to the Theology of Mission*, William B. Eerdmans, Grand Rapids, Mich., 1978, Rev. 1995.

Niles, D. T., *Upon the Earth: The Mission of God and the Missionary Enterprise of the Churches*, McGraw-Hill Book Co., New York, 1962.

Pohl, Christine, *Making Room: Recovering Hospitality as a Christian Tradition*, William B. Eerdmans, Grand Rapids, Mich., 1999.

Potter, Philip, *Life in All Its Fullness*, William B. Eerdmans, Grand Rapids, Mich., 1982. First published by the World Council of Churches, Geneva, Switzerland, 1981.

Robert, Dana L., *American Women in Mission: A Social History of Their Thought and Practice*, Mercer University Press, Macon, Ga., 1997.

Robert, Dana Lee, ed., *Gospel Bearers, Gender Barriers: Missionary Women in the Twentieth Century*, American Society of Missiology Series, Orbis Books, Maryknoll, N.Y., 2002.

Sanneh, Lamin, *Translating The Message: The Missionary Impact on Culture*, Orbis Books, Maryknoll, N.Y., 1989.

Sider, Ronald J., *Good News and Good Works: A Theology for the Whole Gospel*, Baker Books, Grand Rapids, Mich., 1993.

Shenk, Wilbert R., *Changing Frontiers of Mission*, American Society of Missiology Series, Orbis Books, Maryknoll, N.Y., 1999.

——. *Write the Vision: The Church Renewed*, Christian Mission and Modern Culture Series, Trinity Press International, Harrisburg, Pa., 1995.

Thangaraj, M. Thomas, *The Common Task: A Theology of Christian Mission*, Abingdon Press, Nashville, 1999.

Thomas, Norman, *Classic Texts in Mission and World Christianity: A Reader's Companion to David Bosch's* Transforming Mission, American Society of Missiology Series, Orbis Books, Maryknoll, N.Y., 1995.

United Methodism and American Culture Series:

>   Vol. 1: Richey, Russell E., Dennis M. Campbell, and William B. Lawrence, eds., *Connectionalism: Ecclesiology, Mission, and Identity*, Abingdon Press, Nashville, 1997.

>   Vol. 2: Lawrence, William B., Dennis M. Campbell, and Russell E. Richey, eds., *The People(s) Called Methodist: Forms and Reforms of Their Life*, Abingdon Press, Nashville, 1998.

>   Vol. 3: Campbell, Dennis M., William B. Lawrence, and Russell E. Richey, eds., *Doctrines and Discipline*, Abingdon Press, Nashville, 1999.

>   Vol. 4: Richey, Russell E., William B. Lawrence, and Dennis M. Campbell, eds., *Questions for the Twenty-First Century Church*, Abingdon Press, Nashville, 1999.

United Methodist Church History of Mission Series:

>   Vol. 1: Daugherty, Ruth A., *The Missionary Spirit*, General Board of Global Ministries, New York, 2004.

>   Vol. 2: Sledge, Robert W., *"Five Dollars and Myself,"* General Board of Global Ministries, New York, 2005.

>   Vol. 3: Gesling, Linda, *Mirror and Beacon*, General Board of Global Ministries, New York, 2005.

>   Vol. 4: O'Malley, J. Steven, *"On the Journey Home,"* General Board of Global Ministries, New York, 2003.

>   Vol. 5: Harman, Robert J., *From Missions to Mission*, General Board of Global Ministries, New York, 2005.

Vol. 6: Cole, Charles E., ed., *Initiatives for Mission: 1980–2002*, General Board of Global Ministries, New York, 2003.

Vol. 7: Cole, Charles E., ed., *Christian Mission in the Third Millennium*, General Board of Global Ministries, New York, 2004.

Walls, Andrew F., *The Missionary Movement in Christian History*, Orbis Books, Maryknoll, N.Y., 1996.

——. *The Cross-Cultural Process in Christian History*, Orbis Books, Maryknoll, N.Y., 2002.

Women's Division: Ten Best Books on the History of United Methodist Women on CD-ROM, Women's Division, General Board of Global Ministries, The United Methodist Church, New York, N.Y., 1999.

Song Selections to Further Your Study and Reflection

Key:

UMH = *The United Methodist Hymnal*, The United Methodist Publishing House, Nashville, 1989.

TFWS = *The Faith We Sing*, Nashville, Abingdon Press, 2000.

GP1 = *Global Praise 1*, S T Kimbrough, Jr. and Carlton R. Young, eds., General Board of Global Ministries, New York, 1996, Rev. 1999.

GP2 = *Global Praise 2*, S T Kimbrough, Jr. and Carlton R. Young, eds., General Board of Global Ministries, New York, 2000.

GP3 = *Global Praise 3*, S T Kimbrough, Jr., Carlton R. Young, Jorge Lockward, and Barbara Day Miller, eds., General Board of Global Ministries, New York, 2004.

Song Suggestions for Essay 1:

UMH	57	"O For a Thousand Tongues to Sing"
TFWS	2162	"Grace Alone"
GP3	95	"More Than We Know"

Song Suggestions for Essay 2:

UMH	440	"Let There Be Light"
TFWS	2155	"Blest Are They"
GP1	60	"The Right Hand of God"

Song Suggestions for Essay 3:

UMH	560	"Help Us Accept Each Other"
TFWS	2237	"As a Fire Is Meant for Burning"
GP2	34	"For Everyone Born"

Song Suggestions for Essay 4:

UMH	593	"Here I Am, Lord"
TFWS	2172	"We Are Called"
GP2	113	"Enviado Soy de Dios" ("Sent Out in Jesus' Name")

Song Suggestions for Essay 5:

UMH	427	"Where Cross the Crowded Ways of Life"
TFWS	2004	"Praise the Source of Faith and Learning"
GP1	65	"Tua Palavra Na Vida" ("Your Word in Our Lives")

Song Suggestions for Essay 6:

UMH	571	"Go, Make of All Disciples"
TFWS	2153	"I'm Gonna Live So God Can Use Me"
GP2	111-112	"Det Kan Va en Tant" ("It Can Be a Girl")

Song Suggestions for Essay 7:

UMH	572	"Pass It On"
TFWS	2155	"Blest Are They"
GP2	115	"Nurtured By the Spirit"

Song Suggestions for Essay 8:

UMH	356	"Pues Si Vivimos" ("When We Are Living")
TFWS	2178	"Here Am I"
GP1	17	"Child of Joy and Peace"

Song Suggestions for Essay 9:

UMH	444	"O Young and Fearless Prophet"
TFWS	2177	"Wounded World that Cries for Healing"
GP3	159	"Du Satte Dig Selv" ("You Came Down to Earth")

Song Suggestions for Essay 10:

UMH	548	"In Christ There Is No East or West"
TFWS	2181	"We Need a Faith"
GP2	103	"Sound a Mystic Bamboo Song"

Song Suggestions for Essay 11:

UMH	561	"Jesus, United by Thy Grace"
TFWS	2224	"Make Us One"
GP1	56	"Shukuru Allah" ("Let the People Know")

Song Suggestions for Essay 12:

UMH	192	"There's a Spirit in the Air"
TFWS	2095	"Star Child"
GP2	43	"Whose Child Is This?"

Song Suggestions for Essay 13:

UMH	432	"Jesu, Jesu"
TFWS	2176	"Make Me a Servant"
GP2	119	"There Arc Tables in Our City"

Song Suggestions for Essay 14:

UMH	583	"Sois la Semilla" ("You Are the Seed")
TFWS	2220	"We Are God's People"
GP1	15	"Cançao da Caminhada" ("If Walking Is Our Vocation")

Song Suggestions for Essay 15:

UMH	547	"O Church of God, United"
TFWS	2223	"We Are One in the Spirit"
GP2	114	"Jesus Christ Sets Free to Serve"

Song Suggestions for Essay 16:

UMH	428	"For the Healing of the Nations"
TFWS	2190	"Bring Forth the Kingdom"
GP2	123-124	"Min Himmel" ("My Heaven")

Song Suggestions for Essay 17:

UMH	434	"Cuando el Pobre" ("When the Poor Ones")
TFWS	2174	"What Does the Lord Require of You"
GP3	148-149	"Somos Pueblo Que Camina" ("We Are People On a Journey")

Song Suggestions for Essay 18:

UMH	383	"This Is a Day of New Beginnings"
TFWS	2238	"In the Midst of New Dimensions"
GP3	153	"In Mission Together"

Song Suggestions for Essay 19:

UMH	634	"Now Let Us from This Table Rise"
TFWS	2260	"Let Us Be Bread"
GP3	148-149	"Somos Pueblo Que Camina" ("We Are People On a Journey")

Song Suggestions for Essay 20:

UMH	550	"Christ, from Whom All Blessings Flow"
TFWS	2243	"We All Are One in Mission"
GP1	15	"Canção da Caminhada" ("If Walking Is Our Vocation")

Song Suggestions for Essay 21:

UMH	399	"Take My Life, and Let It Be"
TFWS	2044	"My Gratitude Now Accept, O God"
GP3	146	"Reamo Leboga" ("We Give Our Thanks to God")

Internet Resource Pages for Mission Studies and Missiology

Academy of Mission Renewal: http://academyofmissionrenewal.org

American Society of Missiology: http://www.asmweb.org

Association of Professors of Mission: http://www.asmweb.org/apm

Center for Global Christianity and Mission, Boston University School of Theology: http://www.bu.edu/sth/cgcm

Church World Service – USA: http://www.churchworldservice.org

General Board of Global Ministries: http://gbgm-umc.org

Global Praise program of Global Ministries: http://globalpraise.org

International Association for Mission Studies: http://www.missionstudies.org

Overseas Ministries Study Center: http://www.omsc.org
An independent ecumenical organization supported by Global Ministries for missiological studies.

Rethinking Mission: www.rethinkingmission.org
Cooperative effort of USPG: (British) Anglicans in World Mission, the Methodist Church of Great Britain and Ireland, and the Selly Oak Centre for Mission Studies.

United Methodist Women: www.umwmission.org

World Council of Churches: http://www.oikoumene.org
Specifically the programs on "Unity, mission, evangelism, and spirituality," including "Towards 2010" on the 100th anniversary celebration of the 1910 Edinburgh World Mission Conference.

Yale Divinity School Library:
http://www.library.yale.edu/div/MissionsResources.htm
A site for the archives and mission books of the best North American library collection for Protestant mission studies.

STUDY GUIDE
FOR
FAITHFUL WITNESSES

By Diana L. Hynson
Director of Learning and Teaching Ministries
General Board of Discipleship of The United Methodist Church

INTRODUCTION

"Mission education" will help pastors and other leaders in the church become acquainted with the heart of mission as flowing from the heart of God. More than just something we do, it is more appropriately viewed as a part of our Christian identity. We "do" mission because our lives belong to God, whose mission is to transform us into the beloved children we were created to be. In turn, we place our lives in service to the same mission as God's agents in a needy world.

This study hopes to help immerse you in a contemporary understanding of mission, yet it recognizes that both clergy and lay leaders are immersed in ministry already. To respect and accommodate the full schedule of its suggested participants, this study is presented in three schedule formats, with an Appendix of extra activities, resources, and suggestions for alternatives.

Format

Faithful Witnesses is a versatile study! In this resource you have three different formats for leading a group. The suggested number of contact hours is given in the Continuing Education Unit equivalent.

☑ Six sessions of 2½ hours each (1.5 CEUs)

☑ Retreat of 2½ days (1.2 CEUs)

☑ One-day event (.5 CEUs).

All formats will include, in the appropriate way:

☑ learning goals

☑ a list of supplies and instructions for preparation

☑ worship/study with the Scriptures that provides some theological foundation for the session

☑ creative activities and instructions to facilitate the learning goals

☑ a time for synthesis, reflection, and action plan

☑ a closing.

Six Sessions

The six-session format will maximize the experience and is the suggested plan. Each session plan lays out a complete step-by-step process for a 2½ hour session, which will have 15 contact hours overall.

Each session will require advance reading of the essays by both leader and participants. There are four or five essays in each chapter that convey considerable content, theological reflection, Scripture, and anecdotes of mission experience. Participants will gain greatly by having read the text before each session, including Session 1. For the best result, ask session attendees to read before the first session and each subsequent one. They must bring their Bibles to the study sessions.

In addition to the reading, the leader will be asked to provide some visuals or supplies that may not be easily gathered before dashing out the door. Leaders will need to be proactive and prepared. The activities are not difficult, but they involve more than the typical "read and discuss" or lecture format of many adult resources.

This format will maintain the best continuity as a weekly study, but could also be used for continuing education at monthly district meetings, or in other settings where pastors and lay leadership have the opportunity to gather regularly. *If sessions are more than two weeks apart, it will be vitally important to include some time for review at the beginning of Sessions 2-6, which will probably elongate the session.*

Retreat

The retreat format is organized in a "mid-day to mid-day" pattern, starting at about 1:00 p.m. on Day One, a whole day (about 9:00 a.m.–5:30 p.m.) on Day Two, finishing by around noon on Day Three. This format provides for two full days' worth of time together. Since it is a retreat setting, the schedule builds in free time, with about 12 contact hours. This pattern offers three fewer contact hours than the six-week format, but also concentrates the time and maintains continuity from session to session. Furthermore, it minimizes variations in attendance, which would be a consideration in the multi-session format. A suggested schedule is included at the beginning of the session plan.

The list of what to prepare for and have on hand is also included with the suggested schedule. If your retreat is "off-site," it will be very important to be sure that everything is assembled and available when you arrive on site.

Securing a retreat setting requires more logistical work than arranging for a "class-length" space. Be sure to pre-register as many participants as possible so that you can plan accurately for meals, snack food for breaks, rooming arrangements, and carpooling. Consider folding in the cost of the study resource with the registration fee so that you can purchase them in bulk and send copies in advance for participants to do the necessary reading.

Prior to the retreat, notify participants about what to bring, including Bibles; what time to arrive; where to go; and how to get situated in a room. Check on any special conditions that require extra attention or accommodation, such as accessibility or dietary needs.

One-Day Event

In the One-Day event, you will be introduced to five essays within this collection of 21. While there is much more content and considerably more compelling stories in the other essays, the selected five essays will provide a "taste and see" experience for your group in about five contact hours. The strength of this model is that it offers a basic primer on mission for participants, which may whet their appetite for the longer study. We hope that it will encourage you and the other participants to lead the Six-Session study, so group members get the full impact of what mission is and how they can live missional lives.

The essays considered in this One-Day event represent one "bite" from each of the five chapters. The rest of the "menu" is there for you to draw on, should you choose to adapt or augment this plan. Essay 2 introduces the concept of *missio Dei* to form the foundation for the others. Essay 6 (Scripture/Goal 1: Make Disciples) describes a witness to being "on fire in mission." Essay 11 (Tradition/Goal 2: Christian Community) focuses on the analogy of the body of Christ, organized for life (and therefore for ministry), and the body of the United Methodist Connection (also organized for life and ministry). Essay 17 (Experience/Goal 4: Peace With Justice) concentrates on the issues inherent in being in mission with and for those who are most in need of kindness and justice. Essay 20 (Reason/Goal 3: Alleviate Suffering) illustrates the interconnectedness of local and global realities that call all of us to mission wherever we are. Feel free to draw on the content and stories from any of the other essays as you prepare.

Content and Approach

The text is arranged in five parts: an introduction and a section for each of the emphases of what we affectionately call the Wesleyan Quadrilateral (Scripture, tradition, experience, and reason). Within those divisions, mission is considered through the lens of the four ministry goals of the General Board of Global Ministries; briefly, making disciples, creating Christian community, alleviating suffering, and working for peace with justice. The text works horizontally, if you will, across the quadrilateral, addressing the four goals. This study approaches the essays in this arrangement, starting with Chapter Two.

See-Judge-Act is an implicit approach in the reflection/action segment of the session. The four or five activities will help surface the issues and in the final assessment activity, participants will be asked to analyze using this model. The appendix suggests other approaches to the text. *See* means that participants will look carefully at their own context and current reality—what *is*. *Judge* means that this current reality will be evaluated through the lens of Scripture. What does our sacred Writ say and mean in this context? How well do we as Christians acquit ourselves at this time and place in light of the Scriptures? *Act* is our tangible response. If we take a hard look at our current reality and discover that our Scriptures show us to be lacking, for example, how are we called to action and what will that action be? We describe this approach as Reflection/Action.

Within the See-Judge-Act model, teaching suggestions will tap into the seven predominant intelligences: interpersonal, intrapersonal, verbal/linguistic, visual/spatial, logical/mathematical, body/kinesthetic, and musical. These intelligences are described in the Appendix. Our typical teaching methods, especially with adults, are weighted heavily on verbal activities, that require a lot of listening (as in lectures) or "read and discuss." This curriculum uses multiple methods to tap into the learning strengths of all the participants.

We know from brain research that we can only absorb so much at a time and that it is crucial to change pace about every 20 minutes. The activities are arranged so that participants have a mix of passive and active exercises, get to move around, change focus, and spend both time alone and time in groups. While you will no doubt want and need to adapt the curriculum plan to suit your context and group, you are encouraged not to skip over activities that use an intelligence other than your strongest ones. Someone else in the group will need just that activity, because it is the most comfortable for their preferred way of learning. Using the multiple approaches and changes of pace will greatly facilitate and optimize the learning experience.

Reflection/Action

Each session, regardless of the format, must include time for participants to process what they have experienced and to formulate some next steps. There is a temptation, especially if the session runs long, to skip this step, because "We can do this on the way home (or later than that)." Make time during the session to ensure that it is done. Otherwise, participants do not get the full benefit of the experience.

Appendix

The Appendix includes all the handouts necessary for each of the three formats. They are reproducible pages that should be copied in advance for each participant. The handouts for the Six-Session and Retreat formats are very similar and are marked according to activity (such as **1.3**) and format (**6-S** or **R**). The One-Day format includes some selection/adaptation of the activities in the Six-Session format, but it is different enough that most of those handouts are separated for ease in copying. The Readers Theater and Panel Discussion instructions are included with the Six-Session format, and are clearly marked.

Other educational helps are included in the Appendix after the handout section.

Planning and Preparation

For Participants

If you are a participant in a *Six-Session study*, read all the essays in the appropriate part before a session. Read the Scriptures, including verses before and after the quotation or citation, to see the biblical foundation for the essays under consideration. In the *Retreat setting* or *One-Day event*, read all the essays in advance. There is far more content in the essays than will be considered in any format, so mark portions of the text that are meaningful to you or that raise questions. Be sure to bring your Bible to each session.

For Leaders

If you are leading the study, read all the essays before you begin. If you are leading the long study, reread the essays that you will teach in the given session. Flag portions of the text that you want to explore. If they are mentioned in the teaching plan, note the activity on your flag. If not, jot down which activity you will use to present that text.

Each session provides instructions for preparation, including assembling items for the focal point of the room. Be sure to allow time to obtain what you need, as they are generally used as educational tools as well. Nearly every activity is done in table groups, so set up the meeting space accordingly. Participants will need to bring a Bible to each session.

The sessions make use of music (one of the seven core intelligences) at least twice. All the selections of songs are in *The United Methodist Hymnal*, with alternative selections in *Global Praise 1*, *Global Praise 2*, *Global Praise 3*, or *The Faith We Sing* songbooks, because they are available to most groups. The songbooks are abbreviated in the Study Guide as "UMH," "GP1," "GP2," "GP3," and "TFWS," respectively. The songs are chosen because they are familiar and singable, even without accompaniment, but the session will be enhanced if there is a pianist and piano. The Appendix includes more music selections from the various hymnals and songbooks published within The United Methodist Church. Feel free to adapt if those hymnals are available.

Consider sharing leadership, either within each session or from session to session. The change in leadership is another method of changing the pace and visual impact of the session. In addition, it will share the teaching and preparation responsibility. Be sure that each leader knows what the other is doing and going to do during a session, so that leadership is excellent and consistent throughout the study.

Local Church Study

Publicize the study opportunity through the channels that best reach the group you want to attend, such as district or conference e-letters, e-zines, group email lists, or websites. Not everyone has access to electronic communication, so you may need print publicity as well. If you are leading this in your congregation, add bulletin notices, posters, church email or website, and personal notes or calls.

Planning Team

Regardless of the setting, have at least a few other people to help prepare, publicize, and lead. The team will also be responsible for other details necessitated by the format: securing the place, negotiating and reserving retreat space, arranging for food and transportation, providing the essays in advance to participants, determining any registration fee, handling the finances and budget, and attending to hospitality issues at the learning site.

The team may also wish to plan for follow up. As participants gain energy and momentum for mission, they may need further guidance on how to put more specific actions to their convictions. Having an infrastructure in place, even as simple as a designated conference staff person to call, will ensure a more concrete response to God's call for all to be in mission.

CURRICULUM PLAN
FOR A SIX-SESSION STUDY

SESSION ONE
THE WHY, WHAT, WHERE, WHEN, AND HOW OF MISSION

Learning Goals:

☑ To understand mission as God's Mission, in which all are called to participate.

☑ To develop a theology of Mission.

☑ To see oneself in the biblical call.

Prepare or Have on Hand:

☑ An item small enough to hold in one hand, such as a cross, icon, or unbreakable figurine (Activity 1.2).

☑ A tent peg at the focal point; if possible, one for each group (Activity 1.13; 1.18).

☑ Copies of the handouts (Activity 1.3; 1.13; 1.15; see Appendix).

☑ Copies of *The United Methodist Hymnal*, *Global Praise 1*, and *The Faith We Sing* songbooks for each person (Activity 1.8; 1.11; 1.18).

☑ Poster board, tape, and markers (Activity 1.9; 1.12).

Welcome and Opening Devotion (20 minutes)

1.1   Welcome everyone. Mention the necessary hospitality issues (how to handle breaks, location of restrooms, getting snacks or beverages, and so on).

1.2   Hold the icon and take no more than 14 seconds to say something about yourself. Then give the icon to the next person to do the same and so on around the room. Close the introductions with a brief prayer.

1.3   Form small groups of four or five people. Read aloud John 3:1-17, then distribute the handout. Ask participants to skim the passage again, then discuss these questions:

As you think about yourself and your understanding of the kingdom of God, are you more like:

❖ Nicodemus, coming to Jesus in the cover of darkness?

❖ Nicodemus, questioning Jesus about how one enters the kingdom?

❖ One who is born of the Spirit?

❖ One who wonders how Jesus' teaching can be so?

❖ One who testifies to heavenly things?

❖ One who focuses on the condemnation of the world?

1.4   As time allows, invite comments from the whole group about any new insights, then close with prayer.

Mission as God's Mission (20 minutes)

1.5   Form five groups, each with a subgroup and two recorders, and assign a different essay (Essays 1-5) to each group. The subgroup will examine the Scripture references in each of the essays and help its group members support their answer theologically.

1.6   In 15 minutes, ask each group to skim the essay, highlight the major points, and formulate a brief theological answer to the question presented at the beginning of the essay (for example, Essay 1: Why Mission Theology, Anyway?).

1.7   In very quick "popcorn" style, invite the groups to read their presenting questions and brief answers. Ask the recorders to write down the other groups' responses.

Theology of Mission (40 minutes)

1.8   In the same small groups, distribute hymnals and songbooks and have participants continue to work with the whole group responses (Activity 1.8), to formulate a theology of mission statement that includes the Why, What, Where, When, Who, and How of mission. Keep the statement to only two or three paragraphs. Take 20-25 minutes.

1.9   When the statement is finished, find at least one hymn or song that supports your theology statement. Post a list of the hymns and songs on newsprint.

1.10   Have groups read or post their statements. Sing one or more of the hymns or songs.

Break (10 minutes)

Inclusion in the Biblical Call (20 minutes)

1.11   Start the singing of a second hymn or song as a way to gather the group. Re-form the small groups. In those smaller groups, suggest that they divide the review and reading in 1.13 and 1.14, then do the discussion together.

1.12   Review the comments on grace (Essay 1), *missio Dei* and the "four significant consequences" described by Philip Potter (Essay 2), and the sections on Call and Journey (Essay 4). List the main points on newsprint.

1.13   Then read • Isaiah 6:1-8; • Luke 9:23-27 and 10:1-11, 17-20; and • John 1:14-16 and 3:16-17. Use the tent peg as a "talking stick" and discuss these questions:

   ❖ How do you see the call of the prophet and disciples as mission? What does it mean to you to pick up your cross (or tent peg) and follow?

   ❖ How does the Incarnation and saving activity of God through Jesus Christ call you to ministry? Is this different, in your mind, than a call to mission? If so, how?

   ❖ Where and how do you see yourself called to mission?

1.14   If time allows, have one person in each group tell about their own call to ministry and how that has influenced their understanding of mission.

Reflection/Action (30 minutes)

1.15   Encourage participants to work alone first, then compare notes later if they wish. Spend several minutes in silence journaling, keeping these questions in mind:

   ❖ How am I living out God's call to mission?

   ❖ Which Scriptures speak most compellingly to me about my call to mission?

   ❖ What is God's word of grace to me today?

   ❖ How has my "mission tent" moved? How would I like it to move?

❖ What one action will I take in the next week to live out that word of grace?

❖ Who will be my partner in action and/or accountability?

1.16 If you want to take the last 5 or 10 minutes to debrief and compare, do so.

Closing (10 minutes)

1.17 Ask participants to read the Chapter Two essays and remind them to bring a Bible to the next session. Look at the Prepare list to have preparations in place for the session.

1.18 Close by reading Luke 17:20-21; followed by UMH #593: "Here I Am, Lord," GP1 #60: "The Right Hand of God," or TFWS #2172: "We Are Called" (or another from your list). Hold up the tent peg and offer a benediction.

SESSION TWO
SCRIPTURE

Learning Goals:

☑ To understand the meaning of witness.

☑ To view leader development as a call to mission.

☑ To develop a theology of care.

☑ To understand and eliminate barriers to the kingdom.

Prepare or Have on Hand:

☑ Several candles and matches; one for each table group
   (Activity 2.1; 2.5; 2.18).

☑ Copies of *The United Methodist Hymnal*, *Global Praise 1*, *Global Praise 2*,
   and *The Faith We Sing* songbooks for each participant
   (Activity 2.4; 2.7; 2.18).

☑ Copies of the handouts (Activity 2.6; 2.8; 2.15; see Appendix).

☑ A small loaf of bread or pita on a plate at each table, placed before the
   session begins (Activity 2.11; 2.18) and juice for Communion (Closing).

Welcome and Opening Devotion (20 minutes)

2.1   Welcome everyone and do a brief round of introductions if there are new
      persons present. Distribute handouts to each table; place them face down
      for now. Create a focal point for your devotions with the candles and
      light them.

2.2   Read aloud Isaiah 58:6-11 for *lectio divina*. For the first reading, ask
      participants to listen for and jot down any words, phrases, or images that
      capture their attention. Pause for a minute, then invite any who wish to
      respond briefly. Read the passage again. This time ask participants to
      reflect on what that word or image means to them and how it makes them
      feel. Pause for another minute, then ask for any other brief comments.
      Read the passage a third time. With this reading, participants should note
      how they perceive God speaking to them through those words and
      images. After another minute, allow time for further response from the
      group. After the last comment, allow one more minute of silence to rest
      in the reading and hearing of the Word.

2.3   Sing together UMH #427: "Where Cross the Crowded Ways of Life," GP1 #17: "Child of Joy and Peace," or TFWS #2237: "As a Fire Is Meant for Burning." Then open a time of prayer, ask for bidding prayers, and conclude the prayer. Move the candles so that there is one at each table group.

The Meaning of Witness (20 minutes)

2.4   Form table groups. Review Essay 6, paying particular attention to "The Fire of Mission" and "Being Sent." Take a few minutes to bring out the main points.

2.5   Pick up a candle in one of the groups and describe one burning need anywhere in the world that has captured your heart. Have the small group members do the same, one by one, by placing the candle in front of themselves, speaking to a need, and moving the candle carefully to the next person. (If there are *any* concerns about participants doing this safely, do not pass the candles.)

2.6   Distribute the handout. Read aloud, or have group members read Matthew 5:14-16. Reflect on the Scripture and on the burning needs mentioned, then discuss these questions:

   ❖ How does the need you see compel you to witness?

   ❖ On what "lamp stand" do you need to place your lamp—what witness are you on fire to offer? When you do, what is the consequence?

   ❖ How do you or have you hidden your light? What has been the consequence?

   ❖ How do you describe "good works [that] give glory to your Father in heaven"?

Leader Development for Mission (20 minutes)

2.7   Sing together UMH #413: "A Charge to Keep I Have," GP2 #113: "Sent Out in Jesus' Name," or TFWS #2218: "You Are Mine."

2.8   Read Isaiah 43:1, then Luke 5:1-11. Have groups examine the characters, emotions, and movement of the Luke story. Skim over Essay 7 as well, and discuss these questions:

   ❖ What does it mean to you that God calls you by name and that you were created for a purpose? What is your purpose? How do you know?

❖ What mentors, teachers, or leaders recognized your potential as a leader?

❖ As you examine your congregation or area of service, who are the leaders or potential leaders whom you can nurture?

❖ How does the *missio Dei* draw you and others into leadership in mission for the sake of the world community?

Break (10 minutes)

A Theology of Care (20 minutes)

2.9   When the group has gathered, gain their attention by calling out, "The Lord be with you." Read aloud the Berdyaev quote in Essay 8, "The Spirituality of Bread."

2.10 Invite participants to follow along while you read aloud Matthew 25:31-46. Have them skim through Essay 8 to note the major points, and then look at any of the numerous personal stories in Essays 6-8 (or any previous ones).

2.11 Direct group members to pass the plate of bread in turn, referring to what they believe would be "bread" for any of the persons in the stories or in their own mission experience. Ask them to express their theology of care in their own words.

Eliminating Barriers to the Kingdom (20 minutes)

2.12 Begin this activity with the observation that caring is vitally important, but is still not enough. Read the first three paragraphs of Essay 9, concluding with the Bonhoeffer quote ("like a stick into the spokes of the wheel").

2.13 Have everyone stand up for a forced-choice exercise. Indicate that you will all move to a place on an imaginary continuum to indicate your level of participation in certain activities. Designate one side of the room as "No, never" and the other side as "Yes, always." The imaginary line connecting the sides is the range of middle ground. Ask these questions:

❖ When you see wrong or evil in federal, state, or local governance, how often do you name those evils? (People move between Never and Always.)

❖ How often do you call those leaders to account through letters, email, phone calls, letters to the editor, peaceful protests, or other means? (Move.)

❖ How often do you work directly (not just with monetary contributions) to help the victims of injustice or evil? (Move.)

❖ How often do you take the risk of placing yourself like a stick in the spokes of the wheel of injustice? (Move.)

2.14 Debrief the experience by discussing any insights, feelings, or new convictions about joining opinion with action in breaking barriers of injustice.

Reflection/Action (30 minutes)

2.15 Invite everyone to sit down to begin their reflection/action. Have groups review the session, keeping these questions in mind:

❖ What have I seen about the needs of the world that stands in contrast to my own context? What realities cry out for justice and witness?

❖ Given my understanding of the Scripture, how is God judging the church's leaders who are called to be on fire for mission? How might I be evaluated as a "stick in the spokes of the wheel" of injustice?

❖ What is God's word of grace to me today?

❖ What one action will I take in the next week to live out that word of grace?

❖ Who will be my partner in action and/or accountability?

2.16 If you want to take the last 5 or 10 minutes to debrief and compare, do so.

Closing (10 minutes)

2.17 *For Next Session:* Ask participants to read the Chapter Three essays and to bring their Bibles. Look at the Prepare list to have your preparations in place.

2.18 Bring the bread and candles back to the main focal point and prepare the Communion table. Remind the group that this table breaks down the barriers among us. Begin the liturgy for Communion with the prayer of Thanksgiving (*UM Hymnal*, page 9), or invite an appropriate pastoral leader to do it, as necessary.

2.19 After all have communed, sing together UMH #344: "Lord, You Have Come to the Lakeshore," GP2: #115: "Nurtured by the Spirit," or TFWS #2153: "I'm Gonna Live So God Can Use Me" (or a Communion hymn of your choice), then close with a benediction.

SESSION THREE
TRADITION

Learning Goals:

☑ To examine the context(s) for mission.

☑ To understand the United Methodist Connection for mission.

☑ To embrace compassion for the children "in calamity."

☑ To cultivate a ministry of servanthood.

Prepare or Have on Hand:

☑ A large map of the world with pushpins or sticky notes (Activity 3.3).

☑ A small bucket ("glue pot") for the focal point and paper plates with cleaned chicken bones for each table group (Activity 3.1; 3.11).

☑ Copies of *The United Methodist Hymnal*, *Global Praise 1*, *Global Praise 2*, *Global Praise 3*, and *The Faith We Sing* songbooks for each participant (Activity 3.3; 3.10; 3.19).

☑ Copies of the handouts (Activity 3.6; 3.9; 3.11; 3.15; see Appendix).

☑ Newsprint or poster paper and markers/blank letter-size paper (Activity 3.8; 3.13).

Welcome and Opening Devotion (20 minutes)

3.1   Place the bucket and the plates of bones as a focal point before people arrive. Welcome everyone and briefly introduce any newcomers.

3.2   Read Matthew 28:16-20.

3.3   Sing together UMH #571: "Go, Make of All Disciples," GP2 #111: "It Can Be a Girl," or TFWS #2239: "Go Ye, Go Ye Into the World." While the group is singing, have participants go to the map, a few at a time, and put a pushpin or sticky note on every state and country they have visited for any reason. Also sing UMH #581: "Lord, Whose Love Through Humble Service" and UMH #577: "God of Grace and God of Glory" if you need more time.

3.4   When the map is complete, lead a bidding prayer for the needs of the places represented. After each petition, all respond with, "Lord, hear our prayer." Close with the Lord's Prayer.

Context(s) for Mission (20 minutes)

3.5   Distribute the handouts. Have participants sit together based on an area of the world they have visited, including the United States, in groups of up to six. (Some will have been many places; ask them to move accordingly, so that groups have about the same number of people.) Make the areas as large (Latin America) or as small (Caribbean, Central America, northern South America) as necessary to maintain some balance.

3.6   Ask groups to review Essay 10, especially the information on contextualization and "What Is Context?" Then compare experiences and learnings about culture and context within the areas. Invite them to tell stories, briefly, of insights gained when they understood any cultural biases they may have held. Then ask:

   ❖ In what ways have you seen the US church imposing its cultural biases on another Christian context, or been unaware that there were cultural distinctions to make for effective ministry and relationships?

   ❖ How does the call to "make of all disciples" need to be interpreted in cultures other than your own to form responsible partnerships?

The United Methodist Connection (20 minutes)

3.7   Divide the group in two. Group One will read 1 Corinthians 12:12-27; Group Two, John 15:1-8. Have them discuss what these images mean for the identity of the Christian community, and how they might describe the connections within the Methodist tradition. Encourage them to go into detail.

3.8   Pass out blank paper and markers. Ask each person to make a different sign for one of the connections within the Connection, then stand and arrange themselves as either the body or the vine and branches of the Connection. Debrief a bit so that everyone knows and understands what each part or branch signifies, and how far those connections extend.

3.9   Return to table groups to skim Essay 11 and identify the main points. Then discuss these questions:

   ❖ How is Methodism "organized to beat the Devil"? How well do we do?

❖ What is your experience of mission within the Connection? What experience do you have with partner relationships between a local church or annual conference with another (usually foreign) church or conference?

❖ What blessings have you experienced or heard about that have been bestowed on the US church by conferences outside the US?

Break (10 minutes)
(Put a plate of bones at each table group.)

Children "in Calamity" (20 minutes)

3.10 Gather the group together by singing "Jesus Loves the Little Children" or UMH #191: "Jesus Loves Me," GP1 #40: "Star—Child," or TFWS #2092: "Like a Child." Then read the first anecdote in Essay 12 about the child in the Rocinha daycare center. Pause for 30 seconds and read the second anecdote about the street children in São Paulo. Pause another 30 seconds.

3.11 Read Mark 10:13-16. Ask participants to look at the "chicken seeds" at their table and the "glue pot" at the room's focal point. Discuss these questions:

❖ Try to imagine children you know having to sniff glue and hoard "chicken seeds" in order to have the most basic of their needs met. What would you be willing to do to protect children you love from such calamity?

❖ Examine the scene in Mark 10 (assuming Jesus was speaking about small children). What was the child's position in that society? How does that differ from what we expect, even demand, in our culture?

❖ Of the 73 million children in the US, 57 percent (41.2 million) live in low-income or poor families. (See data from the National Center for Children in Poverty at http://www.nccp.org/pub_lic06b.html.) What does the gospel claim of you to care for the millions of children in the US and elsewhere whom you don't know?

3.12 Have group members skim over the "Blessing Children" stories in the rest of Essay 12 and talk about what practical ideas for mission and ministry they provide.

A Ministry of Servanthood (20 minutes)

3.13 Continue working with the stories in Essays 12 and 13 filtered through two central questions:

❖ What do these stories do to your soul?

❖ What are the justice issues? List responses on newsprint.

3.14 Ask participants to identify three Scriptures (at each table group) that speak to the call of servanthood to meet the needs of the "least of these." As members of God's "Commission on Peace With Justice," have them write out their own "Peace With Justice mandates."

Reflection/Action (30 minutes)

3.15 Review the activities and discuss these questions:

❖ What vision of current reality has emerged concerning the needs of the world, especially for children? How does this compare or contrast to your own immediate context? the context in other US areas?

❖ What has been the call of Scripture for mission? How does the vision of this current reality tug at your soul?

❖ What ideas have emerged from the stories or your experience that address the needs?

❖ What do your justice mandates lead you to think, feel, and do?

❖ What one thing will you do in the next week(s) to obey those marching orders?

❖ Who will be your partner(s) in action and accountability?

3.16 If you want to take the last 5 or 10 minutes to debrief and compare, do so.

Closing (10 minutes)

3.17 *For Next Session:* Ask participants to read the essays in Chapter Four and to bring their Bibles. Look at the Prepare list to have your preparations in place.

3.18 Close by reading Philippians 2:1-11. Offer prayer for all the "children of calamity" in the world who cling to "chicken seeds."

3.19 Sing together UMH #584: "Lord, You Give the Great Commission," GP2 #43: "Whose Child Is This?" or TFWS #2178: "Here Am I," then offer a benediction.

SESSION FOUR
EXPERIENCE

Learning Goals:

☑ To understand functional connectionalism.

☑ To establish mission partnerships.

☑ To claim the foundations of abundance.

☑ To establish mission based in peace with justice.

Prepare or Have on Hand:

☑ If possible, have an UMVIM veteran or missionary do a 10-minute opening devotion by telling his or her experience as one who is actively working
out of his or her gifts (Ephesians 4:1-16). The devotional address should
also include what the impact has been on the persons served as well as on
the mission worker. As an alternative, use the video "Here I Am, Lord," produced by Global Ministries, that was sent to all pastors in a 2005 mailing.
Check also with your conference office or resource center.

☑ Bring symbols of the gifts that are employed by mission workers, such as a
Bible, curriculum, stethoscope, small farm or gardening implement, small
tool, food item, woven basket, and so on for the focal point in the room.
Have at least one for each table group (Activity 4.2; 4.7; 4:21).

☑ Recruit four people to do a simple Readers Theater. Make copies of the
script. *Be sure to give them time to practice before the session* (Activity 4.5;
see Appendix).

☑ Copies of the handouts (Activity 4.5; 4.18).

☑ Copies of *The United Methodist Hymnal*, *Global Praise 2*, *Global Praise 3*,
and *The Faith We Sing* songbooks for each person (Activity 4.3; 4.9; 4.20).

☑ Newsprint and markers (Activity 4.17).

☑ Create a Process Statement Chart of four comments: • "But first we"; • "And
then we"; • "And while that is happening"; • "But before that" (Activity 4.13).

Welcome and Opening Devotion (20 minutes)

4.1   Welcome everyone and introduce newcomers.

4.2   Read Ephesians 4:1-16. Introduce the guest. If you do not have a guest, form a circle around the focal point/display of symbols. Invite participants to join hands and form a "circle of gifts." Say, "Each of you is gifted by God and is a gift to the world." Go around the circle, one by one, and have persons say and complete the sentence, "I will build up the body of Christ by [using the gift of…]." Start by modeling the process for participants.

4.3   Sing together UMH #87: "What Gift Can We Bring," GP2 #102: "The Church Is Like a Table," or TFWS #2243: "We All Are One in Mission." Close with Prayer 69, "For True Singing."

Functional Connectionalism (20 minutes)

4.4   In table groups, take 5-8 minutes to skim through Essay 14. Note the main points and agree on your definition of "functional connectionalism." Distribute handouts.

4.5   Present the Readers Theater. Afterward, discuss these questions:

❖ What is your experience with how the connectionalism and/or organization of The United Methodist Church functions to accomplish the *missio Dei*?

❖ What can you do within the Connection that would be difficult or impossible without it?

❖ What opportunities have you had to be educated in the *missio Dei*? What opportunities are you providing for others to cultivate mission leaders?

❖ Which of the five activities (see Mission Education Emphases in the text) have been implemented in your church or ministry area?

Mission Partnerships (20 minutes)

4.6   Ask participants to read John 15:8-17 and review the "Partnering" stories in Essay 15 ("Partnering in Spirituality" and following).

4.7   Send one person from each table group to bring back one of the items from the display. Have them use it as a discussion starter to tell about experiences of UM or ecumenical partnerships that have provided for ministry illustrated by that item. (The conversation is not limited to examples using that item.) For example, using the food item, begin with experiences of food pantries, crop/farming education. Using the basket, begin with experiences of micro-lending programs that aid local commerce.)

4.8   Discuss how "bearing fruit together" yields a "harvest," and what that "harvest" has been. Ask: How have ecumenical or denominational partnerships strengthened, developed, and renewed communities in need?

Break (10 minutes)

Foundations of Abundance (20 minutes)

4.9   Gather people back from the break by singing UMH #95: "Praise God from Whom All Blessings Flow," GP2 #20: "¡Gracias, Señor!" or TFWS #2036: "Give Thanks."

4.10 Ask group members to skim through the stories in Essay 16, starting with "A Haven of Hope." Ask: How are they reflections of shared abundance? Have each group choose one of the anecdotes and make up an alternative ending to the story, as if those in a position to be in mission worked from an attitude of scarcity. What might the difference be?

4.11 Have participants read John 10:1-18 and the first section of Essay 16, "Coming Home to Abundant Life." Focus on Dr. Potter's four aspects of caring: safety, living in community, universal abundance, and God as the source of abundance. Spend time with the Scripture and how it exemplifies the call to the faith community to enliven those aspects of care for all. Discuss the difference it makes when those in ministry act out of a stance of abundance.

Peace With Justice (20 minutes)

4.12 Invite everyone to stand together and read aloud Micah 6:6-8. Remain standing for one minute of silence in prayer and solidarity for those who enjoy neither peace nor justice.

4.13 Ask table groups then to be seated and take about five minutes to review the beginning of Essay 17, through the exegetical comments (up to "Loving Kindness in the Midst of Despair"). Display the Process Statement Chart.

4.14 Ask for three volunteers. Two will take notes from the conversation to follow. The third will start the activity by reading aloud "Loving Kindness in the Midst of Despair" as one example of working for peace with justice.

4.15   Next, identify together a world "hot spot" where peace and justice are much needed, and with which group members are at least somewhat acquainted. Explain what comes next by reading aloud the instruction in 4.16.

4.16   "I will start a conversation about the process of working for peace with justice in that hot spot. The rest of you, as you are led, will add your own comments by introducing it with one of the sentence starters on the Process Statement Chart. For example, 'The desperate situation in [Iraq] is much in need of God's peace.' Someone else will add, '*But before that* we must address the religious strife in the region.' Another may add, '*And while that is happening*, we must engage our US leaders to do _____ about the escalation of military conflict.' And so on."

4.17   Allow the conversation to go where it will for several minutes, while the note takers record on newsprint the main ideas shared by the group. Then spend some time reflecting on the process in terms of the issues of human will, the interface between the religious community and other structures that influence such situations, scriptural mandates, complexity in dealing with justice issues, and so on. (Obviously, the point is not to solve this.)

Reflection/Action (30 minutes)

4.18   In table groups, have participants first review:

❖ What have you seen through your experience and examination of the text and Scriptures concerning how the Church: 1) is equipped for mission; 2) works with partners; 3) advocates for and shares abundance; and 4) strives for peace with justice for all?

❖ How do the Scriptures seem to evaluate our efforts? What do they call us to be and to do?

❖ What spiritual growth opportunities have you experienced (or would be available to you) by engagement with a ministry of abundance?

❖ If you have planned for or implemented any of the five activities (Mission Education Emphases), what has been the effect?

❖ What one or two things can you do to engage in a partnership or educate others for mission?

❖ With whom and how will you hold yourself accountable for these commitments?

Closing (10 minutes)

4.19 *For Next Session:* Ask participants to read the Chapter Five essays and to bring their Bibles. Look at the Prepare list to be sure all your preparations are in place.

4.20 Read Luke 4:14-19, then sing together UMH #434: "Cuando el Pobre" ("When the Poor Ones"), GP3 #161: "You Came Down to Earth," or TFWS #2177: "Wounded World Cries for Healing."

4.21 Ask one person at each table to hold up the symbol while you lead a bidding prayer for those in great need of peace and justice. Close with a benediction.

SESSION FIVE
REASON

Learning Goals:

☑ To become acquainted with missionary methods.

☑ To appreciate the sacramental foundation of Mission.

☑ To learn to think and act "glocally."

☑ To cultivate mission stewardship.

Prepare or Have on Hand:

☑ Fresh loaves of bread; juice for Communion (Activity 5.1; 5.9; 5.25).

☑ Recruit extra readers for a total of three or six, including yourself (Activity 5.2). If at all possible, have an equal number of men and women.

☑ Copies of *The United Methodist Hymnal*, *Global Praise 1*, *Global Praise 2*, *Global Praise 3*, and *The Faith We Sing* songbooks for each participant (Activity 5.4; Closing).

☑ Copies of the handouts (Activity 5.8; 5.10; 5.16; 5.17; 5.21; 5.22).

☑ Select volunteers for the panel discussion (Activity 5.15) and give them advance time to think about their roles.

☑ Make "stewardship chits" (Activity 5.19). Cut up colored index cards into small pieces (about 1" x 1") so that there are chits in three colors in sufficient quantity that each participant can have ten of each. Green (for example) will indicate **Money** or material resources. Blue represents personal **Interest** and yellow represents personal **Energy**. (Participants can make their own by tearing paper and putting an appropriate symbol on them— "$," "Int," and "En"—to distinguish which is which.)

Welcome and Opening Devotion (15 minutes)

5.1   Welcome everyone. Create a focal point with the bread and cup.

5.2   Have the readers seated and evenly placed around the meeting room. They will stand up, in turns, to read Isaiah 43:16-21 verse by verse. Have them remain standing through the reading. (The first reader does 43:16, the second 43:17, and so on.) They should read loudly, clearly, and expressively so that everyone can hear them well.

5.3   Invite group members to call out a new thing that they perceive the Lord doing.

5.4   Sing together UMH #730: "O Day of God, Draw Nigh," GP2 #123: "Min Himmel" ("My Heaven"), or TFWS #2284: "Joy in the Morning."

5.5   Close with a prayer of celebration for all the new things that you see God is doing, and for what God will bring in time.

5.6   If participants are not already in table groups, ask them to form the groups now.

Missionary Method (20 minutes)

5.7   Have group members skim over Essay 18, with special focus on the last section, "Sending the 70." They should also read Luke 10:1-12, 17-20.

5.8   Distribute the handout. Have the groups divide the passage and the questions related to it. Ask them to work independently for a few minutes to jot down ideas from the questions, then to discuss the passage within the group. For the last 5-8 minutes of this time, invite responses from all of the groups.

❖ *Luke 10:1-2:* • Who, in contemporary terms, are "the harvest"? • Who, do you think, are the laborers? • How do we decide which laborers go to which harvest, if there are not enough for the entire "harvest"?

❖ *Luke 10:3-6:* • What is the "way" like today? • Are the "laborers" still like lambs among wolves? Why, or why not? • What sense do these traveling instructions make now? What did they mean for the disciples? • How do the current "laborers" establish peace? What issues are important in establishing peace?

❖ *Luke 10:7-8:* • What was the meaning of these instructions in hospitality to the disciples? • What are the hospitality issues now? • Who should pay the wages? • What are the implications if "the harvest" is unable to pay?

❖ *Luke 10:9-12:* • How do we now say, "The kingdom has come near"? • If we invest in mission in a particular area, what should be done if there is resistance or rejection? • What does that suggest for "laborers" who are expecting to "harvest"? • If the mandate of God is to go to all nations, how do we deal with "shaking the dust"?

❖ *Luke 10:17-20:* • How would you describe the power of God given to the "laborers" then and now? • What are the power issues today inherent in mission? • What are the consequences of succeeding (or not), and how is success to be measured?

❖ *Ask everyone:* • What does this passage teach us about the missionary method? • Is the biblical method appropriate in the complex world of the 21st century? • What models do you know from our Methodist history? • What new things are being done or need to be done? • What new insights come to mind if you consider yourself part of the "harvest," rather than one of the "laborers"?

Sacramental Foundation of Mission (15 minutes)

5.9 Ask a participant from each table to get a plate of bread.

5.10 Ask group members to mention what is the "bread of life" in cultures and regions with which they are familiar (rice in Asia, for example). Then invite personal stories that illuminate the sacramental nature of mission. For example:

❖ When have you shared table fellowship with persons of another culture? How did that meal influence the relationships of those present?

❖ When have you shared or witnessed a joyous rite of passage made possible by mission activity?

❖ What Scriptures empower and encourage you to share the bread of life and/or to regard mission activity as sacramental? (Note those in Essay 19.)

5.11 If participants do not have firsthand knowledge, invite them to skim through the personal stories in Essays 18 and 19 and use them to work on the suggested questions in 5.10. Pay particular attention to the closing story in Essay 19: "Will There Be Enough Bread?"

5.12 If time permits, discuss this final question: • What "food" do you need for your journey if you "go out" in mission?

Break (10 minutes)

5.13 Gather participants from the break by singing through UMH #628: "Eat This Bread," GP2 #42: "Jeder Braucht Brot" ("Lord, We Need Bread"), or TFWS #2267: "Taste and See" two or three times.

Think and Act Glocally (25 minutes)

5.14 Invite table groups to review Essay 20 carefully, up to "Health and School Kits…," to be sure they understand what is meant by a "glocal" church and "glocal" mission. (Watch out for false dichotomies. What is global to us is local to someone else; "glocal" refers to this intersection.)

5.15 Have a panel discussion with five volunteers who will assume certain roles.

5.16 Give the panel members the handout explaining their role. The panel volunteers include a moderator, a "multinational" business executive, a "receiving" bishop, a missionary, and a layperson in the mission area.

5.17 After the panel presentation, discuss these questions as you have time:

❖ What does thinking and acting "glocally" mean to you now?

❖ How does the church's presence "glocally" compare and contrast with what you know of the global business environment?

❖ How can the church speak to the world about "glocal" issues?

❖ What is your part in "glocalization," and what does that mean to you?

Mission Stewardship (25 minutes)

5.18 Form table groups and have members skim over Essay 21. Throughout the essays, you have read numerous anecdotes about how missional enterprises and experiences have made a difference in peoples' lives. Take five minutes (no more just now) to ask which stories, from any essays, have been most compelling.

5.19 Distribute the "stewardship chits." Ask each person to select one of the stories (or other mission opportunity). Think about what time and investment would be necessary to make a meaningful difference in that mission opportunity and how much passion there is to make that difference.

5.20 Do a "moment of truth" exercise with the chits. Each chit represents a unit of personal energy, personal interest, or local church material resources, and the *total* number is what each pastor and layperson has to invest in *every* ministry activity over the course of a month—preaching, teaching, pastoral care, work with children or youth, administration, leadership or participation in various ministry areas, visiting, counseling, and so on. Have each person divide up the chits as they feel appropriately indicates their commitments in ministry. They can discuss their choices and decisions.

5.21 Then discuss these questions:

❖ Given the mission theological statement you worked on in Session 1, the essays, and the Scriptures you have studied, how well have you done on your stewardship in mission?

❖ Missionaries and mission projects (through the Advance, UMCOR, Women's Division of Global Ministries, and so on) need constant support. Were those needs considered?

❖ What sort of balance is appropriate, do you think, between supporting the denominational efforts and personal and local mission? How do you decide?

Reflection/Action (20 minutes)

5.22 Invite the groups to begin their reflection/action. Review the session, keeping these questions in mind:

❖ What have I seen or discovered about my own commitments to the *missio Dei*? In the "divine economy" of all Christians working from their strengths and passions, are my commitments appropriate?

❖ What has the Scripture called me to do towards the "harvest"? How have the Scriptures judged my efforts, interests, and theology of mission?

❖ What has been God's word of grace to me today?

❖ What one action will I take in the next week to live out God's call of mission?

❖ Who will be my partner in action and/or accountability?

Closing (15 minutes)

5.23 *For Next Session:* Ask participants to review all notes, especially their theology of mission statements, and bring them to the next session. They will
be working also with the actions to which they have committed week by
week, and will need their Bibles. Strongly encourage them to browse the
Advance projects through Global Ministries (http://new.gbgm
-umc.org/about/advance) and to bring printouts of information on projects that capture their interest. Look at the Prepare list to be sure all your
preparations are in place.

5.24 Sing together UMH #127: "Guide Me, O Thou Great Jehovah," GP1 #5:
"As Your Children, Lord," or TFWS #2255: "In the Singing."

5.25 Prepare the cup and ready the table. Begin the celebration of Communion
using the liturgy, beginning with the Invitation on page 7 in the *UM
Hymnal.* During the offering, ask a member of each table group to bring
forward his or her plate of bread.

5.26 After the thanksgiving prayer on page 11, sing together UMH #587:
"Bless Thou the Gifts," GP3 #47: "Temesgean Eyesus" ("Thank You,
Jesus"), or TFWS #2258: "Sing Alleluia to the Lord" (or other
Communion hymn) and close with the Dismissal With Blessing.

SESSION 6
STRATEGIZING FOR MISSION

Learning Goals

☑ To synthesize and evaluate the mission education experience.

☑ To establish and clarify desired results for mission.

☑ To commit to next steps for mission—local, national, and/or global.

Prepare or Have on Hand:

☑ If possible, have a computer available that has internet access, so that participants can check on various Advance projects through Global Ministries (http://new.gbgm-umc.org/about/advance).

☑ Assemble a collection of at least a few of the visuals that were used in Sessions 1-5: icon, tent peg, candles, map, bucket, bones, symbols of mission, stewardship chits (Activity 6.1; 6.7).

☑ Copies of *The United Methodist Hymnal, Global Praise 2, Global Praise 3,* and *The Faith We Sing* songbooks for each participant (Activity 6.3; 6.9; Closing).

☑ Newsprint and markers (Activity 6.8).

☑ Art supplies (Activity 6.11).

☑ Copies of the handouts (Activity 6.8; 6.11; 6.12; 6:19).

☑ Five volunteer Scripture readers (Closing). Give them Handout 6.19 *before* the session begins.

Welcome and Opening Devotion (15 minutes)

6.1 Place at your focal point a collection of the visuals that were used in Sessions 1-5.

6.2 Welcome group members and explain that the purpose of this session is to bring together the threads of the previous ones, to develop strategies and goals for mission.

6.3 Sing together UMH #465: "Holy Spirit, Truth Divine," GP3 #105: "Gracious Spirit," or TFWS #2120: "Spirit, Spirit of Gentleness."

6.4   Read Matthew 9:16-17. Ask if there is a brief response to what the "new wine" might be.

6.5   Read the quote from the Willingen Conference (Essay 2, "Those who are sought…"). Allow 30 seconds of silence, then read the quote by Newbigin (Essay 3, "…the whole base of mission…").

6.6   Close with prayer for discernment and guidance in forging your own sense of mission and the actions that flow from it.

Reflection on the Mission Study Experience (25 minutes)

6.7   Ask participants to come forward, as they feel led, and hold up one of the items from the focal point that evokes a commitment to mission or illustrates a need that has touched them deeply. Use the items, or reference to any of the previous teaching activities, to begin the discussion of what the group members have experienced and thought in the past five sessions.

6.8   As necessary, you may also use these reflection questions. Record responses on newsprint.

❖ What was your greatest "Aha!" moment (something that surprised, clarified, amazed, delighted)? What was your greatest "Uh-Oh" moment (something that dismayed, disappointed, discouraged, warned)?

❖ What experience, learning, or insight was the most powerful for you? Why?

❖ What sense of hope or encouragement did this experience engender? Why?

❖ What sense of need did this experience evoke? Why?

❖ As you experienced and learned from the sessions, how did the Theological Task (Scripture, Tradition, Experience, and Reason) intersect with the mission goals (make disciples, strengthen Christian community, alleviate suffering, seek peace with justice)? Did that have any impact on your insights and/or commitments to the *missio Dei*?

❖ Did you commit to any actions as asked at the end of each session? If so, did you follow through? If not, why not? If so, what was the result?

Break (10 minutes)

Establish Desired Results for Mission (40 minutes)

6.9   Bring participants back from the break by singing stanzas 1 and 2 of UMH #437: "This Is My Song," GP2 #118: "We've Packed for the Journey," or TFWS #2220: "We Are God's People."

6.10 Invite participants to arrange themselves in logical affinity groups (for example, members of the same congregation, neighborhood, district, church size) in which they could/would engage in strategic thinking for mission.

6.11 Ask group members to envision what they desire as an outcome before thinking about what to do. Have art supplies available and invite them to draw an art or word picture of their desired outcome. (Look for examples of outcomes in the Appendix.) Refer them to Advance information.

6.12 Then move to some planning steps. If group members feel overwhelmed or stuck, play "I care, but I can't help." Choose one of the big outcomes and ask the first person in the group to help identify one S.M.A.R.T. goal (something Specific, Measurable, Attainable, Reasonable, and Timely). The responder need not include every S.M.A.R.T. aspect; just brainstorm. If the person is at a loss, the response is, "I care, but I can't help." If the person passes in this way, he or she *must* at least indicate an authentic barrier or offer a reason why helping is not possible. Then the next person gives an idea or responds similarly. If the planning steps proceed first by naming barriers and then figuring out how to address them, do it that way. Or, start with the outcome and work backward to identify what must be in place at each stage. Be sure, though, to keep your eyes on the good outcomes and not get mired in the "I Can'ts." (See the Appendix for other planning helps.)

6.13 By the end of this period, encourage groups to have at least one S.M.A.R.T. outcome. Ask each group to post their outcome on newsprint.

Commit to Next Steps (40 minutes)

6.14 Have groups spend the next segment of time refining that outcome statement by identifying the next steps they will take and by when. Distribute blank paper and markers, and have group members write on separate pages each step they have identified and when it might be accomplished.

Recognize that some steps are sequential and some are concurrent. Encourage them to be as detailed as they can in 30 minutes. When they are done, group members should divide up the steps consecutively.

6.15 Draw an imaginary timeline around the room, starting with Next Week, then In Two Weeks, In One Month, In Three Months, In Six Months, In One Year. Ask everyone to stand at the appropriate place on the visual timeline with their steps, and to indicate what they are, in turn. As you move through each time segment, participants will need to mention what outcome they were working on.

6.16 Most likely there will be a great amount of creativity and vision expressed in those proposed steps, even if the progress they imagine takes some time to come to fruition. Note which groups have similar outcome statements and encourage them to maintain contact for support and accountability.

Closing (20 minutes)

6.17 Ask everyone to pick up a *UM Hymnal* and gather in a circle so that they can see the items at the focal point. (If anyone needs to sit down, invite them to have a chair at their place in the circle. Tuck the Next Step sign in the *UM Hymnal* for the time being. Have the Scripture readers evenly spaced in the circle.)

6.18 Say Prayer 446, "Serving the Poor," antiphonally by reading a brief phrase that participants will repeat.

6.19 The volunteers will read their Scriptures in turn. Allow 20 or 30 seconds of silence between each reading: • Micah 6:8; • John 3:16; • Matthew 16:24; • Matthew 22:37-39; • Matthew 28:19-20.

6.20 Invite group members to say a word or phrase that summarizes their experience with and/or their commitment to mission as a result of the study.

6.21 Sing together UMH #463: "Lord, Speak to Me," GP2 #98: "Yo Quiero Ser" ("I Want to Be"), or TFWS #2130: "The Summons." During the singing, have group members place their Next Step signs at the focal point.

6.22 Close with prayer for the "new wine" and God's commission to be faithful, serving disciples and a benediction.

CURRICULUM PLAN FOR A TWO- TO THREE-DAY RETREAT

SUGGESTED SCHEDULE

The various segments have a suggested time frame that does not exactly match the proposed schedule. A little flexibility is built in because you will find that some activities may take more or less time as you adapt them for your group.

Day One

Part One

1:00 Welcome and Opening Devotions
1:45 Mission as God's Mission
2:45 Biblical Foundations
3:40 Reflect on Part One
4:00 Break/Dinner

Part Two

6:00 Leaders for Witness and Mission
6:45 Break
7:00 Theology of Care and Inclusion
8:00 Reflection on Part Two
8:25 Closing

Day Two

Part Three

9:00 Opening Devotions
9:30 Context(s) for Mission
10:00 The United Methodist Connection
10:30 Break
10:45 A Ministry of Servanthood
11:30 Reflect on Part Three
11:45 Lunch/Break

Part Four

1:00 Connectionalism and Partnerships
1:45 Foundations of Abundance
2:15 Break
2:30 Peace with Justice
3:15 Reflection on Part Four

Part Five

3:30 Missionary Method
4:00 Think and Act Glocally
4:35 Break (10 minutes)
4:45 Mission Stewardship
5:15 Reflection on Part Five
5:30 Break for the Day

(option for evening prayer)

Day Three

Part Six

9:00 Morning Devotions
9:30 Reflection on the Study Experience
10:00 Establish Desired Results
10:45 Break
11:00 Commit to Next Steps
11:45 Closing Worship
12:15 Adjourn

218

RETREAT PLAN

Learning Goals:

☑ To develop a theology of mission as God's mission that is both personal and inclusive.

☑ To cultivate caring and compassionate servant leadership for mission and witness that overcomes and eliminates barriers to God's kingdom.

☑ To examine the context(s) for mission.

☑ To understand the United Methodist Connection and how it accomplishes ministry and mission.

☑ To learn to think and act "glocally" and justly.

☑ To synthesize and evaluate the mission-education experience and establish next steps for local, national, and/or global mission.

Prepare or Have on Hand:

Items for the focal point will change between the various parts of the agenda, but the final segment suggests a collection of all or most of them. Other items needed for a specific time are noted according to Activity number.

☑ Copies of handouts (Activity 1.4; 1.13; 1.15; 2.4; 2.11; 3.6; 3.9; 3.11; 3.15; 4.2; 4.15; 5.3; 5.7; 5.8; 5.12; 5.13; 6.8; 6.12; 6.13; 6.17).

☑ Copies of *The United Methodist Hymnal, Global Praise 1, Global Praise 2, Global Praise 3*, and *The Faith We Sing* songbooks for each person (Activity 1.5; 1.10; 1.17; 2.1; 2.13; 3.3; 3.10; 3.18; 4.1; 4.8; 5.1; 5.4; 5.15; 6.3; 6.9).

☑ Newsprint or poster board and markers (Activity 1.10; 1.12; 3.13; 4.14).

☑ Blank writing paper (Activity 3.8; 6.14).

☑ Candles and matches (Focal point each day and Activity 2.1; 2.3).

☑ An item small enough to hold in one hand, such as a cross, icon, or unbreakable figurine (Activity 1.3).

☑ A bowl of water and pitcher (Activity 1.4).

☑ A tent peg, and if possible, one for each group (Focal point, Day 1; Activity 1.1; 1.13).

☑ A large map of the world with pushpins or sticky notes (Activity 3.3).

☑ A small bucket and paper plates with cleaned chicken bones for each table group and a small bucket ("glue pot") for the focal point (Day 2; Activity 3.11).

☑ Symbols of the gifts that are employed by mission workers, such as a Bible, curriculum, stethoscope, small farm or gardening implement, small tool, food item, woven basket, and so on (Focal point, Day 2; Activity 4.4; 4.15; 6.1).

☑ Create a Process Statement Chart of four comments: • "But first we"; • "And then we"; • "And while that is happening"; • "But before that" (Activity 4.10).

☑ Recruit four volunteers to present a Readers Theater (Activity 4.2) and five others to act out a panel discussion (Activity 5.7). Make copies of the scripts and instructions (see Appendix). Be sure to give volunteers time to practice ahead of time.

☑ Make "stewardship chits." Cut up colored index cards into small pieces (about 1" x 1") so that there are chits in three colors in sufficient quantity that each participant can have ten of each. Green (for example) will indicate **Money** or material resources. Blue represents personal **Interest** and yellow represents personal **Energy**. Or, participants can make their own by tearing paper and putting an appropriate symbol on them—"$," "**Int**," and "**En**"— to distinguish which is which (Activity 5.10).

☑ A plate of bread, such as pita, for each table group and a chalice of juice (Focal point, Day 3; Activity 2.1; 2.7; 6.1).

DAY ONE (APPROXIMATELY 1:00 P.M.–8:30 P.M.)
PART ONE

Welcome and Opening Devotions (40 minutes)

1.1   Place a tent peg (or some kind of substitute) and *Hymnals* on each table. Light the candles at your focal point. Distribute the handout pages.

1.2   Welcome everyone. Mention the necessary hospitality issues (how to handle breaks, location of restrooms, getting snacks or beverages, and so on).

1.3   Begin introductions by holding the icon and take no more than 14 seconds to say something about yourself. Then give the icon to the next person to do the same, and so on around the room. Close the introductions with a brief prayer.

1.4   Form small groups of four or five people. Read aloud John 3:1-17 and refer to the handout. Ask participants to skim the passage again, then take about 10 minutes to discuss these questions:

As you think about yourself and your understanding of the kingdom of God, are you more like:

❖ Nicodemus, coming to Jesus in the cover of darkness?

❖ Nicodemus, questioning Jesus about how one enters the kingdom?

❖ One who is born of the Spirit?

❖ One who wonders how Jesus' teaching can be so?

❖ One who testifies to heavenly things?

❖ One who focuses on the condemnation of the world?

1.5   Lead in the reaffirmation of baptism with The Baptismal Covenant IV in the *UM Hymnal* (page 50).

Mission as God's Mission (60 minutes)

1.6   Form five groups, each with a subgroup and two recorders, and assign a different essay (Essays 1-5) to each group. The subgroup will examine the Scripture references in each of the essays and help its group members support their answer theologically.

1.7   In 15 minutes, ask each group to skim the essay, highlight the major points, and formulate a brief theological answer to the question presented at the beginning of the essay (for example, Essay 1: Why Mission Theology, Anyway?).

1.8   In very quick "popcorn" style, invite the groups to read their presenting questions and brief answers. Ask the recorders to write down the other groups' responses.

1.9   Have participants continue to work with the whole group responses just recorded to formulate a theology of mission statement that includes the Why, What, Where, When, Who, and How of mission. Keep the statement to only two or three paragraphs. Take 20-25 minutes.

1.10 When the statement is finished, find at least one hymn that supports your theology statement. Post a list of the hymns on newsprint.

1.11 Have groups read or post their statements. Sing one or more of the hymns.

Biblical Foundations (45 minutes)

1.12 Review the comments on grace (Essay 1), *missio Dei* and the "four significant consequences" described by Philip Potter (Essay 2), and the sections on Call and Journey (Essay 4). List the main points on newsprint.

1.13 Then read: • Isaiah 6:1-8; • Luke 9:23-27 and 10:1-11, 17-20; and • John 1:14-16 and 3:16-17. Use the tent peg as a "talking stick" and discuss these questions:

   ❖ How do you see the call of the prophet and disciples as mission? What does it mean to you to pick up your cross (or tent peg) and follow?

   ❖ How does the Incarnation and saving activity of God through Jesus Christ call you to ministry? Is this different, in your mind, than a call to mission? If so, how?

   ❖ Where and how do you see yourself called to mission?

1.14 If time allows, have one person in each group tell about their own call to ministry and how that has influenced their understanding of mission.

Reflect on Part One (20 minutes)

1.15   Encourage participants to work alone first, then compare notes later if they wish. Spend a few minutes in silence journaling, keeping these questions in mind:

   ❖ How am I living out God's call to mission?

   ❖ Which Scriptures speak most compellingly to me about my call to mission?

   ❖ What is God's word of grace to me today?

   ❖ How has my "mission tent" moved? How would I like it to move?

   ❖ What one action will I take in the next week to live out that word of grace?

   ❖ Who will be my partner in action and/or accountability?

1.16   Remind participants that they will cover the Chapter Two essays (6-9) during the evening segment. Look at the Prepare list to have preparations in place for the session.

1.17   Close by reading Luke 17:20-21; followed by UMH #593: "Here I Am, Lord," GP1 #60: "The Right Hand of God," or TFWS #2172: "We Are Called." Hold up the tent peg and offer a benediction. Extinguish the candles.

Break (2 hours)

PART TWO

Leaders for Witness and Mission (45 minutes)

2.1   Place a candle and a small pita loaf at each table and relight the candles. Sing Hymn 583, "You Are the Seed" ("Sois la Semilla").

2.2   Have the table groups review Essay 6, paying particular attention to "The Fire of Mission" and "Being Sent." Take a few minutes to bring out the main points.

2.3   Pick up a candle in one of the groups and describe one burning need anywhere in the world that has captured your heart. Have participants do the same in their small groups, by placing the candle in front of themselves, one by one, speaking to a need, and moving the candle carefully to the next person. (If there are *any* concerns about participants doing this safely, do not pass the candles.)

2.4   Read aloud, or have the group members read Matthew 5:14-16. Reflect on the Scripture and on the burning needs mentioned, then discuss the following questions:

❖ How does the need you see compel you to witness?

❖ On what "lamp stand" do you need to place your lamp—what witness are you on fire to offer? When you do, what is the consequence?

❖ How do you or have you hidden your light? What has been the consequence?

❖ How do you describe "good works [that] give glory to your Father in heaven"?

2.5   Read Isaiah 43:1, then Luke 5:1-11. Have groups examine the characters, emotions, and movement of the Luke story. Skim over Essay 7 as well, and discuss these questions:

❖ What does it mean to you that God calls you by name and that you were created for a purpose? What is your purpose? How do you know?

❖ What mentors, teachers, or leaders recognized your potential as a leader?

❖ As you examine your congregation or area of service, who are the leaders or potential leaders whom you can nurture?

❖ How does the *missio Dei* draw you and others into leadership in mission for the sake of the world community?

Break (15 minutes)

A Theology of Care and Inclusion (50 Minutes)

2.6   When the group has gathered, gain their attention by calling out, "The Lord be with you." Read aloud the Berdyaev quote in Essay 8, "The Spirituality of Bread." Have group members skim through Essay 8 to note the major points, and then look at any of the numerous personal stories in Essays 6-8 (or any previous ones).

2.7   Have group members read Matthew 25:31-45. Next pass the plate of bread in turn, referring to what they believe would be "bread" (whatever is needed for sustenance) for any of the persons in the stories, or in their own mission experience. Ask them to express their theology of care in their own words.

2.8   Follow that discussion with the observation that caring is vitally important, but is still not enough. Read the first three paragraphs of Essay 9, concluding with the Bonhoeffer quote ("like a stick into the spokes of the wheel").

2.9   Have everyone stand up for a forced-choice exercise. Indicate that you will all move to a place on an imaginary continuum to indicate your level of participation in certain activities. Designate one side of the room as "No, never" and the other side as "Yes, always." The imaginary line connecting the sides is the range of middle ground. Ask these questions:

❖ When you see wrong or evil in federal, state, or local governance, how often do you name those evils? (People move between Never and Always.)

❖ How often do you call those leaders to account through letters, email, phone calls, letters to the editor, peaceful protests, or other means? (Move.)

❖ How often do you work directly (not just with monetary contributions) to help the victims of injustice or evil? (Move.)

❖ How often do you take the risk of placing yourself like a stick in the spokes of the wheel of injustice? (Move.)

2.10   Debrief the experience by discussing any insights, feelings, or new convictions about joining opinion with action in breaking barriers of injustice.

Reflection on Part Two (25 minutes)

2.11   Invite everyone to sit down to begin their reflection on the session, keeping these questions in mind:

❖ What have I seen about the needs of the world that stands in contrast to my own context? What realities cry out for justice and witness?

❖ Given my understanding of the Scripture, how is God judging the church's leaders who are called to be on fire for mission? How might I be evaluated as a "stick in the spokes of the wheel" of injustice?

❖ What is God's word of grace to me through these activities and experiences?

❖ What one action will I take in the next week to live out that word of grace?

❖ Who will be my partner in action and/or accountability?

Closing (10 minutes)

2.12 *For Day Two:* Remind participants that you will cover Chapters Three, Four, and Five (Essays 10-21). Look at the Prepare list to have your preparations in place.

2.13 Have participants break and eat the loaf while you offer prayer for all those whose physical "bread of life" is insecure. Sing together UMH #344: "Lord, You Have Come to the Lakeshore," GP2 #115: "Nurtured by the Spirit," or TFWS #2153: "I'm Gonna Live So God Can Use Me," then close with a benediction.

DAY TWO (APPROXIMATELY 9:00 A.M.–5:30 P.M.)
PART THREE

Opening Devotion (30 minutes)

3.1   Place the bucket and the plates of bones and the "glue pot" as a focal point before people arrive. Put up the world map and have the pushpins or sticky notes available. Be sure hymnals, songbooks, and the Day Two handouts are at each table.

3.2   Welcome everyone and offer a brief invocation. Read Matthew 28:16-20.

3.3   Sing together UMH #571: "Go, Make of All Disciples," GP2 #111: "It Can Be a Girl," or TFWS #2239: "Go Ye, Go Ye, Into the World." While the group is singing, have participants go to the map, a few at a time, and put a pushpin or sticky note on every state and country they have visited for any reason. (Also sing UMH #581: "Lord, Whose Love Through Humble Service" and UMH #577: "God of Grace and God of Glory" if you need more time.)

3.4   When the map is complete, lead a bidding prayer for the needs of the places represented. After each petition, all respond with, "Lord, hear our prayer." Close with the Lord's Prayer.

Context(s) for Mission (25 minutes)

3.5   Have participants sit together based on an area of the world they have visited, including the United States, in groups of up to six. (Some will have been many places; ask them to move accordingly, so that groups have about the same number of people.) Make the areas as large (Latin America) or as small (Caribbean, Central America, Northern South America) as necessary to maintain some balance.

3.6   Ask groups to review Essay 10, especially the information on contextualization and "What Is Context?" Then compare experiences and learnings about culture and context within the areas. Invite them to tell stories, briefly, of insights gained when they understood any cultural biases they may have held. Then ask:

   ❖ In what ways have you seen the US church imposing its cultural biases on another Christian context, or been unaware that there were cultural distinctions to make for effective ministry and relationships?

227

❖ How does the call to "make of all disciples" need to be interpreted in cultures other than your own to form responsible partnerships?

The United Methodist Connection (25 minutes)

3.7   Divide the group in two. Group One will read 1 Corinthians 12:12-27; Group Two, John 15:1-8. Have them discuss what these images mean for the identity of the Christian community, and how they might describe the connections within the Methodist tradition. Encourage the groups to go into detail.

3.8   Pass out blank paper and markers. Ask each person to make a different sign for one of the connections within the Connection, then stand and arrange themselves as either the body or the vine and branches of the Connection. Debrief a bit so that everyone knows and understands what each part or branch signifies, and how far those connections extend.

3.9   Return to table groups to skim Essay 11 and identify the main points. Then discuss these questions:

❖ How is Methodism "organized to beat the Devil"? How well do we do?

❖ What is your experience of mission within the Connection? What experience do you have with partner relationships between a local church or annual conference with another (usually foreign) church or conference?

❖ What blessings have you experienced or heard about that have been bestowed on the US church by conferences outside the US?

Break (10 minutes)
(Put a plate of bones at each table group.)

A Ministry of Servanthood (40 minutes)

3.10   Gather the group together by singing "Jesus Loves the Little Children," UMH #191: "Jesus Loves Me," GP1 #40: "Star—Child," or TFWS #2092: "Like a Child." Then read the first anecdote in Essay 12 about the child in the Rocinha daycare center. Pause for 30 seconds and read the second anecdote about the street children in São Paulo. Pause another 30 seconds.

3.11   Mark 10:13-16. Ask participants to look at the "chicken seeds" at their table and the "glue pot" at the room's focal point. Discuss these questions:

❖ Try to imagine children you know having to sniff glue and hoard "chicken seeds" in order to have the most basic of their needs met. What would you be willing to do to protect children you love from such calamity?

❖ Examine the scene in Mark 10 (assuming Jesus was speaking about small children). What was the child's position in that society? How does that differ from what we expect, even demand, in our culture?

❖ There are 73 million children in the United States. Of them, 57 percent (41.2 million) live in low-income or poor families. (See data from the National Center for Children in Poverty at http://www.nccp.org/pub_lic06b.html.) What does the gospel claim of you to care for the millions of children in the US and elsewhere whom you don't know?

3.12 Have group members skim over the "Blessing Children" stories in the rest of Essay 12 and talk about what practical ideas for mission and ministry they provide.

3.13 Continue working with the stories in Essays 12 and 13 filtered through two central questions: • What do these stories do to your soul? • What are the justice issues? List responses on newsprint.

3.14 Ask participants to identify three Scriptures (at each table group) that speak to the call of servanthood to meet the needs of the "least of these." As members of God's "Commission on Peace With Justice," have them write out their own "Peace With Justice mandates."

Reflection on Part Three (20 minutes)

3.15 Review the activities and discuss these questions:

❖ What vision of current reality has emerged concerning the needs of the world, especially for children? How does this compare or contrast to your own immediate context? the context in other US areas?

❖ What has been the call of Scripture for mission? How does the vision of this current reality tug at your soul?

❖ What ideas have emerged from the stories or your experience that address the needs?

❖ What do your justice mandates lead you to think, feel, and do?

❖ What one thing will you do in the next week(s) to obey those marching orders?

❖ Who will be your partner(s) in action and accountability?

3.16 Remind participants that you will cover Parts Four and Five in the afternoon. Look at the Prepare list to have your preparations in place. Your volunteers for the Readers Theater and panel discussion will be needed at the next session.

3.17 Close by offering prayer for all the "children of calamity" in the world who cling to "chicken seeds," and give thanks for the coming meal.

3.18 Sing together UMH #584: "Lord, You Give the Great Commission," GP2 #43: "Whose Child Is This?" or TFWS #2178: "Here Am I," then offer a benediction.

Break (75 minutes)

(Place the symbols of gifts employed by mission workers at your focal point. Encourage your Readers Theater volunteers to practice and give the panel members their assigned roles, if you haven't done that earlier.)

PART FOUR

Connectionalism and Partnerships (45 minutes)

4.1 Gather together by singing UMH #589: "The Church of Christ, in Every Age," UMH #555: "Forward Through the Ages," GP2 #102: "The Church Is Like a Table," or TFWS #2243: "We All Are One in Mission." In table groups, take 5-8 minutes to skim through Essay 14. Note the main points and agree on your definition of "functional connectionalism." Distribute handouts.

4.2 Present the Readers Theater. Afterward, discuss these questions:

❖ What is your experience with how the connectionalism and/or organization of The United Methodist Church functions to accomplish the *missio Dei*?

❖ What can you do within the Connection that would be difficult or impossible without it?

❖ What opportunities have you had to be educated in the *missio Dei*? What opportunities are you providing for others to cultivate mission leaders?

❖ Which of the five activities (see Mission Education Emphases in the text) have been implemented in your church or ministry area?

4.3   Ask participants to read John 15:8-17 and review the "Partnering" stories in Essay 15 ("Partnering in Spirituality" and following).

4.4   Send one person from each table group to bring back one of the items from the display. Have them use it as a discussion starter to tell about experiences of UM or ecumenical partnerships that have provided for ministry illustrated by that item. (The conversation is not limited to examples using that item.) For example, using the food item, begin with experiences of food pantries, crop/farming education. Using the basket, begin with experiences of micro-lending programs that aid local commerce.)

4.5   Discuss how "bearing fruit together" yields a "harvest," and what that "harvest" has been. Ask: How have ecumenical or denominational partnerships strengthened, developed, and renewed communities in need?

Foundations of Abundance (20 minutes)

4.6   Ask group members to skim through the stories in Essay 16, starting with "A Haven of Hope." Ask: How are they reflections of shared abundance? Have each group choose one of the anecdotes and make up an alternative ending to the story, as if those in a position to be in mission worked from an attitude of scarcity. What might the difference be?

4.7   Have participants read John 10:1-18 and the first section of Essay 16, "Coming Home to Abundant Life." Focus on Dr. Potter's four aspects of caring: safety, living in community, universal abundance, and God as the source of abundance. Spend time with the Scripture and how it exemplifies the call to the faith community to enliven those aspects of care for all. Discuss the difference it makes when those in ministry act out of a stance of abundance.

4.8   Close this activity by singing UMH #95: "Praise God from Whom All Blessings Flow," GP2 #20: "¡Gracias, Señor!" or TFWS #2036: "Give Thanks."

Break (15 minutes)

Peace With Justice (45 minutes)

4.9   Invite everyone to stand together and read aloud Micah 6:6-8. Remain standing for one minute of silence in prayer and solidarity for those who enjoy neither peace nor justice.

4.10   Ask table groups then to be seated and take about five minutes to review the beginning of Essay 17, through the exegetical comments (up to "Loving Kindness in the Midst of Despair"). Display the Process Statement Chart.

4.11   Ask for three volunteers. Two will take notes from the conversation to follow. The third will start the activity by reading aloud "Loving Kindness in the Midst of Despair" as one example of working for peace with justice.

4.12   Next, identify together a world "hot spot" where peace and justice are much needed, and with which group members are at least somewhat acquainted. Explain what comes next by reading aloud the instruction in 4.13.

4.13   "I will start a conversation about the process of working for peace with justice in that hot spot. The rest of you, as you are led, will add your own comments by introducing it with one of the sentence starters on the Process Statement Chart. For example, 'The desperate situation in [Iraq] is much in need of God's peace.' Someone else will add, '*But before that* we must address the religious strife in the region.' Another may add, '*And while that is happening,* we must engage our US leaders to do _____ about the escalation of military conflict.' And so on."

4.14   Allow the conversation to go where it will for several minutes, while the note takers record on newsprint the main ideas shared by the group. Then spend some time reflecting on the process in terms of the issues of human will, the interface between the religious community and other structures that influence such situations, scriptural mandates, complexity in dealing with justice issues, and so on. (Obviously, the point is not to solve this.)

Reflection on Part Four (15 minutes)

4.15   In table groups, have participants first review:

❖ What have you seen through your experience and examination of the text and Scriptures concerning how the Church: 1) is equipped for mission; 2) works with partners; 3) advocates for and shares abundance; and 4) strives for peace with justice for all?

❖ How do the Scriptures seem to evaluate our efforts? What do they call us to be and to do?

❖ What spiritual-growth opportunities have you experienced (or would be available to you) by engagement with a ministry of abundance?

❖ If you have previously planned for or implemented any of the five activities (Mission Education Emphases), what has been the effect?

❖ What one or two things can you do to engage in a partnership or educate others for mission?

❖ With whom and how will you hold yourself accountable for these commitments?

4.16   Ask one person at each table to hold up the symbol while you lead a bidding prayer for those in great need of peace and justice. Close with a benediction.

PART FIVE

Missionary Method (20 minutes)

5.1   Gather participants from the break by singing together UMH #730: "O Day of God, Draw Nigh," GP2 #123: "Min Himmel" ("My Heaven"), or TFWS #2284: "Joy in the Morning."

5.2   Have group members skim over Essay 18, with special focus on the last section, "Sending the 70." They should also read Luke 10:1-12, 17-20.

5.3   Turn to the handout. Have the groups divide the Luke passage and the questions related to it. Ask them to work independently for a few minutes to jot down ideas from the questions, then to discuss the passage within the group. For the last few minutes of this time, invite responses from all the groups.

❖ *Luke 10:1-2:* • Who, in contemporary terms, are "the harvest"? • Who, do you think, are the laborers? • How do we decide which laborers go to which harvest, if there are not enough for the entire "harvest"?

❖ *Luke 10:3-6:* • What is the "way" like today? • Are the "laborers" still like lambs among wolves? Why, or why not? • What sense do these traveling instructions make now? What did they mean for the disciples? • How do the current "laborers" establish peace? What issues are important in establishing peace?

❖ *Luke 10:7-8:* • What was the meaning of these instructions in hospitality to the disciples? • What are the hospitality issues now? • Who should pay the wages? • What are the implications if "the harvest" is unable to pay?

❖ *Luke 10:9-12:* • How do we now say, "The kingdom has come near"? • If we invest in mission in a particular area, what should be done if there is resistance or rejection? • What does that suggest for "laborers" who are expecting to "harvest"? • If the mandate of God is to go to all nations, how do we deal with "shaking the dust"?

❖ *Luke 10:17-20:* • How would you describe the power of God given to the "laborers" then and now? • What are the power issues today inherent in mission? • What are the consequences of succeeding (or not) and how is success to be measured?

❖ *Ask everyone:* • What does this passage teach us about the missionary method? • Is the biblical method appropriate in the complex world of the 21st century? • What models do you know from our Methodist history? • What new things are being done or need to be done? • What new insights come to mind if you consider yourself part of the "harvest," rather than one of the "laborers"?

Think and Act Glocally (35 minutes)

5.4   Sing through UMH #628: "Eat This Bread," GP2 #42: "Jeder Braucht Brot" ("Lord, We Need Bread"), or TFWS #2267: "Taste and See," two or three times.

5.5   Invite table groups to review Essay 20 carefully, up to "Health and School Kits…," to be sure they understand what is meant by a "glocal" church and "glocal" mission. (Watch out for false dichotomies. What is global to us is local to someone else; "glocal" refers to this intersection.)

5.6   Have a panel discussion with five volunteers who will assume certain roles.

5.7   Give the panel members the handout explaining their role. The panel volunteers include a moderator, a "multinational" business executive, a "receiving" bishop, a missionary, and a layperson in the mission area.

5.8   After the panel presentation, discuss these questions as you have time:

  ❖ What does thinking and acting "glocally" mean to you now?

  ❖ How does the church's presence "glocally" compare and contrast with what you know of the global business environment?

  ❖ How can the church speak to the world about "glocal" issues?

  ❖ What is your part in "glocalization," and what does that mean to you?

Break (10 Minutes)

Mission Stewardship (35 minutes)

5.9   Re-form the table groups and have members skim over Essay 21. Throughout the essays, you have read numerous anecdotes about how missional enterprises and experiences have made a difference in peoples' lives. Take five minutes (no more just now) to ask which stories, from any essays, have been most compelling.

5.10 Distribute the "stewardship chits." Ask each person to select one of the stories (or other mission opportunity). Think about what time and investment would be necessary to make a meaningful difference in that mission opportunity and how much passion there is to make that difference.

5.11 Do a "moment of truth" exercise with the chits. Each chit represents a unit of personal energy, personal interest, or local church material resources, and the *total* number is what each pastor and layperson has to invest in *every* ministry activity over the course of a month—preaching, teaching, pastoral care, work with children or youth, administration, leadership or participation in various ministry areas, visiting, counseling, and so on. Have each person divide up the chits as they feel appropriately indicates their commitments in ministry. They can discuss their choices and decisions.

5.12 Then discuss these questions:

  ❖ Given the mission theological statement you worked on in Session 1, the essays, and the Scriptures you have studied, how well have you done on your stewardship in mission?

  ❖ Missionaries and mission projects (through the Advance, UMCOR, Women's Division of Global Ministries, and so on) need constant support. Were those needs considered?

❖ What sort of balance is appropriate, do you think, between supporting the denominational efforts and personal and local mission? How do you decide?

Reflection on Part Five (15 minutes)

5.13 Invite the groups to begin their reflection/action. Review the session, keeping these questions in mind:

❖ What have I seen or discovered about my own commitments to the *missio Dei*? In the "divine economy" of all Christians working from their strengths and passions, are my commitments appropriate?

❖ What has the Scripture called me to do towards the "harvest"? How have the Scriptures judged my efforts, interests, and theology of mission?

❖ What has been God's word of grace to me in this segment?

❖ What one action will I take in the next week to live out God's call of mission?

❖ Who will be my partner in action and/or accountability?

5.14 *For Next Session:* Ask participants to review all notes, especially their theology of mission statements and the commitments they have considered during the reflection times. Look at the Prepare list to be sure all your preparations are in place.

5.15 Sing together UMH #127: "Guide Me, O Thou Great Jehovah," GP1 #5: "As Your Children, Lord," or TFWS #2255: "In the Singing." Offer a prayer of thanks for the day and for the evening meal.

(Option for Evening Prayer)

DAY THREE (APPROXIMATELY 9:00 A.M.–12:00 P.M.)
PART SIX

Opening Devotion (15 minutes)

6.1   Place at your focal point a collection of the visuals that were used in Sessions 1-5. Prepare the table with elements for the closing Communion.

6.2   Welcome group members and explain that the purpose of this session is to bring together the threads of the previous ones, to develop strategies and goals for mission.

6.3   Sing together UMH #465: "Holy Spirit, Truth Divine," GP3 #105: "Gracious Spirit," or TFWS #2120: "Spirit, Spirit of Gentleness."

6.4   Read Matthew 9:16-17. Ask if there is a brief response to what the "new wine" might be.

6.5   Read the quote from the Willingen Conference (Essay 2, "Those who are sought…"). Allow 30 seconds of silence, then read the quote by Newbigin (Essay 3, "…the whole base of mission…").

6.6   Close with prayer for discernment and guidance in forging your own sense of mission and the actions that flow from it.

Reflection on the Mission Study Experience (25 minutes)

6.7   Ask participants to come forward, as they feel led, and hold up one of the items from the focal point that evokes a commitment to mission or illustrates a need that has touched them deeply. Use the items, or reference to any of the previous teaching activities, to begin the discussion of what the group members have experienced and thought in the past five sessions.

6.8   As necessary, you may also use these reflection questions. Record responses on newsprint.

❖ What was your greatest "Aha!" moment (something that surprised, clarified, amazed, delighted)? What was your greatest "Uh-Oh" moment (something that dismayed, disappointed, discouraged, warned)?

❖ What experience, learning, or insight was the most powerful for you? Why?

❖ What sense of hope or encouragement did this experience engender? Why?

❖ What sense of need did this experience evoke? Why?

❖ As you experienced and learned from the sessions, how did the Theological Task (Scripture, Tradition, Experience, and Reason) intersect with the mission goals (make disciples, strengthen Christian community, alleviate suffering, seek peace with justice)? Did that have any impact on your insights and/or commitments to the *missio Dei*?

Establish Desired Results for Mission (40 minutes)

6.9   Bring participants back from the break by singing stanzas 1 and 2 of UMH #437: "This Is My Song," GP2 #118: "We've Packed for the Journey," or TFWS #2220: "We Are God's People."

6.10 Invite participants to arrange themselves in logical affinity groups (for example, members of the same congregation, neighborhood, district, church size) in which they could or would engage in strategic thinking for mission.

6.11 Ask group members to envision what they desire as an outcome before they do any thinking about what to do. Have art supplies available and invite them to draw an art or word picture of their desired outcome. (Look for examples of outcomes in the Appendix.)

6.12 Then move to some planning steps. If group members feel overwhelmed or stuck, play "I care, but I can't help." Choose one of the big outcomes and ask the first person in the group to help identify one S.M.A.R.T. goal (something Specific, Measurable, Attainable, Reasonable, and Timely). The responder need not include every S.M.A.R.T. aspect; just brainstorm. If the person is at a loss, the response is, "I care, but I can't help." If the person passes in this way, he or she *must* at least indicate an authentic barrier or offer a reason why helping is not possible. Then the next person gives an idea or responds similarly. If the planning steps proceed first by naming barriers and then figuring out how to address them, do it that way. Or, start with the outcome and work backward to identify what must be in place at each stage. Be sure, though, to keep your eyes on the good outcomes and not get mired in the "I Can'ts." (See the Appendix for planning helps and examples of outcomes.)

6.13 By the end of this period, encourage groups to have at least one S.M.A.R.T. outcome. Ask each group to post their outcome on newsprint.

Break (15 minutes)

Commit to Next Steps (40 minutes)

6.14 Have groups spend the next segment of time refining that outcome statement by identifying the next steps they will take and by when. Distribute blank paper and markers, and have group members write on separate pages each step they have identified and when it might be accomplished. Recognize that some steps are sequential and some are concurrent. Encourage them to be as detailed as they can in 30 minutes. When they are done, group members should divide up the steps consecutively.

6.15 Draw an imaginary timeline around the room, starting with Next Week, then In Two Weeks, In One Month, In Three Months, In Six Months, In One Year. Ask everyone to stand at the appropriate place on the visual timeline with their steps, and to indicate what they are, in turn. As you move through each time segment, participants will need to mention what outcome they were working on.

6.16 Most likely there will be a great amount of creativity and vision expressed in those proposed steps, even if the progress they imagine takes some time to come to fruition. Note which groups have similar outcome statements and encourage them to maintain contact for support and accountability.

Closing (30 minutes)

6.17 Ask everyone to pick up a *UM Hymnal* and gather in a circle so that they can see the items at the focal point. If anyone needs to sit down, invite them to have a chair at their place in the circle. Tuck the Next Step sign in the *Hymnal* for the time being. Have the Scripture readers evenly spaced in the circle.

6.18 Say Prayer 446, "Serving the Poor," antiphonally, by reading a brief phrase that participants will repeat.

6.19 The volunteers will read their Scriptures in turn. Allow 20 or 30 seconds of silence between each reading: • Micah 6:8; • John 3:16; • Matthew 16:24; • Matthew 22:37-39; • Matthew 28:19-20.

6.20 Invite group members to say a word or phrase that summarizes their experience with and/or their commitment to mission as a result of the study.

6.21 Sing together UMH #463: "Lord, Speak to Me," GP2 #98: "Yo Quiero Ser" ("I Want to Be"), or TFWS #2130: "The Summons." During the singing, have the group members place their Next Step signs at the focal point.

6.22 Celebrate Communion together using the liturgy beginning on page 12 of the *UM Hymnal.*

6.23 Close with prayer for the "new wine" and God's commission to be faithful, serving disciples, and a benediction.

CURRICULUM PLAN
FOR A ONE-DAY EVENT
9:00 A.M.– 3:30 P.M.

Learning Goals:

☑ To understand mission as God's mission, in which all are called to make a witness and to be a witness.

☑ To recognize the interconnectedness of our denomination within the body of Christ and how that helps us organize for ministry.

☑ To heighten awareness of the justice issues inherent in mission, and to urge us to loving action.

☑ To see how ministry that is global for some is local for others, and to prompt us to action from our own context.

Prepare or Have on Hand:

☑ Read through at least Essays 2, 6, 11, 17, and 20. Highlight or list the main points in each essay so that you can better guide and shape the activities, especially for those who have not read the essays before attending.

☑ A candle and matches for each table group. Have one candle at the focal point and a candle at each table with matches (Activity 1.1; 1.4; 2.2; 4 1).

☑ An item small enough to hold in one hand, such as a cross, icon, or unbreakable figurine (Activity 1.2).

☑ Copies of the handouts (Activity 2.3; 2.5; 3.2; 3.5; 5.3; 5.5; 6.3; see Appendix).

☑ Copies of *The United Methodist Hymnal, Global Praise 1, Global Praise 2, Global Praise 3*, and *The Faith We Sing* songbooks for each person (Activity 1.4; 2.6; 3.3; 4.1; 6.3; 6.5).

☑ Poster board or newsprint, tape, and markers (Activity 2.4; 2.7; 4.7; 4.10; 5.1).

☑ Recruit four people to do a simple Readers Theater. Make copies of the script (in the Appendix). *Be sure to give them time to practice before the session* (Activity 3.2).

☑ Select five other people for the panel discussion and give them advance time to think about their roles (Activity 5.2; See Appendix).

☑ A large map of the world (and pushpins or sticky notes) on display as people enter the room (Activity 3.3).

☑ Create a Process Statement Chart of four comments: • "But first we"; • "And then we"; • "And while that is happening"; • "But before that" (Activity 4.3).

☑ Small plates of fresh bread (pita works well) and juice for Communion; enough for each table group to have a plate of bread. Place all of them at your focal point at first (Activity 6.1; 6.5).

Welcome and Opening Bible Reflection (20 minutes)

1.1 Welcome everyone and have them form table groups. Mention the necessary hospitality issues (how to handle breaks, location of restrooms, getting snacks or beverages, and so on). Distribute handouts to each table; place them face down for now. Create a focal point for your devotions with *all* the elements and the lighted candles.

1.2 Hold the icon and take no more than 14 seconds to say something about yourself. Then give the icon to the next person to do the same and so on around the room. Welcome any latecomers, and introduce the *lectio divina.*

1.3 Read aloud Isaiah 58:6-11 for *lectio divina.* For the first reading, ask participants to listen for and jot down any words, phrases, or images that capture their attention. Pause for a minute, then invite any who wish to respond briefly. Read the passage again. This time ask participants to reflect on what that word or image means to them and how it makes them feel. Pause for another minute, then ask for any other brief comments. Read the passage a third time. With this reading, participants should note how they perceive God speaking to them through those words and images. After another minute, allow time for further response from the group. After the last comment, allow one more minute of silence to rest in the reading and hearing of the Word.

1.4 Allow five minutes for comments from the whole group about any new insights. Sing together UMH #427: "Where Cross the Crowded Ways of

Life," GP1 #17: "Child of Joy and Peace," or TFWS #2237: "As a Fire Is Meant for Burning." Then open a time of prayer, ask for bidding prayers, and conclude the prayer. Move the candles so that there is one at each table group.

Understanding Mission and Witness (75 minutes)

2.1   Review Essay 6, paying particular attention to "The Fire of Mission" and "Being Sent." Take a few minutes to bring out the main points.

2.2   Pick up a candle in one of the groups and describe one burning need anywhere in the world that has captured your heart. Have the small group members do the same, one by one, by placing the candle in front of themselves, speaking to a need, and moving the candle carefully to the next person. (If there are *any* concerns about participants doing this safely, do not pass the candles.)

2.3   Turn over the handout. Read aloud, or have group members read Matthew 5:14-16. Reflect on the Scripture and on the burning needs mentioned in the essay, then discuss these questions in the small groups:

❖ How does the need you see compel you to witness?

❖ On what "lamp stand" do you need to place your lamp—what witness are you on fire to offer? When you do, what is the consequence?

❖ How do you or have you hidden your light? What has been the consequence?

❖ How do you describe "good works [that] give glory to your Father in heaven"?

2.4   Ask for responses from the groups, "popcorn" style. Record the responses on newsprint.

2.5   Have group members skim through Essay 2 and to look for the following key points:

❖ A definition or explanation of "*missio Dei.*"

❖ The consequences of the assertion that "mission is God's, not ours."

❖ The difference between theocentric and ecclesiocentric mission.

❖ The call to be the authentic body of Christ.

2.6   Ask the table groups next to formulate their own theology of mission statement by pulling together the Scripture readings and reflection and the essay information. When the statement is finished, have them select at least one, preferably two or three, hymns that support their statement.

2.7   When groups are done, list the hymns on newsprint.

Ministry Through the Connection (60 minutes)

3.1   Remind group members that The United Methodist Church is both connectional and global. The function of the Connection enables us to be effective in ministry across the globe. Have everyone skim Essay 11.

3.2   Present the Readers Theater. Afterward, discuss these questions:

❖ How is Methodism "organized to beat the Devil"? How well do we do?

❖ What is your experience with how the connectionalism and/or organization of The United Methodist Church functions to accomplish the *missio Dei*?

❖ What is your experience of mission within the Connection? What experience do you have with partner relationships between a local church or annual conference with another (usually foreign) church or conference?

❖ What can you do within the Connection that would be difficult or impossible without it?

❖ What opportunities have you had to be educated in the *missio Dei*? What opportunities are you providing for others to cultivate mission leaders?

❖ What blessings have you experienced or heard about that have been bestowed on the US church by conferences outside the US?

3.3   Turn attention to the world map. Invite participants to come to the maps in groups of three or four to put a pushpin or sticky note on all the areas of the world they have visited, for any reason, including the United States. (For "movement music" and theological support, sing several of the hymns from the newsprint list.)

3.4   When the map is complete, invite them to tell stories, briefly, of insights gained about the culture of the places they have visited, especially if they came to understand any cultural biases they may have held.

3.5   Then talk about the contexts for mission, using these questions:

❖ What were the circumstances of your visit (tourist, family visit, mission trip)?

❖ If you were a tourist, did you see the "real" country or community?

❖ If you went to mission areas, what did you see? How was it different from what a tourist may see?

❖ In what ways, if any, have you seen the US church imposing its cultural biases on another Christian context or been unaware that there were cultural distinctions to make for effective ministry and relationships?

❖ How does the call to "make of all disciples" need to be interpreted in cultures other than your own to form responsible partnerships?

3.6   Close the discussion with a bidding prayer for the needs of the places that were represented.

Break for Lunch (45 Minutes)

❖ Be sure the panel members have the description of their roles, if they have not received this information earlier (Activity 5.2).

❖ Offer a prayer of thanksgiving and extinguish the candles.

Justice and Loving Action Through Mission (75 minutes)

4.1   Gather people back from the break by standing and singing UMH #428: "For the Healing of the Nations," GP3 #161: "You Came Down to Earth," or TFWS #2177: "Wounded World That Cries for Healing." Have someone at each table relight the candle.

4.2   Invite everyone to remain standing while you read aloud Micah 6:6-8. Continue standing for one minute of silence in prayer and solidarity for those who enjoy neither peace nor justice.

4.3   Ask table groups then to be seated and take about five minutes to review the beginning of Essay 17, through the exegetical comments (up to "Loving Kindness in the Midst of Despair"). Display the Process Statement Chart.

4.4   Ask for three volunteers. Two will take notes from the conversation to follow. The third will start the activity by reading aloud "Loving Kindness in the Midst of Despair" as one example of working for peace with justice.

4.5   Next, identify together a world "hot spot" where peace and justice are much needed, and with which group members are at least somewhat acquainted. Explain what comes next by reading aloud the instruction in 4.6.

4.6   "I will start a conversation about the process of working for peace with justice in that hot spot. The rest of you, as you are led, will add your own comments by introducing it with one of the sentence starters on the Process Statement Chart. For example, 'The desperate situation in [Iraq] is much in need of God's peace.' Someone else will add, '*But before that* we must address the religious strife in the region.' Another may add, '*And while that is happening,* we must engage our US leaders to do _____ about the escalation of military conflict.' And so on."

4.7   Allow the conversation to go where it will for several minutes, while the note takers record the main ideas shared by the group. Then spend some time reflecting on the process in terms of the issues of human will, particularly the attitude of either abundance or scarcity that motivates behavior. Discuss also the interface between the religious community and other structures that influence such situations, scriptural mandates, complexity in dealing with justice issues, and so on. (Obviously, the point is not to solve this.)

4.8   Bring this segment to a close by offering prayer for peace with justice for the area under discussion.

4.9   Now ask participants to reflect on two other Scriptures that speak to the call of servanthood to meet the needs of the "least of these." Have group members read Isaiah 61 and Luke 6:20-36, and refer again to the examples of loving kindness in Essay 17. As members of God's "Commission on Peace With Justice," have them write out their own "Peace With Justice mandates."

4.10 As you have time, record a few of the specific mandates.

Living Locally, Working "Glocally" (60 minutes)

5.1   Have group members skim through Essay 20, up to "Health and School Kits…." Together, list the main points on newsprint. Be sure everyone understands what is meant by a "glocal" church and "glocal" mission. (Watch out for false dichotomies. What is global to us is local to someone else; "glocal" refers to this intersection.)

5.2   Have a panel discussion with five volunteers who will assume the roles of moderator, a "multinational" business executive, a "receiving" bishop, a missionary, and a layperson in the mission area. If you have more than 20-25 participants, consider having two parallel panels in different parts of the room.

5.3   Invite the moderator to introduce the discussion and give the panel 15-20 minutes. Be sure the moderator limits each speech to 60-90 seconds at a time. After the panel presentation, discuss these questions for no more than 10 minutes:

❖ What does thinking and acting "glocally" mean to you now?

❖ How does the church's presence "glocally" compare and contrast with what you know of the global business environment?

❖ How can the church speak to the world about "glocal" issues?

❖ What is your part in "glocalization," and what does that mean to you?

5.4   Now that some opinions and ideas have surfaced about glocalization, reflect on them again through the lens of Scripture. Ask everyone to read Luke 10:1-12, 17-20.

5.5   Refer to the handout. Divide the passage and its related questions among the table groups. Ask them to work independently for a few minutes to jot down ideas from the questions, then to discuss the passage within the group. For the last 5-8 minutes of this time, invite responses from all the groups.

❖ *Luke 10:1-2:* • Who, in contemporary terms, are "the harvest"? • Who, do you think, are the laborers? • How do we decide which laborers go to which harvest, if there are not enough for the entire "harvest"?

247

❖ *Luke 10:3-6:* • What is the "way" like today? • Are the "laborers" still like lambs among wolves? Why, or why not? • What sense do these traveling instructions make now? What did they mean for the disciples? • How do the current "laborers" establish peace? What issues are important in establishing peace?

❖ *Luke 10:7-8:* • What was the meaning of these instructions in hospitality to the disciples? • What are the hospitality issues now? • Who should pay the wages? • What are the implications if "the harvest" is unable to pay?

❖ *Luke 10:9-12:* • How do we now say, "The kingdom has come near"? • If we invest in mission in a particular area, what should be done if there is resistance or rejection? • What does that suggest for "laborers" who are expecting to "harvest"? • If the mandate of God is to go to all nations, how do we deal with "shaking the dust"?

❖ *Luke 10:17-20:* • How would you describe the power of God given to the "laborers" then and now? • What are the power issues today inherent in mission? • What are the consequences of succeeding (or not) and how is success to be measured?

❖ *Ask everyone:* • What does this passage teach us about mission in a global community? • Is the biblical method appropriate in the complex world of the 21st century? • What models do you know from our Methodist history? • What new insights come to mind if you consider yourself part of the "harvest," rather than one of the "laborers"?

Reflection and Closing (45 Minutes)

6.1 Make the transition from the last activity to the reflection time by asking a person from each group to get a plate of bread and place it on their table. Take no more than 10 minutes for steps 6.1–6.3.

6.2 Ask group members to mention what is the "bread of life" in cultures and regions with which they are familiar (rice in Asia, for example). Then invite one brief personal story from each group that illuminates the sacramental nature of mission.

6.3 Begin the celebration of Communion using the liturgy beginning with the Great Thanksgiving on page 9 of the *UM Hymnal*, through the consecration of the elements on page 11. When the bread is broken, ask a person at each table to break their loaf. The consecrated bread, next to the symbol of the Light of the world at each table, will serve as a reminder of why we engage in mission. Pause at this point to reflect on the day using the following questions:

❖ What was your greatest "Aha!" moment (something that surprised, clarified, amazed, delighted)? What was your greatest "Uh-Oh" moment (something that dismayed, disappointed, discouraged, warned)?

❖ What experience, learning, or insight was the most powerful for you? Why?

❖ What sense of hope or encouragement did this experience engender? Why?

❖ What sense of need did this experience evoke? Why?

❖ As you experienced and learned from the sessions, how did Scripture, Tradition, Experience, and Reason intersect with the mission goals (make disciples, strengthen Christian community, alleviate suffering, seek peace with justice)?

❖ Did that have any impact on your insights and/or commitments to the *missio Dei*?

❖ Given your theology of mission statement and your mission mandates, to what action has this experience called you? What outcome do you want?

❖ What first S.M.A.R.T. step (specific, measurable, attainable, reasonable, and timely) will you take, and by when? Who will be your partner in support and accountability?

6.4 Give participants 20 minutes to work on the reflection with the encouragement to continue to reflect and refine later.

6.5 Then resume the Communion liturgy. Sing together UMH #620: "One Bread, One Body," GP2 #42: "Jeder Braucht Brot" ("Lord, We Need Bread"), or TFWS #2267: "Taste and See," while forming a circle around your focal point (if the group size is manageable). Have groups bring their plate of bread and place it with the other consecrated elements.

6.6 At the close of the hymn, offer the elements by intinction. Close with a prayer for God's commission to be faithful, serving disciples followed by a benediction.

APPENDIX

HANDOUTS FOR THE SIX-SESSION FORMAT [6-S] AND RETREAT [R] FORMAT

SESSION/SEGMENT ONE

Activity 1.3/6-S   **Activity 1.4/R**

Read John 3:1-17. As you think about yourself and your understanding of the kingdom of God, are you more like:

❖ Nicodemus, coming to Jesus in the cover of darkness?

❖ Nicodemus, questioning Jesus about how one enters the kingdom?

❖ One who is born of the Spirit?

❖ One who wonders how Jesus' teaching can be so?

❖ One who testifies to heavenly things?

❖ One who focuses on the condemnation of the world?

❊❊❊❊❊❊❊❊❊❊❊❊❊❊❊❊❊❊❊❊❊❊❊❊❊❊❊❊❊❊

Activity 1.13/6-S   **Activity 1.13/R**

Read: • Isaiah 6:1-8; • Luke 9:23-27 and 10:1-11, 17-20; and • John 1:14-16 and 3:16-17. Use the tent peg as a "talking stick" and discuss these questions:

❖ How do you see the call of the prophet and disciples as mission? What does it mean to you to pick up your cross (or tent peg) and follow?

❖ How does the Incarnation and saving activity of God through Jesus Christ call you to ministry? Is this different, in your mind, than a call to mission? If so, how?

❖ Where and how do you see yourself called to mission?

❊❊❊❊❊❊❊❊❊❊❊❊❊❊❊❊❊❊❊❊❊❊❊❊❊❊❊❊❊❊

Activity 1.15/6-S. Reflection/Action Questions   **Activity 1.15/R**

❖ How am I living out God's call to mission?

❖ Which Scriptures speak most compellingly to me about my call to mission?

❖ What is God's word of grace to me today?

❖ How has my "mission tent" moved? How would I like it to move?

❖ What one action will I take in the next week to live out that word of grace?

❖ Who will be my partner in action and/or accountability?

SESSION/SEGMENT TWO

Activity 2.6/6-S   **Activity 2.4/R**

Read Matthew 5:14-16. Discuss these questions:

❖ How does the need you see compel you to witness?

❖ On what "lamp stand" do you need to place your lamp—what witness are you on fire to offer? When you do, what is the consequence?

❖ How do you or have you hidden your light? What has been the consequence?

❖ How do you describe "good works [that] give glory to your Father in heaven"?

✳ ✳

Activity 2.8/6-S   **Activity 2.5/R**

Read Isaiah 43:1 and Luke 5:1-11. Examine the characters, emotions, and movement of the Luke story.

❖ What does it mean to you that God calls you by name and that you were created for a purpose? What is your purpose? How do you know?

❖ What mentors, teachers, or leaders recognized your potential as a leader?

❖ As you examine your congregation or area of service, who are the leaders or potential leaders whom you can nurture?

❖ How does the *missio Dei* draw you and others into leadership in mission for the sake of the world community?

✳ ✳

Activity 2.15/6-S. Reflection/Action Questions   **Activity 2.11/R**

❖ What have I seen about the needs of the world that stands in contrast to my own context? What realities cry out for justice and witness?

❖ Given my understanding of the Scripture, how is God judging the church's leaders who are called to be on fire for mission? How might I be evaluated as a "stick in the spokes of the wheel" of injustice?

❖ What is God's word of grace to me today?

❖ What one action will I take in the next week to live out that word of grace?

❖ Who will be my partner in action and/or accountability?

SESSION/SEGMENT THREE

Activity 3.6/6-S
Activity 3.6/R

❖ In what ways have you seen the US church imposing its cultural biases on another Christian context, or been unaware that there were cultural distinctions to make for effective ministry and relationships?

❖ How does the call to "make of all disciples" need to be interpreted in cultures other than your own to form responsible partnerships?

* *

Activity 3.9/6-S
Activity 3.9/R

❖ How is Methodism "organized to beat the Devil"? How well do we do?

❖ What is your experience of mission within the Connection? What experience do you have with partner relationships between a local church or annual conference with another (usually foreign) church or conference?

❖ What blessings have you experienced or heard about that have been bestowed on the US church by conferences outside the US?

* *

Activity 3.11/6-S
Activity 3.11/R

Read Mark 10:13-16. Focus on the "chicken seeds" and the "glue pot." Discuss.

❖ Try to imagine children you know having to sniff glue and hoard "chicken seeds" in order to have the most basic of their needs met. What would you be willing to do to protect children you love from such calamity?

❖ Examine the scene in Mark 10 (assuming Jesus was speaking about small children). What was the child's position in that society? How does that differ from what we expect, even demand, in our culture?

❖ There are 73 million children in the US. Of them, 57 percent (41.2 million) live in low-income or poor families. (See data from the National Center for Children in Poverty at http//www.nccp.org/pub_lic06b.html.) What does the gospel claim of you to care for the millions of children in the US and elsewhere whom you don't know?

* *

Activity 3.15/6-S. Reflection/Action Questions   **Activity 3.15/R**

❖ What vision of current reality has emerged concerning the needs of the world, especially for children? How does this compare or contrast to your own immediate context? the context in other US areas?

❖ What has been the call of Scripture for mission? How does the vision of this current reality tug at your soul?

❖ What ideas have emerged from the stories or your experience that address the needs?

❖ What do your justice mandates lead you to think, feel, and do?

❖ What one thing will you do in the next week(s) to obey those marching orders?

❖ Who will be your partner(s) in action and accountability?

SESSION/SEGMENT FOUR

Activity 4.5/6-S　　　　**Activity 3.2/One-Day**　　　　**Activity 4.2/R**

Preparation for Readers Theater

Each speaker should have a sign indicating his or her role. Write out the character's name with a broad-tipped marker on an 8½" x 11" sheet of paper or card stock. Fasten the signs to the blouse or shirt with pins, or by fixing a length of string, necklace style. Highlight the different parts on each script ahead of time so readers can easily identify their lines.

Instruction to Readers

Readers are assigned according to *height*. General Board of Global Ministries is the tallest, then Annual Conference, District, and Local Church. Use minimal movement, but convey the action through vocal and facial expression, volume, pace, and gesture. You may *ad lib* a bit so long as the script remains intact. Do your best to look up, rather than being buried in the script. Watch for the places in the script where you speak together or in quick succession. Be conversational. Address each other as the script indicates, not by personal name.

Begin

[*District and Annual Conference are standing next to each other. General Board of Global Ministries is a step or two away. Local Church approaches District and Annual Conference.*]

Local Church (LC): A funny thing happened on the way to my planning retreat. I was thinking that I'm not really happy with the small amount of time I have given to mission trips, and God told me to talk to you two about foundational conferencism, whatever that is.

District (D): Never heard of it. Are you sure you were directed to me? I do mission trips, a food bank, and a clothing closet, but I don't know what you're talking about.

Annual Conference (AC): [*With a slight grin*] What a goofy term. I do mission trips, flood buckets, health kits; support a missionary couple; and partner with a central conference, but I think you're having a nightmare, not a vision. There's no such thing as foundational conferencism.

LC [*Defensively*]: That's what I heard!

D: I bet it's not!

LC: Is too!

AC: Is not!

LC: Is too! Is too!

General Board of Global Ministries (GBGM): [*Steps closer, speaking soothing-ly*] Hold on. Hold on. We're all on the same side here. I might be able to help. [*To LC*]: Could you have heard the term "functional connectionalism?

LC: That's it! [*More subdued*]. Well, I was close. [*With more energy*]. But I still don't know what it means or why I'm supposed to talk to District and Annual Conference about it. Do you two know what this is?

D: Uh.

AC: Mmmm. It's on the tip of my tongue….

GBGM: I think you know what it is, but haven't used that term before. Want a clue?

[*LC, D, AC speak at the same time:*]

LC: Yes, please.

D: Yep, you bet.

AC: Get on with it!

GBGM: LC, you said you do mission trips. How do you do that?

LC: I send information to my members about a particular need in a specific area. Those who are interested and have the dates available will contribute some funds and work with the other members to raise the rest of the funds. They get the word out to other churches in the area, and sometimes a few of their members will ask to join us, which is always great. We have several announcements in worship, and the outreach committee keeps the information and need in front of the congregation with posters, calls, email, website, and such. And when we're ready to go, the congregation has a consecration and blessing of the participants in the worship service. When we get back, we give a brief report in a worship service and a longer one, with pictures and stories, in a special presentation during Sunday school or a mid-week gathering time.

GBGM: OK, hold that thought. District, you said you did trips and have a way to distribute food and clothing. How do you do that?

D: Well, I do all that much the same way as LC said. I use my various communication tools to reach out from the District to the Local Churches. We have a committee on outreach, and they act as a kind of speakers' bureau, that travels by invitation to cluster meetings and to local churches. I have some money budgeted and the rest comes from special offerings that the speakers raise. A few of the volunteers who run the pantry and the food bank are recruited by my committee, but most are invited by way of the Local Churches. The churches sign up for a week or a month or some regular turn and then ask their folks to help out, like on the third Thursday, or every Tuesday.

GBGM: That's wonderful. Now, let's hold that thought, too. Annual Conference, you said you do several wonderful mission ministries. How do you get those flood buckets and health kits assembled?

AC: To make a long story short....

D and LC: [*Quickly and smiling*] Too late!

AC: [*Smiling*] Very funny. I use essentially the same methods as my pals District and Local Church.

GBGM: And where do you send the buckets and kits?

AC: To a collection center run by UMCOR.... [*With a look of sudden recognition*] Hey, that's you!

GBGM: [*Smiling modestly*] Well, not all of me. How about your support of the missionaries and your partnership with a central conference?

AC: Same kind of approach. During the year, I use all the channels we mentioned, plus special events. I try to have a representative at my annual meeting, and there is typically a special offering.

GBGM: And where do you send those funds and receive information about partnerships, missionaries, needs, and so on?

AC: Some of it is direct contact, and some of it goes through you.

GBGM: Do you notice a pattern here?

LC: I can't do it alone; I need my people.

D: I sure couldn't do my thing without you, Local Church.

AC: And I could do barely anything without the two of you.

Permission is granted to photocopy this page for use in educational settings.

GBGM: For my part, I rely very deeply on all three of you as I coordinate mission, send relief, get out the word on all the tremendous needs, and interpret this ministry to and through all of you.

LC: So, are you ultimately the one in charge of all this?

GBGM: Organizationally, that would be General Conference, but General Conference is pretty busy and only comes around every four years. My partner agencies and I work to keep all the denominational plates spinning in the meantime, but without you, I would be next to nothing. Now, the next to last question: Why do you do what you do?

[*AC, D, and LC respond in quick succession:*]

AC: There is tremendous need in the world,

D: and in our nation,

LC: and in our communities.

AC: But more than that, God places an ache in my heart, and a great blessing, when I see my brothers and sisters in need. I just have to participate, both to give and to receive.

D: God has claimed me too. I see the need, and I also know how much I can learn from others, both nearby and in what seem like faraway, exotic places.

LC: God calls to me as well. Jesus the Christ came to save and redeem the whole world, and I just have to respond to that radical love. It's what makes me what I am, even if my influence seems small in the great scheme of things.

GBGM: [*Nodding with approval*] So the last question is, What is functional connectionalism?

AC: God sent the Son for the sake of the whole world to work with and through each of us.

D: As the community of faith, we can do and be more than each of us acting alone.

LC: So we value and depend on each other, and we're all in this together!

GBGM: [*With great gusto*] YES! You got it!

Everyone claps (and hug or shakes hands, if that would be acceptable in this group).

SESSION/SEGMENT FOUR

Activity 4.5/6-S   Activity 4.2/R

❖ What is your experience with how the connectionalism and/or organization of The United Methodist Church functions to accomplish the *missio Dei*?

❖ What can you do within the Connection that would be difficult or impossible without it?

❖ What opportunities have you had to be educated in the *missio Dei*? What opportunities are you providing for others to cultivate mission leaders?

❖ Which of the five activities (see Mission Education Emphases in the text) have been implemented in your church or ministry area? (More on these later.)

❊❊❊❊❊❊❊❊❊❊❊❊❊❊❊❊❊❊❊❊❊❊❊❊❊❊❊❊❊❊❊

Activity 4.18/6-S. Action/Reflection Questions   Activity 4.15/R

❖ What have you seen through your experience and examination of the text and Scriptures concerning how the Church: 1) is equipped for mission; 2) works with partners; 3) advocates for and shares abundance; and 4) strives for peace with justice for all?

❖ How do the Scriptures seem to evaluate our efforts? What do they call us to be and to do?

❖ What spiritual-growth opportunities have you experienced (or would be available to you) by engagement with a ministry of abundance?

❖ If you have planned for or implemented any of the five activities (Mission Education Emphases), what has been the effect?

❖ What one or two things can you do to engage in a partnership or educate others for mission?

❖ With whom and how will you hold yourself accountable for these commitments?

SESSION/SEGMENT FIVE

Activity 5.8/6-S   **Activity 5.3/R**

Read Luke 10:1-12, 17-20.

❖ *Luke 10:1-2:* • Who, in contemporary terms, are "the harvest"? • Who, do you think, are the laborers? • How do we decide which laborers go to which harvest, if there are not enough for the entire "harvest"?

❖ *Luke 10:3-6:* • What is the "way" like today? • Are the "laborers" still like lambs among wolves? Why, or why not? • What sense do these traveling instructions make now? What did they mean for the disciples? • How do the current "laborers" establish peace? What issues are important in establishing peace?

❖ *Luke 10:7-8:* • What was the meaning of these instructions in hospitality to the disciples? • What are the hospitality issues now? • Who should pay the wages? What are the implications if "the harvest" is unable to pay?

❖ *Luke 10:9-12:* • How do we now say, "The kingdom has come near"? • If we invest in mission in a particular area, what should be done if there is resistance or rejection? • What does that suggest for "laborers" who are expecting to "harvest"? • If the mandate of God is to go to all nations, how do we deal with "shaking the dust"?

❖ *Luke 10:17-20:* • How would you describe the power of God given to the "laborers" then and now? • What are the power issues today inherent in mission? • What are the consequences of succeeding (or not) and how is success to be measured?

❖ *For everyone:* • What does this passage teach us about missionary method? • Is the biblical method appropriate in the complex world of the 21st century? • What models do you know from our Methodist history? • What new things are being done or need to be done? • What new insights come to mind if you consider yourself part of the "harvest," rather than one of the "laborers"?

* *

Activity 5.10/6-S

❖ When have you shared table fellowship with persons of another culture? How did that meal influence the relationships of those present?

❖ When have you shared or witnessed a joyous rite of passage made possible by mission activity?

❖ What Scriptures empower and encourage you to share the bread of life and/or to regard mission activity as sacramental? (Note those in Essay 19.)

SESSION/SEGMENT FIVE

Activity 5.16/6-S   **Activity 5.2/One-Day**   **Activity 5.7/R**

Moderator

You will begin the panel discussion by briefly introducing the other participants and asking the first question to get the conversation started. Your role will be to monitor the conversation, make sure each person gets a balanced share of the discussion, and introduce new questions as the discussion warrants. Be sure to limit each speech to 60-90 seconds at a time. You may synthesize the comments of the group as needed, especially if they seem stuck somewhere.

"Multinational" Business Executive

You represent a business that has international offices, and that employs persons who have come from the United States to head international offices and local persons from the host country. You may determine how the staff is configured between US "imports" and local persons in the leadership, management, and "rank and file" operations. You may also determine the service or product of your business and must disclose it to the moderator before you are introduced. You must determine the business practices that you find acceptable and be honest about them in the panel discussion.

"Receiving" Bishop

You are the resident Methodist bishop in one host country in which the multinational business is located. You have a special concern that all business practices, including those "imported" from the US and elsewhere, respect the workers, provide appropriate wages, use environmental resources wisely, and are "good neighbors" to the community in which the business operates.

Missionary

You are sent by the General Board of Global Ministries and work with a team (of the realistic size you determine) of other missionaries (including non-UM) in the area. You speak the local language. You were there before the company started doing business there and have some perspective on how life was before and now, relative to the presence of that business.

Layperson in the Mission Area

You are a local worker, employed by this business. You may determine your gender, the size of your family (if any), and what your work was prior to this employment. You speak English, though you may decide what your proficiency level is. You are a member of a church in the Methodist tradition, and you may indicate how long you have been a member and whether you have previously practiced a faith other than Christianity.

✳✳✳✳✳✳✳✳✳✳✳✳✳✳✳✳✳✳✳✳✳✳✳✳✳✳✳✳✳✳✳

Activity 5.17/6-S. Questions after the Panel   Activity 5.8/R

- ❖ What does thinking and acting "glocally" mean to you now?
- ❖ How does the church's presence "glocally" compare and contrast with what you know of the global business environment?
- ❖ How can the church speak to the world about "glocal" issues?
- ❖ What is your part in "glocalization," and what does that mean to you?

✳✳✳✳✳✳✳✳✳✳✳✳✳✳✳✳✳✳✳✳✳✳✳✳✳✳✳✳✳✳✳

Activity 5.21/6-S   Activity 5.12/R

- ❖ Given the mission theological statement you worked on in Session 1, the essays, and the Scriptures you have studied, how well have you done on your stewardship in mission?
- ❖ The General Board of Global Ministries needs constant support of missionaries and Advance Special gifts. Were those needs considered?
- ❖ What sort of balance is appropriate, do you think, between supporting the denominational efforts and personal and local mission? How do you decide?

✳✳✳✳✳✳✳✳✳✳✳✳✳✳✳✳✳✳✳✳✳✳✳✳✳✳✳✳✳✳✳

Activity 5.22/6-S. Reflection/Action Questions   Activity 5.13/R

- ❖ What have I seen or discovered about my own commitments to the *missio Dei*? In the "divine economy" of all Christians working from their strengths and passions, are my commitments appropriate?
- ❖ What has the Scripture called me to do towards the "harvest"? How have the Scriptures judged my efforts, interests, and theology of mission?
- ❖ What has been God's word of grace to me today?
- ❖ What one action will I take in the next week to live out God's call of mission?
- ❖ Who will be my partner in action and/or accountability?

SESSION/SEGMENT SIX

Activity 6.8/6-S   Activity 6.8/R

❖ What was your greatest "Aha!" moment (something that surprised, clarified, amazed, delighted)? What was your greatest "Uh-Oh" moment (something that dismayed, disappointed, discouraged, warned)?

❖ What experience, learning, or insight was the most powerful for you? Why?

❖ What sense of hope or encouragement did this experience engender? Why?

❖ What sense of need did this experience evoke? Why?

❖ As you experienced and learned from the sessions, how did the Theological Task (Scripture, Tradition, Experience, and Reason) intersect with the mission goals (make disciples, strengthen Christian community, alleviate suffering, seek peace with justice)? Did that have any impact on your insights and/or commitments to the *missio Dei*?

❖ Did you commit to any actions as asked at the end of each session? If so, did you follow through? If not, why not? If so, what was the result? **[For 6-Session only.]**

* *

Activity 6.11/6-S. Examples of Outcomes   Activity 6.13/R

❖ A congregation, cluster, or district having a relationship with a missionary or Mission Initiative conference.

❖ Seeing X% of the congregation thinking about and engaged in local mission as an expression of the grace of God from their church into the community.

❖ A church council that always operates from a framework of Matthew 25:31-46 before it decides on any future ministry and as an evaluation of current ministry.

❖ A district committed to teaching some form of this academy for X% of the churches, so that they will begin to think and act "glocally."

❖ The annual conference committed and empowered as a "glocal" neighbor in all its areas of ministry.

* *

Activity 6.12/6-S. Planning Helps　　　　　　　**Activity 6.12/R**

❖ What is God calling us to be and do? How can we share this calling so that it is appealing and compelling?

❖ What gifts and strengths do we possess? What would happen if everyone interested worked only from strengths?

❖ Who are our chosen and natural leaders? Who has passion for ministry whom we have not invited?

❖ What training and equipping resources are available?

❖ What tangible resources are or could be available?

❖ What organizations already do what we want to do? What other partners are available?

❖ What barriers must be overcome? What one step can be taken first?

❖ What is the best and worst that could happen with a given strategy?

❖ S.M.A.R.T. Example: We will host a mission fair (specific) during the summer (timely) to acquaint our congregation with mission theology, specific ministries in our church, and those through the UMC (attainable, reasonable). One measure of outcome is the people who make a tangible commitment to mission theology and activity (measurable).

＊＊＊＊＊＊＊＊＊＊＊＊＊＊＊＊＊＊＊＊＊＊＊＊＊＊＊＊＊＊＊＊

Activity 6.19/6-S. Distribute Only to the Readers　　　**Activity 6.17/R**

Read your Scriptures in turn. Allow 20 or 30 seconds of silence between each reading.

Reader 1: The Great Requirement—Micah 6:8

Reader 2: The Great Redemption—John 3:16

Reader 3: The Great Commitment—Matthew 16:24

Reader 4: The Great Commandment—Matthew 22:37-39

Reader 5: The Great Commission—Matthew 28:19-20

HANDOUTS FOR THE ONE-DAY FORMAT

Activity 2.3

Read aloud, or have group members read Matthew 5:14-16. Reflect on the Scripture and on the burning needs mentioned in the essay, then discuss these questions in the small groups:

❖ How does the need you see compel you to witness?

❖ On what "lamp stand" do you need to place your lamp—what witness are you on fire to offer? When you do, what is the consequence?

❖ How do you or have you hidden your light? What has been the consequence?

❖ How do you describe "good works [that] give glory to your Father in heaven"?

Activity 3.2. Readers Theater (See Activity 4.5/6-S)

Activity 3.2

Discuss these questions after the Readers Theater:

❖ How is Methodism "organized to beat the Devil"? How well do we do?

❖ What is your experience with how the connectionalism and/or organization of The United Methodist Church functions to accomplish the *missio Dei*?

❖ What is your experience of mission within the Connection? What experience do you have with partner relationships between a local church or annual conference with another (usually foreign) church or conference?

❖ What can you do within the Connection that would be difficult or impossible without it?

❖ What opportunities have you had to be educated in the *missio Dei*? What opportunities are you providing for others to cultivate mission leaders?

❖ What blessings have you experienced or heard about that have been bestowed on the US church by conferences outside the US?

Activity 3.5

Talk about the contexts for mission, using these questions:

❖ What were the circumstances of your visit (tourist, family visit, mission trip)?

❖ If you were a tourist, did you see the "real" country or community?

❖ If you went to mission areas, what did you see? How was it different from what a tourist may see?

❖ In what ways, if any, have you seen the US church imposing its cultural biases on another Christian context or been unaware that there were cultural distinctions to make for effective ministry and relationships?

❖ How does the call to "make of all disciples" need to be interpreted in cultures other than your own to form responsible partnerships?

Activity 5.2. Roles for Panel Members (See Activity 5.16/6-S)

Activity 5.3

After the panel presentation, discuss these questions for no more than 10 minutes:

❖ What does thinking and acting "glocally" mean to you now?

❖ How does the church's presence "glocally" compare and contrast with what you know of the global business environment?

❖ How can the church speak to the world about "glocal" issues?

❖ What is your part in "glocalization," and what does that mean to you?

Activity 5.5

Read Luke 10:1-12, 17-20. Discuss the questions associated with the portion of Scripture you have been assigned.

❖ *Luke 10:1-2:* • Who, in contemporary terms, are the "harvest"? • Who, do you think, are the "laborers"? • How do we decide which laborers go to which harvest, if there are not enough for the entire "harvest"?

❖ *Luke 10:3-6:* • What is the "way" like today? • Are the "laborers" still like lambs among wolves? Why, or why not? • What sense do these traveling instructions make now? What did they mean for the disciples? • How do the current "laborers" establish peace? What issues are important in establishing peace?

❖ *Luke 10:7-8:* • What was the meaning of these instructions in hospitality to the disciples? • What are the hospitality issues now? • Who should pay the wages? • What are the implications if the "harvest" is unable to pay?

❖ *Luke 10:9-12:* • How do we now say, "The kingdom has come near"? • If we invest in mission in a particular area, what should be done if there is resistance or rejection? • What does that suggest for "laborers" who are expecting to "harvest"? • If the mandate of God is to go to all nations, how do we deal with "shaking the dust"?

❖ *Luke 10:17-20:* • How would you describe the power of God given to the "laborers" then and now? • What are the power issues today inherent in mission? • What are the consequences of succeeding (or not) and how is success to be measured?

❖ *For everyone:* • What does this passage teach us about the missionary method? • Is the biblical method appropriate in the complex world of the 21st century? • What models do you know from our Methodist history? • What new things are being done or need to be done?

Activity 6.3

Reflect on the day using these questions:

❖ What was your greatest "Aha!" moment (something that surprised, clarified, amazed, delighted)? What was your greatest "Uh-Oh" moment (something that dismayed, disappointed, discouraged, warned)?

❖ What experience, learning, or insight was the most powerful for you? Why?

❖ What sense of hope or encouragement did this experience engender? Why?

❖ What sense of need did this experience evoke? Why?

❖ As you experienced and learned from the sessions, how did Scripture, Tradition, Experience, and Reason intersect with the mission goals (make disciples, strengthen Christian community, alleviate suffering, seek peace with justice)?

❖ Did that have any impact on your insights and/or commitments to the *missio Dei?*

❖ Given your theology of mission statement and your mission mandates, to what action has this experience called you? What outcome do you want?

❖ What first S.M.A.R.T. step (specific, measurable, attainable, reasonable, and timely) will you take, and by when? Who will be your partner in support and accountability?

ABOUT THE AUTHORS

Dr. John Edward Nuessle is an assistant general secretary at the General Board of Global Ministries of The United Methodist Church. John serves in wide-ranging missional arenas with specific responsibilities for leading the Mission Education and Mission Initiatives staff teams, as well as the team on the Academy of Mission Renewal. Through these mission programs, he works to promote engagement in the United Methodist theology of mission by the whole church, and advance the pioneer evangelism efforts of the denomination. In addition to his work at Global Ministries over half his career, John has held a variety of pastoral appointments during the past 30 years, in multiple rural church charges, suburban settings, a downtown urban pastorate, and as a district superintendent. A native of New York State, John is an ordained elder of the North Central New York Annual Conference and holds M.Div. and D.Min. theological degrees from Drew University at Madison, New Jersey.

Dr. Diana L. Hynson is currently a staff member of the General Board of Discipleship (GBOD), serving as director of Learning and Teaching Ministries and director of Church Vitality Indicator since 2001. Prior to this appointment, Dr. Hynson worked as a development editor of adult resources at the United Methodist Publishing House for over 13 years.

Diana is a member of the Conference Leaders team at GBOD, offering seminars, classes, workshops, and other resources in the area of Christian education and formation, small group ministry, and coaching. She is a member of the Baltimore-Washington Annual Conference and a two-time graduate of Wesley Theological Seminary, holding an M.Div. and a D.Min. in Christian education. Diana has planned and written study materials for other resources, most recently for *Beyond the Roll Book: Sunday School and Evangelism* (Abingdon) and *Lay Speakers Teach Adults* (Discipleship Resources).